the furtwängler sound

6th edition

discography with concert register
compiled by john hunt

contents

The Furtwaengler Sound
Published by John Hunt.
© 1999 John Hunt
reprinted 2009
ISBN 978-1-901395-97-6

Sole distributors:
Travis & Emery,
17 Cecil Court,
London, WC2N 4EZ,
United Kingdom.
(+44) 20 7 459 2129.
sales@travis-and-emery.com

Acknowledgement: these publications have
been made possible by contributions or by
advance 3-volume subscriptions from

Masakasu Abe	Richard Ames
Stefano Angeloni	Stathis Arfanis
Yoshihiro Asada	Jack Atkinson
E. C. Blake	Andreas Brandmair
Peter Buescher	Eduardo Chibas
Siam Chowkwanyun	Robert Christoforides
Robert Dandois	F. De Vilder
Richard Dennis	John Derry
Hans-Peter Ebner	Henry Fogel
Peter Fu	Nobuo Fukumoto
Peter Fulop	James Giles
Jens Golumbus	Jean-Pierre Goossens
Johann Gratz	A. G. Greenburgh
Peter Hamann	James Hansford
Michael Harris	Tadashi Hasegawa
Naoya Hirabayashi	Don Hodgman
Martin Holland	John T. Hughes
Bodo Igesz	Richard Igler
Andrew Keener	Koji Kinoshita
Detlef Kissmann	Bent Klovborg
Kathryn Lanford	John Larsen
Ernst Lumpe	Elisabeth Legge-Schwarzkopf DBE
John Mallinson	Carlo Marinelli
Ryosuke Masuda	Finn Moeller Larsen
Jean-Michel Molkhou	Philip Moores
Bruce Morrison	W. Moyle
Alan Newcombe	Hugh Palmer
Jim Parsons	Laurence Pateman
James Pearson	Johann Christian Petersen
Tully Potter	Patrick Russell
Yves Saillard	Jorge Monteiro dos Santos
Neville Sumpter	Ian Sutcliffe
Yoshihiko Suzuki	Michael Tanner
H. A. Van Dijk	Mario Vicentini
Hiromitsu Wada	Urs Weber
Michael Wierer	Nigel Wood
G. Wright	Ken Wyman

Introduction to the discography

Wilhelm Furtwängler has benefited more than most executant musicians in the historical category from the burgeoning of interest in the gramophone's past. His name features consistently in comparative reviews of the key repertory, be it in record magazines or programmes like "Building a library" on BBC Radio 3. That is a far cry even from the LP era, when dedicated collectors needed to search out particular performances from often expensive import lists, which received scant mention in the musical press.

The main discography in this, my return to the Furtwängler legacy on record for the sixth time, comprises the published recordings. All known unissued tapes join those elusive pre-1940 radio excerpts which stubbornly continue to remain hidden - perhaps we must deem them irretrievably lost - in a separate section of unpublished Furtwängler recordings. Wilhelm Furtwängler as composer at the hands of other interpreters makes his appearance in another separate section, which failed to materialise in time for the fifth (1996) printing of my discography.

The spurious recordings continue to be a source of speculation and interest for the most inquisitive collectors, and some of those even continue to reach publication in editions from unscrupulous pirates, which the newcomer should be warned about. The same warning applies to superficially interesting editions of genuine material from CD labels like Dante/Lys, Arlecchino, Grammofono and Iron Needle - to mention just a few - which blatantly copy existing LPs or, worse still, the carefully engineered CD transfers from legitimate editions like Tahra, Biddulph and the German and French Furtwängler Societies.

Becoming a member of at least one of those Furtwängler Societies cannot be urged too strongly, as the German and French issues from that source are a model of their kind. The Paris-based Société Wilhelm Furtwängler is particularly anxious that the entire archive should be permanently available, and to this end has recently expressed an interest in re-issuing the tapes of Furtwängler's Caracas concert in 1954 (briefly published by the British Society in 1985 and 1992), so that an important example of the conductor's work with an unfamiliar orchestra can be preserved for future study.

An undervalued contribution to the publishing of rare Furtwängler material has come from Akira Tanaka in Japan, firstly with a series of LPs with the prefix "AT" (these included war-time versions of Bruckner 4 and 7, incomplete but of staggering intensity, and still not reissued on CD). There followed a highly valuable series of CDs on the label "Refrain", which curiously suggested a Canadian source - Mr Tanaka no doubt has his reasons! Recent publications in the series are on labels entitled "Elaborations" and "Evangel", and are listed as appropriate in this discography. I can give Mr Tanaka's address to anyone who requests it from me. As far as other Japanese issues are concerned, it can be taken for granted that all issues from the major companies (EMI, Deutsche Grammophon and Decca) are also published (in multiple editions) by their Japanese counterparts - it is therefore not considered necessary to list these. Japanese labels like Seven Seas, which have no Western equivalent, are mentioned, usually in the form of a footnote.

Gratitude must be expressed to the often-criticised EMI who, for the first time in the history of their Furtwängler issues, has in recent years systematically made available on CD all of his "official" HMV legacy, supplemented by a representative selection of the concerts and operas which he performed in Salzburg between 1950 and 1954. Deutsche Grammophon, on the other hand, has opted to rely on its Japanese affiliate to carry out the work, although of course Furtwängler's small body of post-war studio work for the company is now admirably restored in the "DG Originals" series.

Wilhelm Furtwängler's war-time concerts had of course long been available on LPs of variable quality from the Russian Melodiya company, which had stored the original tapes since about 1949. It was, however, not until the fall of the Berlin Wall some 40 years later that restored copies of those tapes were made available to Deutsche Grammophon for publication on CD. In the intervening period, the Russians have also capitalised on the original tapes by publishing many of them on Japanese Melodiya CD (with the prefix MEL) and subsequently on a label called "Russian Compact Disc" (not to be confused with "Russian Disc"). Russian Compact Disc has not, as far as I can ascertain, been available in the UK. Many collectors will, I know, prefer these unequalised incarnations from original tapes with a sound far more immediate than that produced by many Western editions. Unfortunately, Melodiya has not yet developed a matching sense of scholarship, so that the discredited items (Grieg, Haydn, Glazunov and D'Albert) are blatantly included as if they were genuine Furtwängler performances!

To conclude, and in spite of my recommendation for at least some of the Russian Compact Disc issues, I must single out Tahra's recent "Furtwängler: Historic Wartime Archives 1942-1944". This also includes the cream of the Russian tapes, and is a 6-CD set (FURT 1034-1039) but is also available as three separate 2-CD sets. Quality of sound is here even better than previous Tahra editions of the same material.

My thanks must go, as always, to the many Furtwängler collectors who continue to send me details of issues from many parts of the world.

I have just had time to include in this discography a 10-CD anthology of miscellaneous Furtwängler material on the label "History", originating from Israel, of all places. It is retailing in Germany at the amazingly low price of DM 29.-, but transfers are unremarkable and several items are blatantly copied from Tahra originals.

To conclude, I have been asked by many readers to include the recommendations for a preferred edition, which was a feature in the fifth issue of The Furtwängler Sound. Of course this can only be done in cases where such an edition is readily available in domestic catalogues: I see little practical point in recommending something which can only be obtained with great difficulty. It must also be remembered that the recommendations, which appear *in italics,* are purely personal.

JOHANN SEBASTIAN BACH (1685-1750)

brandenburg concerto no 3

✓ berlin   bpo   78: grammophon 95417-95418
1930   78: ultraphon G 19036-19037
78: brunswick 90161-90162
78: decca CA 8013-8014
78: polydor (japan) 45153-60192
45: dg EPL 30 539
lp: dg 2535 827
lp: discocorp RR 431
cd: symposium 1043
cd: grammofono AB 78574
cd: dante LYS 117
cd: music and arts CD 954
cd: history 20.3090/20.3093
cd: koch 3-7059-2

✓ salzburg   vpo   lp: discocorp RR 515
31 august   lp: nippon columbia OZ 7594
1950   cd: refrain (japan) DR 92 0018
also issued on cd in japan by seven seas

cd: emi 7234 5 67422 2.2

brandenburg concerto no 5

vienna 21-22 december 1940	vpo schneiderhan, niedermayer, furtwängler	lp: french furtwängler society SWF 8401-8402 lp: tanaka AT 13-14
✓ salzburg 31 august 1950	vpo boskovsky, niedermayer, furtwängler	lp: discocorp RR 515 lp: nippon columbia OZ 7594 cd: refrain (japan) DR 92 0018 also issued on cd in japan by seven seas *cd: emi 7243 5 67 422 2.2*

orchestral suite no 3

berlin 22 october 1948	bpo	lp: dg LPM 18 856/KL 27-31/2535 806 isuued on cd in japan only by dg

berlin
24 october
1948
	bpo	lp: german furtwängler society
		    F668.164-F668.165
		cd: german furtwängler society
		    TMK 12681
		cd: music and arts CD 708
		also issued on cd in japan by palette

air/orchestral suite no 3

berlin 1929	bpo	78: grammophon 66926/66935/95418 78: brunswick 90050 78: decca CA 8014 45: dg EPL 30 164 lp: dg LPEM 19 078/2535 827 lp: private issue (japan) JP 1101-1102 cd: music and arts CD 954 *cd: koch 3-7059-2*

matthäus-passion

buenos aires 2 may 1950	teatro colon orchestra and chorus n.hoffmann, klose, dermota, greindl, mattiello	lp: tanaka AT 15-16 abridged recording; chorus sings in spanish
vienna 9 april 1952	vpo singakademie seefried, rössl-majdan, patzak, braun, wiener	lp: private issue (japan) GCL 5003 recording comprises part one nos 1-33 only *cd orfeo C834 1184*
vienna 14-17 april 1954	vpo singakademie grümmer, höffgen, dermota, edelmann, fischer-dieskau	lp: cetra LO 508/FE 34 lp: movimento musica 03.008 cd: movimento musica 013.005 cd: priceless D 20899 cd: virtuoso 269.9212 *cd: emi CHS 565 5092* the performance contained cuts, and emi issue further omits the bass arias komm süsses kreuz and mache dich mein herze rein *cd: orfeo C834 1184*

BELA BARTOK (1881-1945)

violin concerto no 2

london	philharmonia	lp: hmv ALP 1121
12-13	menuhin	lp: hmv (france) FALP 313/FALP 30528
september		lp: electrola E 90070/WALP 1121
1953		lp: victor LHMV 3
		lp: angel (argentina) LPC 11593
		lp: emi 1C053 01322/2C053 01322/
		2C051 01322
		cd: priceless D 15100
		cd: emi CDH 769 8042

LUDWIG VAN BEETHOVEN (1770-1827)

symphony no 1

✓ amsterdam   concertgebouw   lp: olympic OL 8120/OL 8124
13 july   orchestra   lp: private issue (japan) JP 1199-1200
1950   lp: dial discos (spain) 50.200
    cd: refrain (japan) DR 92 0033
    cd: tahra FURT 1012-1013

vienna   vpo   lp: hmv ALP 1324
24-30   lp: hmv (france) FALP 30124/
november   FBLP 25023/UVT 3124
1952   lp: electrola E 90132/WALP 1324/
    E 60657/WDLP 663/SME 91412
    lp: victor LHMV 700
    lp: melodiya D 03375-03376
    lp: emi RLS 727/1C149 53432-53439M/
    1C027 00806M/
    2C153 52540-52551/
    2C153 53678-53679
    cd: emi CDC 747 4092/CHS 763 6062/
    CDH 763 0332

vienna   vpo   lp: cetra FE 33
30 november   lp: german furtwängler society
1952   F669.056-F669.057
    cd: arkadia CD 504/CDHP 504
    cd: curcio CON 02
    cd: cetra CDE 1013
    cd: nuova era 013.6305/013.6300
    cd: virtuoso 269.7162
    cd: classical collection CD3-CLC 4006
    cd: music and arts CD 711/*CD 942*
    cd: emblem EF 4003
    some issues incorrectly dated
    29 november 1952

symphony no 1/concluded

✓ stuttgart   sdr orchestra   lp: discocorp RR 511
30 march   lp: french furtwängler society
1954   SWF 8301-8302
                                       lp: nippon columbia OZ 7587
                                       cd: french furtwängler society SWF 931
                                       cd: evangel (japan) FRL 1002
                                       cd: mediaphon/sdr JA 75.100

berlin   bpo   lp: movimento musica 08.001
19 september   lp: victor/jvc (japan) RCL 3333
1954   cd: rodolphe RPC 32522-32534
                                      cd: music and arts CD 792
                                      cd: tahra FURT 1025
                                      furtwängler's final concert; RCL 3333
                                      incorrectly dated 15 january 1953

symphony no 2

london	vpo	lp: emi 1C149 53432-53439M/
3 october		2C051 03649
1948		cd: music and arts CD 942
		cd: emi CHS 763 6062/*CDH 763 1922*

symphony no 3 "eroica"

✓ vienna
19-20
december
1944
	vpo	lp: urania C 7075
		lp: melodiya D 06443-06444/
		    M10 06443 009
		lp: unicorn UNI 104
		lp: turnabout THS 65020
		lp: intercord INT 120.921
		lp: emi 2C051 63332/
		    3C153 53810-53816M
		cd: priceless D 16395
		cd: melodiya MEL 10 00710
		cd: music and arts CD 814/CD 942
		cd: documents LV 919-920
		cd: historical performers HP 2
		cd: urania (japan) URCD 7095
		cd: grammofono AB 78538
		cd: dante LYS 063
		cd: russian compact disc RCD 25001
		cd: preiser 90251
		cd: tahra FURT 1034-1039/
		    FURT 1034-1035/*FURT 1031*
		also issued in japan by toshiba: original
		urania, melodiya, documents and
		grammofono editions incorrectly name
		orchestra as bpo

vienna 10-17 november 1947	vpo	78: hmv DB 6741-6747/ DB 9296-9302 auto lp: discocorp RR 456 lp: private issue (japan) JP 1190-1192 lp: french furtwängler society SWF 7903 lp: emi 3C153 53800-53805M cd: toshiba shinseido SGR 8221 cd: dante LYS 197 *cd: tahra FURT 1027* side 5 of 78rpm recording was re-made on 15 february 1949 and substituted in later pressings of the set

symphony no 3/continued

✓ berlin   bpo   lp: victor/jvc (japan) RCL 3334
20 june   cd: german furtwängler society
1950   MMS 9010
✱   cd: music and arts CD 711
                                cd: tahra FURT 1030

rome   rai roma   lp: olympic OL 8120/OL 8122
19 january   orchestra   lp: cetra FE 6
1952   only issued on cd in japan by seven seas

vienna   vpo   lp: hmv ALP 1060
26-27   lp: hmv (france) FALP 287/
november   FALP 50037/UVT 3037
1952   lp: hmv (italy) QALP 10030
                                lp: electrola E 90050/WALP 1060/
                                   EBE 600 000/STE 90050/
                                   SME 90050/SMVP 8041
                                lp: columbia (austria) VALP 530
                                lp: victor LHMV 1044
                                lp: angel 6018
                                lp: world records SH 375
                                lp: emi 1C149 53432-53439M/
                                   1C027 00810M/3C053 00810/
                                   2C153 52540-52551
                                cd: emi CDC 747 4102/CHS 763 6062/
                                   CDH 763 0332

✓ vienna   vpo   cd: nuova era 013.6314/013.6300
30 november   cd: virtuoso 269.7182
1952

berlin   bpo   lp: rococo 2050
7 december   lp: discocorp RR 520
1952   lp: german furtwängler society
                                   F 666.848M
                                lp: nippon columbia OW 7818/OZ 7584
                                lp: private issue (japan) WFJ 1
                                cd: refrain (japan) DR 93 0065
                                cd: music and arts CD 520
                                also issued in japan by rococo,
                                palette and bruno walter society

symphony no 3/concluded

✓ berlin   bpo   lp: cetra LO 530
8 december   cd: rodolphe RPC 32522-32524/
1952   RPV 32801
                                        cd: arkadia CDWFE 363
                                        cd: emblem EF 4001
                                        cd: music and arts CD 869
                                        cd: tahra FURT 1008-1011/
                                        FURT 1008-1009
                                    also issued in japan by cetra and
                                    seven seas; some editions incorrectly
                                    dated 20 june 1950, 3 or 7 december
                                    1952

✓ lucerne   lucerne   cd: french furtwängler society
26 august   festival   SWF 961-962
1953   orchestra   cd: elaborations (japan) ELA 904-905
                                      cd: music and arts CD 1018

symphony no 4

✓ berlin
27-30
june
1943
	bpo	first performance, without audience
		lp: vox PL 7210
		lp: dg LPM 18 742/2535 813/
		          2730 005
		lp: eterna 820 312
		lp: turnabout TV 4344
		lp: french furtwängler society SWF 7103
		
		second performance, with audience
		cd: dg 427 7772/427 7732
		cd: melodiya MEL 10 00719
		cd: russian compact disc RCD 25010
		cd: grammofono AB 78502
		cd: dante LYS 072
		cd: music and arts CD 824
		also issued by toshiba in japan
		
		version with movements 1 and 2 from
		second performance and movements
		3 and 4 from first performance
		lp: melodiya D 09083-09084
		lp: nippon columbia DXM 103
		lp: olympic OL 8120/OL 8124
		lp: emi 3C153 53810-53816M
		
		all three versions issued by
		dg in japan
		
		movements 1 and 2 only from
		second performance
		lp: french furtwängler society
		          SWF 8801-8803

symphony no 4/concluded

vienna 25-30 january 1950	vpo	78: hmv DB 21099-21103/ DB 9524-9528 auto lp: hmv (france) FALP 116 lp: discocorp RR 437 lp: french furtwängler society SWF 7904 lp: emi 3C153 53800-53805M issued on cd in japan by toshiba; catalogue number FALP 116 also allocated to 1952 HMV version

vienna
1-2
december
1952
	vpo	lp: hmv ALP 1059
		lp: hmv (france) FALP 116/
		    FALP 30032/FALP 30124/
		    UVT 3124
		lp: hmv (italy) QALP 10025
		lp: electrola E 90059/WALP 1059/
		    SME 91412
		lp: columbia (austria) VALP 518
		lp: victor LHMV 1059
		lp: emi MFP 2072/1C027 00806M/
		    1C149 53432-53439M/
		    2C153 52540-52551
		cd: emi CDC 747 4092/CHS 763 6062/
		    CDH 763 1922
		catalogue number FALP 116 also
		allocated to HMV 1950 version

V munich 4 september 1953	vpo	lp: cetra FE 49 lp: victor/jvc (japan) RCL 3333 cd: nuova era 013.6310/013.6300 cd: rodolphe RPC 32522-32524 cd: virtuoso 269.7192 cd: french furtwängler society SWF 892 cd: emblem EF 4005-4006 cd: music and arts CD 792/*CD 942* also issued on cd in japan by seven seas cd: Dahra PURT 1090

symphony no 5

berlin 1926	bpo	78: grammophon 69855-69859 78: brunswick 25005-25009 lp: discocorp RR 431 lp: private issue (japan) NA 121-122 lp: furtwängler society FURT 100 *cd: koch 3-7059-2* also issued on cd in japan by dg and philips shinseido

berlin
8 october-
3 november
1937
	bpo	78: hmv DB 3328-3332/
		        DB 8374-8378 auto
		78: victor M 426/AM 426/DM 426
		lp: emi 2C051 03587/
		        3C153 53800-53805M
		lp: french furtwängler society SWF 7002
		cd: novello NVLCD 904
		cd: music and arts CD 954
		cd: dante LYS 072
		cd: history 20.3090/20.3095
		cd: biddulph WHL 006-007/ WHL 006
		cd: tahra FURT 1032-1033

berlin 13 september 1939	bpo	*cd: tahra FURT 1014-1015* side 7 of this 78rpm radio recording (bars 486-668 of final movement) missing: it is replaced here by the same section of 1937 hmv version

symphony no 5/continued

√ berlin   bpo   lp: melodiya D 05800-05801/
27-30   M10 05800 009
june   lp: unicorn UNI 106
1943   lp: french furtwängler society SWF 7002

berlin bpo

- lp: melodiya D 05800-05801/ M10 05800 009
- lp: unicorn UNI 106
- lp: french furtwängler society SWF 7002
- lp: nippon columbia DXM 157
- lp: turnabout TV 4353/TV 4361/ TV 34478
- lp: ariston ARCL 13029
- lp: emi 3C153 53810-53816M
- cd: dg 427 7752/427 7732
- cd: melodiya MEL 10 00720
- cd: russian compact disc RCD 25011
- cd: grammofono AB 78502
- cd: music and arts CD 824
- cd: dante LYS 065
- cd: tahra TAH 272/FURT 1034-1039/ FURT 1034-1035/FURT 1032-1033
- also issued in japan by toshiba

√ berlin   bpo
25 may
1947

- lp: cetra FE 32
- cd: cetra CDE 1014
- cd: rodolphe RPC 32522-32524
- cd: music and arts CD 789/CD 942
- cd: german furtwängler society TMK 08080
- cd: dante LYS 198
- cd: tahra FURT 1016
- also issued on cd in japan by seven seas

berlin   bpo
27 may
1947

- lp: dg LPM 18 724/88 011/2535 810/ 2721 202/2730 005/2740 260
- lp: eterna 820 280
- lp: heliodor (usa) H 25078/HS 25078
- cd: dg 439 8322
- cd: bellaphon 689.22003
- bellaphon incorrectly dated 25 may 1947

symphony no 5/continued

stockholm 25 september 1950	vpo	lp: discocorp RR 507 lp: private issues (japan) JP 1190-1192/ GC 570 234-570 235 lp: nippon columbia OZ 7585 *cd: music and arts CD 802* <u>also issued on cd in japan by</u> <u>palette and seven seas</u>
copenhagen 1 october 1950	vpo	lp: danacord DACO 114 cd: danacord DACOCD 301 *cd: tahra FURT 1090*
rome 10 january 1952	rai roma orchestra	lp: olympic OL 8120/OL 8126 lp: cetra FE 7 <u>issued on cd in japan only</u> <u>by seven seas</u>

symphony no 5/concluded

vienna
28 february-
1 march
1954
	vpo	lp: hmv ALP 1195
		lp: hmv (france) FALP 260/
		    FALP 30128/UVT 3128
		lp: hmv (italy) QALP 10086
		lp: electrola E 90088/WALP 1195/
		    EBE 600 000/STE 90088/
		    SME 90088/SMVP 8049
		lp: victor LHMV 9
		lp: eterna 820 053
		lp: angel 6018
		lp: emi 1C149 53432-53439M/
		    1C027 00771M/
		    2C153 52540-52551
		cd: emi CDC 747 8032/CHS 763 6062/
		    CDH 769 8032

✓ paris 4 may 1954	bpo	lp: cetra LO 519/FE 45 lp: discocorp RR 522 cd: french furtwängler society SWF 942-943 cd: elaborations (japan) ELA 901 also issued on cd in japan by seven seas

✓ berlin
23 may
1954
	bpo	lp: german furtwängler society
		    F669.310-F669.311
		cd: nuova era 013.6305/013.6300
		cd: virtuoso 269.7192
		cd: music and arts CD 869
		cd: emblem EF 4003
		cd: tahra FURT 1008-1011/
		    FURT 1008-1009/*FURT 1032-1033*

symphony no 6 "pastoral"

✓vienna   vpo   lp: turnabout TV 4408
22-23   lp: nippon columbia DXM 131
december   lp: vox (japan) H 5060
1943   lp: emi ED 29 06661

cd: music and arts CD 954
cd: dante LYS 074
cd: preiser 90199
<u>this was an unpublished electrola 78 rpm</u>
<u>recording; emi lp and toshiba editions</u>
<u>contained an unsanctioned first</u>
<u>movement repeat</u>

✓berlin   bpo   lp: melodiya D 02777-02778/
20-22   M10 02777 004
march   lp: rococo 2077
1944   lp: nippon columbia DXM 155/OZ 7586

lp: french furtwängler society SWF 7104R
lp: discocorp RR 412
cd: french furtwängler society SWF 901
cd: melodiya MEL 10 00712
cd: russian compact disc RCD 25003
cd: history 20.3090/20.3095
cd: dante LYS 064
cd: music and arts WFSA 2001/
    CD 824/CD 942
cd: tahra FURT 1004-1007/
    FURT 1034-1039/FURT 1036-1037
<u>also issued on cd in japan by palette:</u>
<u>FURT 1034-1039 and FURT 1036-1037</u>
<u>incorrectly dated 30 june 1943</u>

berlin   bpo   lp: cetra FE 32
25 may   cd: cetra CDE 1014
1947   cd: rodolphe RPC 32422-32424

cd: german furtwängler society
    TMK 08080
cd: music and arts CD 789
cd: bellaphon 689.22003
cd: tahra FURT 1016
<u>also issued on cd in japan by seven seas</u>

rome   rai roma   lp: olympic OL 8120/OL 8128
10 january   orchestra   lp: cetra FE 5
1952   <u>issued on cd in japan only by seven seas</u>

symphony no 6/concluded

vienna
24-25
november
1952
	vpo	lp: hmv ALP 1041
		lp: hmv (france) FALP 288/
		   FALP 30038/UVT 3038
		lp: hmv (italy) QALP 10034
		lp: electrola E 90040/WALP 1041/
		   SME 90040/SMVP 8038
		lp: columbia (austria) VALP 535
		lp: victor LHMV 1066
		lp: angel (argentina) LPC 11526
		lp: eterna 820 045
		lp: unicorn WFS 9
		lp: emi 1C149 53432-53439M/
		   1C027 00807M/100 8071/
		   2C153 52540-52551
		cd: emi CDC 747 1212/CHS 763 6062/
		   CDH 763 0342

lugano 15 may 1954	bpo	lp: cetra LO 529 lp: discocorp RR 477 cd: ermitage ERM 120 **also issued on cd in japan by seven seas**

berlin
23 may
1954
	bpo	lp: german furtwängler society
		   F669.310-F669.311
		lp: private issue (japan) GHE 86125/
		   TPR 1159
		cd: arkadia CD 504/CDHP 504
		cd: nuova era 013.6303/013.6300
		cd: virtuoso 269.7162
		cd: emblem EF 4004
		cd: music and arts CD 869`
		cd: tahra FURT 1008-1011/
		   FURT 1008-1009

symphony no 7

berlin 31 october- 3 november 1943	bpo	lp: melodiya D 027779-027780 lp: turnabout TV 34509 lp: unicorn WFS 8 lp: french furtwängler society SWF 7105 lp: olympic OL 8120/OL 8129 lp: intercord INT 120.924 lp: emi 3C153 53810-53816M cd: dg 427 7752/427 7732 cd: melodiya MEL 10 00713 cd: russian compact disc RCD 25004 cd: french furtwängler society SWF 941 cd: dante LYS 065 cd: music and arts CD 824 also issued on lp and cd in japan by toshiba and on cd by dg and palette
stockholm 13 november 1948	stockholm po	lp: discocorp RR 505 lp: nippon columbia OZ 7587 cd: dante LYS 198 cd: music and arts CD 793 also issued on cd in japan by seven seas

vienna
18-19
january
1950
	vpo	78: hmv DB 21106-21110/
		    DB 9516-9520 auto
		45: victor WHMV 1008
		lp: hmv (france) FALP 115/
		    FALP 30031/UVT 3031
		lp: hmv (italy) QALP 115
		lp: electrola E 90016/WALP 527/
		    SME 90016/SMVP 8048
		lp: victor LHMV 1008
		lp: angel 6018
		lp: emi 1C149 53432-53439M/
		    1C027 00809M/2C051 03089/
		    2C153 52540-52551
		cd: emi CHS 763 6062/CDH 769 8032
		some japanese issues incorrectly
		dated 25-31 january 1950

symphony no 7/concluded

✓ berlin   bpo   lp: german furtwängler society
14 april   F666.624-F666.625
1953   lp: discocorp RR 476
                                  lp: cetra FE 4
                                  lp: private issue (japan) WFS 2-3
                                  cd: rodolphe RPC 32422-32524
                                  cd: dg 415 6662/427 4012
                                  cd: music and arts CD 942

✓ salzburg   vpo   lp: movimento musica 01.029
30 august   cd: nuova era 013.6313/013.6300
1954   cd: foyer CDS 16007
                                  cd: virtuoso 269.7172
                                  cd: classical collection CD3-CLC 4006
                                  cd: orfeo C293 921B
                                  also issued in japan by seven seas

✓ symphony no 7, rehearsal from second movement

lucerne   lucerne   lp: french furtwängler society SWF 7401
15 august   festival   lp: private issue (japan) JPL 1006
1951   lp: discocorp RR 393
                                  lp: nippon columbia OZ 7597
                                  cd: french furtwängler society
                                    SWF 961-962
                                  cd: music and arts CD 1018
                                  also issued on cd in japan by nippon columbia

symphony no 8

stockholm
13 november
1948
	stockholm po	lp: unicorn WFS 5
		lp: olympic OL 8120/OL 8129
		lp: emi 1C149 53432-53439M/
		    1C053 93533M/3C053 93533/
		    2C153 52540-52551
		lp: ariston ARCL 13035
		cd: music and arts CD 793
		cd: dante LYS 199
		cd: emi CHS 763 6062/*CDH 763 0342*

berlin 14 april 1953	bpo	lp: german furtwängler society F666.624-F666.625 lp: discocorp RR 413 lp: nippon columbia OZ 7585 lp: private issue (japan) WFJ 2-3 lp: cetra FE 48 cd: rodolphe RPC 32522-32524 cd: dg 415 6662/427 4012 *cd: music and arts CD 942*
salzburg 30 august 1954	vpo	lp: cetra LO 530 lp: discocorp RR 522 cd: nuova era 013.6310/013.6300 cd: virtuoso 269.7172 cd: as-disc AS 115 *cd: orfeo C293 921B* also issued in japan by seven seas

32

symphony no 9 "choral"

cd: emi 7243 5 62875

london	bpo	lp: emi ED 27 01231
1 may	philharmonic	cd: dante LYS 073
1937	choir of london	*cd: music and arts CD 818*
	berger,	also issued by toshiba in japan; music
	pitzinger,	and arts incorrectly describes chorus
	w.ludwig,	as kittel choir; prior to publication
	watzke	this was thought to be a 1936
		performance

berlin	bpo	lp: melodiya D 010851-010854/
22-24	kittel choir	M10 10851 009
march	briem,	lp: unicorn UNI 100-101
1942	höngen,	lp: nippon columbia DXM 105-106
	anders,	lp: turnabout TV 4346-4347/
	watzke	TV 4353-4354
		lp: french furtwängler society
		SWF 7003-7004
		lp: everest SDBR 3241
		lp: emi 3C153 53810-53816M
		lp: movieplay (spain) 11.0090-11.0091
		cd: priceless D 13256
		cd: french furtwängler society SWF 891
		cd: music and arts CD 653
		cd: classical disk 880.456
		cd: arkadia CDWFE 357
		cd: melodiya MEL 10 00715
		cd: russian compact disc RCD 25006
		cd: documents LV 919-920
		cd: historical performers HP 6
		cd: grammofono AB 78581
		cd: dante LYS 071
		cd: tahra FURT 1004-1007/
		FURT 1034-1039/ FURT 1036-1037
		also issued in japan by palette and
		toshiba; some lp editions were
		incorrectly pitched; classical disk
		was a poorly engineered conflation
		of this and bayreuth 1951 versions

cd: archipel ARPCD 0270

berlin
19 April
1942

symphony no 9/continued

stockholm 8 december 1943	stockholm po and chorus schymberg, tunnell, bäckelin, s.björling	lp: olympic OL 8120 lp: private issue (japan) JPL 1119-1120 lp: discocorp RR 205 cd: dante LYS 066 cd: music and arts WFSA 2002/CD 2002 also issued on cd in japan by seven seas last movement lp: bjr records BJR 118 excerpt from last movement cd: bis BISCD 421A
✓vienna 7 january 1951	vpo singakademie seefried, anday, patzak, edelmann	lp: cetra FE 33 cd: cetra CDC 1 cd: bellaphon 689.22005 also issued in japan by seven seas *cd: orfeo C834 118Y*

✓ bayreuth
✓ 29 july
1951
	bayreuth
	festival
	orchestra
	and chorus
	schwarzkopf,
	höngen,
	hopf,
	edelmann
		lp: hmv ALP 1286-1287
		lp: hmv (france) FALP 381-382/
		    FALP 30048-30049/COLH 78-79/
		    UVT 3048-3049
		lp: hmv (italy) QALP 10116-10117
		lp: electrola E 90115-90116/
		    WALP 1286-1287/EBE 600 000/
		    STE 90115-90116/SMVP 3048-3049/
		    SME 90115-90116
		lp: victor LM 6043
		lp: angel 4003/6068
		lp: emi RLS 727/1C147 00811-00812/
		    1C149 53432-53439M/
		    2C151 53678-53679/
		    2C153 00811-00812/
		    2C153 52540-52551/
		    3C153 00811-00812
		cd: emi CDC 747 0812/CDH 769 0812/
		    CHS 763 6062/CDM 566 9012
		last movement
		lp: electrola E 80005/WALP 1508/
		    WCLP 1508/SME 80005
		cd: orfeo C754 081B

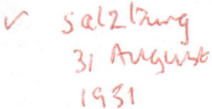

✓ salzburg
31 August
1951

cd: orfeo C533 0018

symphony no 9/continued

✓ vienna 3 february 1952	vpo singakademie güden, anday, patzak, poell	lp: rococo 2109 cd: refrain (japan) DR 91 0003 *cd: orfeo C834 119 Y*
✓ vienna 31 may 1953	vpo singakademie seeefried, anday, dermota, schöffler	lp: discocorp RR 460 lp: nippon columbia OZ 7588 lp: german furtwängler society F669.056-F669.057 cd: rodolphe RPC 32465 cd: arkadia CD 532/CDHP 532 cd: nuova era 013.6301/013.6300 cd: virtuoso 269.7202 cd: dg 435 3252/435 3212 *cd: music and arts CD 942* also issued on cd in japan by seven seas; arkadia and dg editions incorrectly dated 30 may 1953; both arkadia editions name different/incorrect soprano soloists *cd: orfeo C834 118 Y*
✓ bayreuth 8 august 1954	bayreuth festival orchestra and chorus brouwenstijn, malaniuk, windgassen, weber	lp: tanaka AT 07-08 cd: refrain (japan) DR 92 0033 rehearsal performance of third and fourth movements only

symphony no 9/concluded

bayreuth
9 august
1954

bayreuth
festival
orchestra
and chorus
brouwenstijn,
malaniuk,
windgassen,
weber

lp: private issue (japan) W 16
cd: refrain DR 91 0016

lucerne
22 august
1954

philharmonia
lucerne
festival
chorus
schwarzkopf,
cavelti,
haefliger,
edelmann

lp: private issue (japan)
    MF 18862-18863
lp: cetra LO 530
lp: discocorp RR 390
cd: arkadia CDLSMH 34006
cd: rodolphe RPC 32522-32524
cd: music and arts CD 790
cd: tahra FURT 1003
also issued on cd in japan by seven seas
last movement
cd: relief CR 1882
excerpt from last movement
lp: french furtwängler society SWF 7701

piano concerto no 1

✓ lucerne	lucerne	lp: rococo 2106
27 august	festival	lp: french furtwängler society SWF 7401
1947	orchestra	lp: private issue (japan) JPL 1006
	aeschbacher	lp: discocorp RR 205/RR 438
		lp: nippon columbia OZ 7595
		cd: french furtwängler society
		SWF 961-962
		cd: dante LYS 199
		cd: elaborations (japan) ELA 906
		cd: music and arts CD 839/CD 1018
		cd: history 20.3090/20.3094
		cd: tahra FURT 1028-1029

piano concerto no 4

berlin	bpo	lp: unicorn UNI 106
31 october-	hansen	lp: french furtwängler society
3 november		SWF 7005R
1943		lp: nippon columbia DXM 104
		lp: dg 2535 807
		lp: emi 3C153 53010-53016M
		lp: melodiya M10 46067 003
		cd: melodiya MEL 10 00711
		cd: russian compact disc RCD 25002
		cd: french furtwängler society SWF 941
		cd: arkadia CDWFE 365
		cd: music and arts CD 839
		cd: tahra FURT 1034-1039/
		FURT 1034-1035
		also issued in japan on cd by dg and
		on lp and cd by toshiba
rome	rai roma	lp: discocorp RR 441
19 january	orchestra	lp: cetra FE 2
1952	scarpini	lp: nippon columbia OZ 7595
		cd: as-disc AS 373

piano concerto no 5 "emperor"

| london
19-20
february
1951 | philharmonia
fischer | 78: hmv DB 21315-21319/
    DB 9661-9665 auto
lp: hmv ALP 1051/HLM 7027
lp: hmv (france) FALP 121/
    FALP 30034/UVT 3034
lp: hmv (italy) QALP 10024
lp: electrola E 90048/WALP 1051/
    EBE 600 000/STE 90048/
    SME 90048/SMVP 8039
lp: columbia (austria) VALP 536
lp: victor LHMV 4
lp: eterna 820 031
lp: turnabout THS 65072
lp: emi 1C027 00803M/1C045 50023/
    1C047 00803M/29 00013/
    29 00021/2C153 52540-52551/
    3C153 53800-53805M
cd: emi CDH 761 0052 |

grosse fuge, arranged by weingartner

| berlin
10 february
1952 | bpo | lp: dg LPM 18 859/88 023/2535 813
issued on cd by dg in japan only |
| salzburg
30 august
1954 | vpo | lp: discocorp RR 520
lp: nippon columbia OZ 7584
lp: cetra FE 40
cd: virtuoso 269.7322
cd: arkadia CDWFE 363
cd: as-disc AS 373
cd: music and arts CD 520
cd: dg 435 3242/435 3212 |

violin concerto

berlin	bpo	lp: melodiya M10 40929-40930
9-12	röhn	lp: french furtwängler society SWF 7901
january		lp: discocorp IGI 364
1944		cd: as-disc AS 331-332
		cd: melodiya MEL 10 00716
		cd: russian compact disc RCD 25007
		cd: history 20.3090/20.3095
		cd: dg 427 7802/427 7732
		also issued by toshiba in japan

lucerne	lucerne	78: hmv DB 6574-6579/
28-29	festival	DB 9198-9203 auto
august	orchestra	lp: emi 1C027 01570M/
1947	menuhin	3C153 53800-53805M
		lp: french furtwängler society
		2C051 1570
		lp: private issue (japan) JP 1114
		cd: dante LYS 249
		cd: music and arts CD 1018
		cd: testament SBT 1109

cd: history 20.3090

violin concerto/concluded

berlin 30 september 1947	bpo menuhin	lp: cetra FE 1 cd: cetra CDE 1013 cd: german furtwängler society TMK 08080 cd: music and arts CD 708 cd: *tahra FURT 1020*

london
7-8
april
1953
	philharmonia
	menuhin
		lp: hmv ALP 1100
		lp: hmv (france) FALP 314/
		    FALP 30041/UVT 3041
		lp: hmv (italy) QALP 10056
		lp: electrola E 90065/WALP 1100/
		    EBE 600 000/STE 90065/
		    SME 90065/SMVP 8050
		lp: columbia (austria) VALP 537
		lp: eterna 820 547
		lp: victor LHMV 1061
		lp: angel 60135
		lp: emi 1C047 00117M/
		    2C153 52540-52551/
		    3C153 53800-53805M
		cd: movimento musica 051.052
		cd: emi CDC 747 1192/CDH 769 7992/
		    CDM 566 9752

berlin 18 may 1953	bpo schneiderhan	lp: dg LPM 18 855/KL 27-31/88 024/ 2535 809/2730 005 cd: amadeo 431 3452/431 3432 also issued on cd in japan by dg

violin romance no 1

| london
9 april
1953 | philharmonia
menuhin | 45: electrola E 41131/E 41686/
   E 50513/7ERW 5371/7EGW 8597/
   7EGW 8751
lp: hmv ALP 1135/HLM 7015
lp: hmv (france) FALP 312/FBLP 25051
lp: hmv (italy) QALP 10071
lp: electrola E 90074/WALP 1135
lp: angel 60135
lp: angel (argentina) LPC 11582
lp: emi 2C153 52540-52551/
   3C153 53800-53805M
cd: testament SBT 1109 |

violin romance no 2

| london
9 april
1953 | philharmonia
menuhin | 45: electrola E 41686/E 50513/
   7ERW 5371/7EGW 8751
lp: hmv ALP 1135/HLM 7015
lp: hmv (france) FALP 312/FBLP 25051
lp: hmv (italy) QALP 10071
lp: electrola E 90074/WALP 1135
lp: angel (argentina) LPC 11582
lp: emi 2C153 52540-52551/
   3C153 53800-53805M
cd: testament SBT 1109 |

coriolan overture

✓ berlin
27-30
june
1943
	bpo	lp: melodiya D 09867-09868/
		    M10 09867 006
		lp: french furtwängler society SWF 7002
		lp: nippon columbia DXM 103
		lp: discocorp SID 713
		lp: emi 3C153 53810-53816M
		cd: dg 427 7802/427 7732/
		    453 8042/453 7002
		cd: melodiya MEL 10 00718
		cd: russian compact disc RCD 25009
		cd: history 20.3090/20.3095
		cd: grammofono AB 78502
		cd: dante LYS 064
		cd: music and arts CD 826/CD 942
		cd: tahra FURT 1004-1007
		also issued by toshiba in japan:
		concluding pizzicato chords missing
		on original copy tape but restored
		(electronically) on later issues

vienna 25 november 1947	vpo	78: hmv DB 6625 78: victor 11-8036 lp: hmv (france) FBLP 25113 lp: unicorn WFS 9 lp: emi 1C149 53432-53439M/ 1C047 00843M/2C153 52540-52551 cd: dante LYS 249 cd: emi CHS 565 5132
munich 29 october 1951	vpo	lp: decca ECM 684/592.110 cd: nuova era 013.6313/013.6300 cd: elaborations (japan) ELA 906 cd: french furtwängler society SWF 892

egmont overture

berlin 1933	bpo	78: grammophon 67055 78: brunswick 90250 78: decca CA 8170 45: dg EPL 30 540 lp: dg 2535 827 lp: private issue (japan) JP 110-112 cd: symposium 1043 cd: grammofono AB 78574 cd: dante LYS 074 cd: history 20.3090/20.3093 cd: dg 453 7002/453 8042 cd: koch 3-7059-2

berlin
27 may
1947
	bpo	lp: dg LPM 18 724/LPM 18 859/
		    88 008/004 279/2535 810/
		    2721 202/2730 005/2740 260
		cd: nuova era 013.6313/013.6300
		cd: dg 439 8322

munich 4 september 1953	vpo	lp: cetra FE 50 lp: tanaka AT 04/AT 07-08 cd: rodolphe RPC 32522-32524 cd: french furtwängler society SWF 892 cd: melodram CDM 25009 cd: elaborations (japan) ELA 906 cd: music and arts CD 792 AT 04 and CDM 25009 incorrectly described as vienna 24 september 1948 cd: tahra FURT 1091

fidelio

salzburg 3 august 1948	vpo vienna opera chorus schlüter, della casa, schock, patzak, alsen, frantz, edelmann	lp: rococo 1012 cd: melodram CDM 25009 excerpts lp: tanaka AT 07-08 cd: german furtwängler society TMK 10670 nos. 5-8 missing from this recording
salzburg 5 august 1950	vpo vienna opera chorus flagstad, schwarzkopf, dermota, patzak, braun, schöffler, greindl	lp: morgan MOR 5001 lp: mrf records MRF 50 lp: bjr records BJR 112 lp: discocorp IGI 328 lp: cetra FE 44 lp: cls records AMDRL 32819 cd: arkadia CDWFE 304/CDWFE 354 cd: verona 27044-27045 cd: emi CHS 764 9012 excerpts cd: priceless D 16395 excerpts also issued on cd in japan by palette; many issues of this version were dated 22 august 1950, which is probably date on which the recording was broadcast
vienna 12 october 1953	vpo vienna opera chorus mödl, jurinac, schock, windgassen, poell, frick, edelmann	lp: replica RPL 2439-2441 lp: cetra FE 8-10 cd: cetra CDC 12 cd: priceless D 20902 cd: rodolphe RPC 32494 cd: virtuoso 269.7272 excerpts cd: nuova era 013.6300 cd: virtuoso 269.7182

fidelio/concluded

vienna	vpo	lp: hmv ALP 1130-1132/
13-17	vienna	HQM 1109-1110
october	opera chorus	lp: hmv (france) FALP 323-325
1953	mödl,	lp: hmv (italy) QALP 10061-10063
	jurinac,	lp: electrola E 90071-90073/
	schock,	WALP 1130-1132
	windgassen,	lp: victor LHMV 700
	poell,	lp: angel 6022
	frick,	lp: emi 1C147 01105-01107M/
	edelmann	2C153 01105-01107

cd: emi CHS 4962
<u>excerpts</u>
45: hmv 7ER 5036/7ER 5065/7ER 5137
45: hmv (italy) 7ERQ 123
45: electrola E 50042/E 50048/
    7ERW 5036/7ERW 5393
lp: hmv (italy) QALP 10298
lp: hmv (france) FBLP 25113
lp: electrola E 80038/WCLP 600/
    E 60655/WDLP 662/SMVP 8029
lp: melodiya D 033275-033276
lp: world records SH 375
lp: emi XLP 30090/1C047 00832M/
    1C047 00843M/
    1C149 03584-03586M/
    1C149 53432-53439M/
    3C153 53800-53805M
cd: emi CDM 565 9172/CMS 565 9152
<u>HQM 1109-1110 omitted performance</u>
<u>of leonore no 3 overture</u>

fidelio, excerpt (ha welch ein augenblick!)

vienna	vpo	lp: ed smith UORC 242
7 january	vienna	
1942	opera chorus	
	hotter	

leonore no 2 overture

✓ hamburg 9 june 1947	philharmonisches staatsorchester	lp: discocorp RR 511 lp: cetra FE 48 lp: french furtwängler society SWF 8602 cd: nuova era 013.6303/013.6300 cd: french furtwängler society SWF 921-922 cd: elaborations (japan) ELA 906 *cd: music and arts CD 869* *cd: tahra FURT 1091*
berlin 18 october 1949	bpo	lp: DG LPM 18 742/LPM 18 859/ 88 008/2535 807/2730 005 lp: melodiya D 26585-26586 issued on cd in japan only by dg
bremen 11 june 1950	bpo	rehearsal performance lp: tanaka AT 07-08 rehearsal extract lp: french furtwängler society SWF 8602 lp: private issue (japan) GMV 10S lp: tanaka AT 07-08 cd: refrain (japan) DR 92 0031 cd: french furtwängler society SWF 921-922

berlin
4-5
april
1954
	bpo	lp: hmv ALP 1324
		lp: electrola E 90132/WALP 1324/
		    E 70362/WBLP 546/
		    E 70421/WBLP 563
		lp: unicorn WFS 4
		lp: emi 1C149 53432-53439M/
		    1C047 00843M/
		    2C153 52540-52551/
		    3C153 53800-53805M
		cd: emi CHS 565 5132

telefunken recording of the overture scheduled with vpo on 17 october
1944 , and noted in vpo archives, appears not to have taken place

leonore no 3 overture

vienna 2 june 1944	vpo	lp: french furtwängler society SWF 7101 lp: private issue (japan) JP 1190-1192 lp: discocorp RR 460 lp: nippon columbia OZ 7512 cd: rodolphe RPC 32522-32524 cd: dg 435 3242/435 3212 cd: french furtwängler society SWF 901 cd: dante LYS 063 cd: history 20.3090/20.395 *cd: preiser 90251* *cd: music and arts CD 942* many issues incorrectly dated 2 may 1944 or 28 january 1945
lucerne 27 august 1947	lucerne festival orchestra	lp: tanaka AT 04 cd: french furtwängler society SWF 961-962 cd: music and arts CD 1018 *cd: tahra FURT 1028-1029*

leonore no 3 overture/concluded

stockholm 12 november 1948	stockholm po	lp: french furtwängler society SWF 7101 lp: unicorn WFS 5 lp: emi 1C053 93533M/3C053 93533M/ 3C153 53810-53816M cd: rodolphe RPC 32522-32524 cd: bis BISCD 424A cd: emi CMS 565 9152 *cd: music and arts CD 793* <u>rehearsal sequence</u>
stockholm 13 november 1948	stockholm po	lp: unicorn WFS 5 lp: emi 1C053 93533M/3C053 93533M/ 3C153 53810-53816M cd: dante LYS 197 <u>also issued in japan by toshiba</u>
amsterdam 13 july 1950	concertgebouw orchestra	lp: private issue (japan) JP 1199-1200 lp: tanaka AT 09-10 cd: refrain (japan) DR 92 0033 cd: music and arts WFSA 2001/CD 824 *cd: tahra FURT 1012-1013*
turin 3 march 1952	rai torino orchestra	lp: cetra FE 48 <u>issued on cd only in japan by seven seas</u>

<u>additional versions of this overture included in the complete recordings of fidelio listed previously</u>

cavatina from string quartet no 13, version for string orchestra

berlin   bpo   78: telefunken SK 3104
15 october   45: telefunken UV 115
1940   lp: telefunken LS 6025
                                    lp: capitol (usa) H 8130
                                    lp: rococo 2013
                                    lp: private issue (japan) JP 1101-1102
                                    lp: tanaka AT 07-08
                                    lp: french furtwängler society SWF 7702
                                    cd: french furtwängler society SWF 901
                                    cd: teldec 9031 764352
                                    cd: music and arts CD 954
                                    cd: tahra FURT 1012-1013

HECTOR BERLIOZ (1803-1869)

la damnation de faust

lucerne 26 august 1950	lucerne festival orchestra and chorus schwarzkopf, vroons, hotter, pernerstorfer sung in german	lp: cetra FE 21 cd: eklipse EKR 60

marche hongroise/la damnation de faust

berlin 1930	bpo	78: grammophon 95411 78: fonit 91025 78: decca CA 8054 78: polydor (japan) S 4040 lp: dg 88 021 *cd: koch 3-7073-2* also issued on cd in japan by dg
vienna 31 march 1949	vpo	lp: emi 1C149 03584-03586M *cd: emi CHS 566 7702* unpublished hmv 78rpm recording

BORIS BLACHER (1903-1975)

concertante musik

berlin	bpo	lp: cetra FE 26
27 april		cd: as-disc AS 370
1954		

JOHANNES BRAHMS (1833-1897)

symphony no 1

berlin
✓23 january
1945
	bpo	lp: french furtwängler society
		    SWF 8801-8803
		lp: tanaka AT 13-14
		cd: refrain (japan) DR 91 0004
		cd: french furtwängler society
		    SWF 951-952
		cd: music and arts CD 805/CD 941
		cd: dante LYS 048/LYS 205
		cd: tahra FURT 1004-1007
		only the last movement survives
		in this recording

salzburg 13 august 1947	vpo	cd: refrain (japan) DR 92 0022
lucerne 27 august 1947	lucerne festival orchestra	lp: french furtwängler society SWF 7601 lp: discocorp RR 393 lp: nippon columbia OZ 7597 cd: french furtwängler society SWF 971-972 cd: dante LYS 209-210 cd: music and arts CD 804/CD 1018 *cd: tahra FURT 1028-1029*

symphony no 1/continued

vienna
17-20
november
1947
	vpo	78: hmv DB 6634-6639/
		    DB 9220-9224 auto
		lp: hmv (france) COLH 97
		lp: electrola E 90992/WALP 545
		lp: unicorn WFS 6
		lp: emi 1C147 50336-50339M/
		    1C149 53420-53426/1C027 01145M/
		    2C153 53420-53426/
		    3C153 53661-53669M
		cd: dante LYS 205
		cd: testament SBT 1142
		cd: history 20. 3090

amsterdam 13 july 1950	concertgebouw orchestra	lp: private issue (japan) JP 1199-1200 cd: music and arts CD 289 cd: refrain (japan) DR 92 0033 *cd: tahra FURT 1012-1013* also issued on cd in japan by seven seas
hamburg 27 october 1951	ndr orchestra	lp: french furtwängler society SWF 8201-8202 lp: victor/jvc (japan) RCL 3335 cd: french furtwängler society SWF 881 cd: nuova era 013.6332-6334 cd: music and arts CD 941 *cd: tahra FURT 1001*

symphony no 1/concluded

vienna 27 january 1952	vpo	lp: emi ED 27 01241 cd: history 20.3090/20.3094 cd: emi CZS 252 3212/CHS 565 5132 also issued in japan by toshiba, palette and flowers: CZS 252 3212 and 20.3090/20.3094 incorrectly dated november 1947
berlin 10 february 1952	bpo	lp: dg 2535 162/2721 202 cd: virtuoso 269.9072 cd: dg 415 6622/415 4022/439 8322
turin 7 march 1952	rai torino orchestra	lp: rococo 2017
berlin 18 may 1953	bpo	lp: discocorp RR 418 lp: everest SDBR 3437 lp: nippon columbia OW 7820 lp: cetra FE 13 cd: elaborations (japan) ELA 902 cd: german furtwängler society TMK 05294
caracas 21 march 1954	venezuela so	lp: furtwängler society FURT 101 cd: furtwängler society FURT 102 awaiting re-issue by french furtwängler society

symphony no 2

vienna 28 january 1945	vpo	lp: french furtwängler society SWF 7301 lp: discocorp SID 713/RR 418 lp: olympic OL 8141 lp: private issue (japan) JP 1128-1129 lp: nippon columbia OW 7821 cd: nuova era 013.6322-6324 cd: french furtwängler society SWF 902 cd: dg 435 3242/435 3212 cd: dante LYS 047 cd: music and arts CD 804/*CD 941* issued in japan by toshiba and dg
berlin 14 september 1947	bpo	*cd: tahra FURT 1008-1011* rehearsal of second movement
london 22-25 march 1948	lpo	78: decca K 1875-1879/ AK 1875-1879 auto 78: london (usa) LA 189 lp: decca LXT 2586/ACL 50/592.109 lp: london (usa) LLP 28/B 19020 cd: dante LYS 204 cd: dutton awaiting publication also issued on cd in japan by seven seas and wing: wing edition claimed to contain an alternative take of the opening of second movement

munich
7 may
1952
	bpo	lp: emi 1C147 50336-50339M/
		    1C149 53420-53426M/
		    1C049 01532M/2C153 53420-53426/
		    3C153 53661-53669M
		cd: virtuoso 269.9072
		cd: emi CZS 252 3212/*CHS 565 5132*

symphony no 3

berlin
18 december
1949
	bpo	lp: hmv (france) FALP 543
		lp: electrola E 90994/WALP 547
		lp: unicorn WFS 4
		lp: emi 1C147 50336-50339M/
		    1C149 53420-53426/1C027 01146M/
		    2C153 53420-53426/
		    3C153 53661-53669M
		cd: virtuoso 269.9072
		cd: emi CZS 252 3212/*CHS 565 5132*

berlin 27 april 1954	bpo	lp: dg 2535 163 lp: longanesi GCL 05 cd: dg 423 5722 *cd: music and arts CD 941*
turin 14 may 1954	bpo	lp: discocorp RR 418 lp: nippon columbia OW 7822 lp: paragon DSV 52101 cd: nuova era 013.6332-6334 also issued on cd in japan by seven seas

symphony no 4

berlin
12-15
december
1943
	bpo	lp: melodiya D 09867-09868/
		    M10 09867 006
		lp: french furtwängler society SWF 7102R
		lp: nippon columbia DXM 107/OW 7823
		lp: rococo 2013
		lp: discocorp RR 418
		lp: emi 3C153 53661-53669M
		cd: melodiya MEL 10 00722
		cd: russian compact disc RCD 25013
		cd: magic talent MT 48059
		cd: arkadia CDWFE 365
		cd: french furtwängler society
		    SWF 951-952
		cd: grammofono AB 78594
		cd: dante LYS 048
		cd: music and arts CD 804/CD 941
		cd: tahra FURT 1034-1039/
		    FURT 1038-1039
		also issued in japan by toshiba; arkadia
		incorrectly dated 1942

berlin 22 october 1948	bpo	*cd: tahra FURT 1025*

symphony no 4/concluded

berlin	bpo	lp: hmv (france) FALP 544

berlin   bpo   lp: hmv (france) FALP 544
24 october   lp: hmv (spain) LXLP 121
1948   lp: electrola E 90995/WALP 548
                             lp: unicorn WFS 1
                             lp: emi 1C147 50336-50339M/
                                   1C149 53420-53426/1C047 01147M/
                                   2C153 53420-53426/
                                   3C153 53661-53669M
                             cd: as-disc AS 331-332
                             cd: virtuoso 269.9072
                             cd: refrain (japan) DR 91 0004
                             cd: emi CZS 252 3212/*CHS 565 5132*
                             as-disc incorrectly dated january 1944;
                             refrain incorrectly dated 22 october
                             1948

london   bpo   vhs video: teldec 4509 950383
2 november   laserdisc: teldec 4509 950386
1948   rehearsal of conclusion of symphony

wiesbaden   bpo   lp: german furtwängler society
10 june   F666.156-F666.157
1949   lp: discocorp RR 394
                             lp: nippon columbia OZ 7598-7599
                             cd: dante LYS 206
                             cd: elaborations (japan) ELA 903
                             cd: *tahra FURT 1021-1022*
                             also issued on cd in japan by seven seas

salzburg   vpo   cd: music and arts CD 258
15 august   cd: nuova era 013.6332-6334
1950

piano concerto no 2

✓ berlin
8 november
1942
	bpo
	fischer
		lp: melodiya D 09883-09884
		lp: unicorn UNI 102
		lp: french furtwängler society SWF 6901
		lp: nippon columbia DXM 108
		lp: emi 1C149 53420-53426/29 09701/
		    2C153 53420-53426/
		    3C153 53661-53669M
		cd: dg 427 7782/427 7732
		cd: priceless D 14236
		cd: melodiya MEL 10 00724
		cd: russian compact disc RCD 25015
		cd: dante LYS 046
		cd: music and arts CD 804
		cd: testament awaiting publication

berlin
✓ 12-15
december
1943
	bpo
	aeschbacher
		lp: melodiya M10 45921 009
		lp: french furtwängler society SWF 8502
		cd: french furtwängler society
		    SWF 951-952
		cd: music and arts CD 941
		cd: dante LYS 049
		cd: tahra FURT 1004-1007/
		    FURT 1034-1039/*FURT 1038-1039*

violin concerto

lucerne	lucerne	78: hmv DB 21000-21004/
29-31	festival	DB 9444-9448 auto
august	orchestra	78: victor DM 1361
1949	menuhin	45: victor WDM 1361
		lp: hmv (france) FALP 122/FALP 30001
		lp: electrola E 90013/WALP 524
		lp: victor LM 1142
		lp: emi HLM 7015/1C047 01239M/
		1C149 53420-53426/2C051 01239M/
		2C153 53420-53426/
		3C153 53661-53669M
		cd: movimento musica 051.052
		cd: emi CZS 252 3212/*CDH 763 4962*
		<u>some editions incorrectly dated</u>
		<u>7 october 1949</u>
turin	rai torino	lp: rococo 2027
7 march	orchestra	lp: nippon columbia DXM 159/OW 7819
1952	de vito	lp: discocorp RR 510
		lp: cetra FE 3
		cd: refrain (japan) MADR 204
		cd: music and arts CD 804
		<u>also issued on cd in japan by seven seas</u>

double concerto

lucerne 24 august 1949	lucerne festival orchestra schneiderhan, mainardi	lp: private issue (japan) W 19 cd: as-disc AS 372 cd: *music and arts CD 1018* also issued on cd in japan by palette

vienna
27 january
1952
	vpo
	boskovsky,
	brabec
		lp: emi 1C149 53420-53426/
		    2C153 53420-53426/
		    3C153 53661-53669M
		lp: cetra FE 16
		cd: curcio CON 05
		cd: emi CZS 252 3212/*CDH 763 4962*

hungarian dance no 1 in g minor

berlin   bpo   78: grammophon 90190
1930   78: brunswick 85034
                               78: decca DE 7006
                               lp: dg 88 021
                               lp: melodiya D 030275-030276
                               cd: symposium 1043
                               cd: dante LYS 204
                               cd: *koch 3-7073-2*

vienna   vpo   78: hmv DB 6976/DB 9729
4 april   78: hmv (australia) ED 1233
1949   45: victor EHA 17
                               lp: unicorn WFS 1
                               lp: emi 1C149 03584-03586M/
                                   1C149 53420-53426/
                                   2C153 53420-53426/
                                   3C153 53661-53669M
                               cd: dante LYS 204
                               cd: emi CZS 252 3212/*CHS 565 5132*

hungarian dance no 3 in f

vienna   vpo   78: hmv DB 6943/DB 9402
4 april   lp: unicorn WFS 1
1949   lp: emi 1C149 03584-03586/
                                   1C149 53420-53426/
                                   2C153 53420-53426/
                                   3C153 53661-53669M
                               cd: dante LYS 204
                               cd: emi CZS 252 3212/*CHS 565 5132*

hungarian dance no 10 in e

berlin   bpo   78: grammophon 90190
1930   78: brunswick 85034
                              78: decca DE 7006
                              lp: dg 88 021
                              lp: melodiya D 030275-030276
                              cd: symposium 1043
                              cd: dante LYS 204
                              cd: koch 3-7073-2

vienna   vpo   78: hmv DB 6943/DB 9402
4 april   45: victor EHA 17
1949   lp: unicorn WFS 1
                              lp: emi 1C149 03584-03586/
                                      1C149 53420-53426/
                                      2C153 53420-53426/
                                      3C153 53661-53669M
                              cd: dante LYS 204
                              cd: emi CZS 252 3212/*CHS 565 5132*

ein deutsches requiem

lucerne 20 august 1947	lucerne festival orchestra and chorus schwarzkopf, hotter	lp: private issue (japan) W 24 cd: wing (japan) WCD 1-2 cd: french furtwängler society SWF 971-972 <u>second movement</u> lp: private issue (japan) W 22-23 <u>final 2 bars of the work missing:</u> <u>SWF 971-972 gives this both in its</u> <u>original state and also with the</u> <u>identical bars added from the close</u> <u>of the first movement</u>
stockholm 19 november 1948	stockholm po and chorus lindberg-torlind sonnerstedt	lp: unicorn WFS 17-18 lp: orfeus (sweden) 1-73-4/5 lp: emi 1C187 93534-93535M/ 3C153 93534-93535M cd: dante LYS 209-210 cd: emi CZS 252 3212 cd: *music and arts CD 289*
vienna 25 january 1951	vpo singakademie seefried, fischer-dieskau	lp: tanaka AT 01-02 cd: refrain (japan) DR 92 0021 <u>section of sixth movement taken</u> <u>from a performance not conducted</u> <u>by furtwängler</u>

haydn variations

✓ berlin 12-15 december 1943	bpo	lp: melodiya D 010851-010854/ 　　　M10 10851 009 lp: unicorn UNI 100-101 lp: everest SDBR 3252 lp: nippon columbia DXM 104/OS 7076 lp: french furtwängler society 　　　SWF 8203-8204 lp: emi 3C153 53661-53669M cd: priceless D 14236 cd: melodiya MEL 10 00722 cd: russian compact disc RCD 25013 cd: magic talent MT 48059 cd: grammofono AB 78594 cd: dante LYS 049 cd: music and arts CD 805/CD 941 cd: tahra FURT 1034-1039/ 　　　*FURT 1038-1039* also issued in japan by toshiba, palette and seven seas

cds history 20. 3090

vienna 18-23 december 1943	vpo	lp: french furtwängler society SWF 7602 lp: discocorp RR 456 lp: emi ED 29 06661 cd: music and arts CD 804/CD 954 cd: dante LYS 046/LYS 047 *cd: preiser 90199* *cd: tahra FURT 1012-1013* previously unpublished electrola 78 rpm recording; SWF 7602 and FURT 1012/3 contain additional rejected 78rpm takes; CD 804 incorrectly described as berlin 12-15 december 1943; also issued by toshiba in japan

haydn variations/continued

vienna
30 march-
2 april
1949
	vpo	78: hmv DB 6932-6934/
		    DB 9402-9404 auto
		45: victor WHMV 1010
		lp: hmv ALP 1011
		lp: hmv (france) FALP 188
		lp: hmv (italy) QALP 188
		lp: electrola E 90025/WALP 1011/
		    E 70420/WBLP 558
		lp: columbia (austria) VALP 505
		lp: victor LHMV 1010
		lp: emi 1C047 01415M/
		    3C153 53661-53669M
		cd: flowers (japan) BL 024
		cd: dante LYS 206
		cd: emi CZS 252 3212/CHS 565 5132
		CZS 252 3212 and BL 024 incorrectly
		dated 27 january 1952

berlin 20 june 1950	bpo	lp: dg 2535 164 lp: cetra FE 16 cd: dg 415 6622/427 4022 cd: virtuoso 269.9072 also issued on cd in japan by dg and seven seas
hamburg 27 october 1951	ndr orchestra	lp: french furtwängler society SWF 8201-8202 lp: tanaka AT 01-02 cd: as-disc AS 113 cd: french furtwängler society SWF 881 cd: nuova era 013.6332-6334 cd: music and arts CD 941 cd: tahra FURT 1001

haydn variations/concluded

vienna	vpo	lp: emi 1C149 53420-53426M/
27 january		2C153 53420-53426/
1952		3C153 53661-53669M
		cd: *testament SBT 1142*
		also issued in japan by toshiba

paris	bpo	lp: cetra LO 519/FE 45
4 may		cd: curcio CON 14
1954		cd: french furtwängler society
		SWF 942-943
		cd: elaborations (japan) ELA 902
		also issued on cd in japan by seven seas

ANTON BRUCKNER (1824-1896)

symphony no 4 "romantic"

berlin	bpo	lp: tanaka AT 11-12
14-16		acetate recording with gaps in music;
december		last movement incomplete
1941		

stuttgart	vpo	lp: dg 2740 201
22 october		lp: discocorp RR 557
1951		cd: dg 415 6642/427 4032/445 4152

munich   vpo

✓ 29 october

1951

lp: decca ECM 685
cd: priceless D 14228
cd: virtuoso 269.7372
cd: music and arts CD 796
also issued on cd in japan by
palette and seven seas

cd: tahra FURT 1092

symphony no 5

berlin   bpo
25-28
october
1942

lp: melodiya M10 42555-42558
lp: discocorp RR 538
lp: french furtwängler society
  SWF 8203-8204
lp: nippon columbia OZ 7600
cd: bella musica BMF 967
cd: melodiya MEL 10 00714
cd: russian compact disc RCD 25005
cd: dg 427 7742/427 7732
cd: dante LYS 108
cd: music and arts CD 538

salzburg vpo
19 august
1951

lp: rococo 2034
lp: discocorp RR 314/RR 508
lp: german furtwängler society
  F667.497-F667.489M
lp: cetra FE 42
cd: virtuoso 269.7342
cd: arkadia CDWFE 360
cd: emi CDH 565 7502
also issued on cd in japan by seven seas

symphony no 6

berlin   bpo
13-16
november
1943

lp: melodiya M10 47465 005
lp: french furtwängler society
  SWF 8801-8803
lp: private issue (japan) W 28-29
cd: melodiya MEL 10 00720
cd: russian compact disc RCD 25011
cd: dante LYS 106-107
cd: music and arts CD 805
cd: french furtwängler society SWF 963
cd: emi CHS 566 2102
cd: tahra FURT 1004-1007
first movement is missing from
this recording

symphony no 7

berlin 2-4 february 1941	bpo	lp: tanaka AT 11-12 acetate recording with gaps in music; last movement missing
berlin 7 april 1942	bpo	78: telefunken SK 3230-3231 78: ultraphon 922264-922266 lp: rococo 2014 lp: private issue (japan) JP 1101-1102 lp: tanaka AT 11-12 lp: discocorp RR 457 lp: french furtwängler society SWF 7702/SWF 8801-8803 cd: teldec 9031 764352 cd: french furtwängler society SWF 963 cd: dante LYS 106-107 cd: music and arts CD 954 cd: tahra FURT 1004-1007 this recording comprises adagio movement only

berlin
18 october
1949
	bpo	lp: hmv (france) FALP 852-853
		lp: electrola STE 91375-91378/
		    SMVP 8055-8056
		lp: emi HQM 1169/F666.700/
		    1C147 29229-29230
		cd: dante LYS 214
		cd: emi CHS 566 2062

cairo 23 april 1951	bpo	lp: dg 2535 161/2721 202/ 2740 201/2740 260 cd: dg 439 8372/445 4182 cd: music and arts CD 698
rome 1 may 1951	bpo	lp: rococo 2105 lp: discocorp RR 416 lp: nippon columbia OZ 7601 lp: cetra FE 42 cd: arkadia CDWFE 362 cd: music and arts CD 698 also issued on cd in japan by seven seas

symphony no 8

vienna 17 october 1944	vpo	lp: unicorn UNI 109-110 lp: nippon columbia DXM 110-111 lp: dg 2740 201 cd: dante LYS 106-107 cd: grammofono AB 78696-78697 cd: *music and arts CD 764* cd: *dg 445 4152* also issued in japan by toshiba

berlin
14-15
march
1949
	bpo	lp: hmv (france) FALP 850-851
		lp: electrola STE 91375-91378/
		    SMVP 8057-8058
		lp: emi 1C147 29231-29232
		cd: dante LYS 244
		also issued in japan by toshiba
		
		14 march only
		cd: *testament SBT 1143*
		
		15 march only
		lp: rococo 2032
		lp: discocorp RR 457
		lp: nippon columbia OS 7091-7092
		cd: arkadia CDWFE 356
		cd: palladio PD 4135
		cd: german furtwängler society
		    MMS 9103
		cd: originals SH 854
		cd: dante LYS 245
		cd: evangel (japan) FRL 1001
		cd: music and arts CD 624
		cd: *emi CHS 566 2102*

vienna 10 april 1954	vpo	lp: cetra FE 17 cd: arkadia CDWFE 355 cd: emblem (usa) EF 4005-4006

symphony no 9

berlin	bpo	lp: dg KL 27-31/LPM 18 854/
7 october		88 019/2730 005/2740 201
1944		lp: eterna 820 380
		cd: music and arts CD 730
		cd: dante LYS 110
		cd: grammofono AB 78696-78697
		cd: dg 445 4182

JOSE MARIA CASTRO (1892-1964)

obertura para una opera comica

buenos aires	teatro colon	lp: tanaka AT 09-10
5 may	orchestra	cd: refrain (japan) DR 92 0032
1950		

LUIGI CHERUBINI (1760-1842)

anacréon overture

vienna	vpo	78: hmv DB 21493
11 january		78: hmv (argentina) 266601
1951		lp: hmv ALP 1498
		lp: electrola E 90152/WALP 1498/
		E 70361/WBLP 547
		lp: emi 1C149 03584-03586M
		cd: emi CHS 566 7702

CLAUDE DEBUSSY (1862-1918)

nuages et fêtes/nocturnes

rome	bpo	lp: discocorp BWS 708/DIS 708
1 may		lp: cetra FE 15
1951		lp: nippon columbia OZ 7592
		cd: cetra CDE 1044
		cd: music and arts CD 719

ANTONIN DVORAK (1841-1904)

slavonic dance op 46 no 3

berlin	bpo	*cd: tahra FURT 1008-1011*
1930		

WOLFGANG FORTNER (1907-1987)

violin concerto

berlin	bpo	lp: cetra FE 31
19 december	taschner	cd: as-disc AS 370
1949		cd: german furtwängler society
		TMK 12681

CESAR FRANCK (1822-1890)

symphony in d minor

vienna 28 january 1945	vpo	lp: vox PL 7230 lp: melodiya D 021093-021094 lp: french furtwängler society SWF 7302 lp: discocorp RR 403 lp: private issue (japan) JP 1128-1129 cd: french furtwängler society SWF 902 cd: dante LYS 124 cd: arlecchino ARL 140 also issued on cd in japan by dg and seven seas; melodiya catalogue number D 021093-021094 also used for vienna 1953 recording, but both issues were dated 1945
vienna 14-15 december 1953	vpo	lp: decca LXT 2905/ACL 179/ECS 563/ 220.037/592.107/417 2871 lp: london (usa) LL 967/CM 9091/ R 23027 lp: eurodisc KK 70368 lp: melodiya D 021093-021094 lp: nippon columbia DXM 113 cd: decca 417 2872 cd: arlecchino ARL 140 also issued on cd in japan by toshiba and seven seas; melodiya catalogue number D 021093-021094 also used for vienna 1945 recording, but both issues were dated 1945; nippon columbia and seven seas were also incorrectly described as vienna 1945

WILHELM FURTWAENGLER (1886-1954)

symphony no 2

berlin february 1948	bpo	cd: refrain (japan) DR 92 0031 <u>rehearsal extract only from</u> <u>second movement</u>
hamburg 17-18 october 1948	philharmonisches staatsorchester	cd: french furtwängler society SWF 921-922
berlin december 1951	bpo	78: dg LVM 72 159-72 164 lp: dg LPM 18 017-18 018/ LPM 18 114-18 115/2707 086/ 2721 202 lp: private issue (japan) M 2431-2432 cd: dg 439 8372/457 7222
frankfurt 15 december 1952	orchestra of hessischer rundfunk	lp: cetra FE 36 <u>also issued on lp by seven seas; both</u> <u>incorrectly dated 16 december 1952</u>
vienna 22 february 1953	vpo	cd: theatre (japan) 400 3531 cd: orfeo C375 941B
stuttgart 30 march 1954	sdr orchestra	lp: french furtwängler society SWF 8301-8302 cd: mediaphon/sdr JA 75.100

symphonic concerto for piano and orchestra

✓ berlin   bpo   cd: pilz history CD 78004
  19 january   fischer   cd: dante LYS 123
  1939

  berlin   bpo   78: electrola DB 4696-4697
  25 april   fischer   lp: french furtwängler society SWF 7101
  1939   lp: private issue (japan) JP 1101-1102
                                        lp: emi HLM 7027/1C047 01415M
                                        lp: discocorp MLG 74
              adagio only   cd: music and arts CD 954
                                        cd: history 20.3090/20.3093
                                        cd: biddulph WHL 006-007/ *WHL 007*
                                        cd: testament awaiting publication
                                        adagio movement only was recorded:
                                        also issued by toshiba in japan

CHRISTOPH WILLIBALD GLUCK (1714-1787)

alceste overture

✓ berlin 29 october 1942	bpo	78: telefunken SK 3266/T 122/GX 61008 78: capitol (usa) 81001 45: telefunken UV 115 lp: telefunken LS 6025 lp: capitol (usa) H 8130 lp: french furtwängler society SWF 7702 lp: private issue (japan) JP 1101-1102 lp: tanaka AT 09-10 lp: melodiya M10 46683 000 cd: melodiya MEL 10 00724 cd: russian compact disc RCD 25015 cd: history 20.3090/20.3093 cd: dante LYS 117 cd: music and arts CD 954 cd: teldec 9031 764352
berlin 4 september 1951	bpo	cd: german furtwängler society TMK 05294
berlin 5 september 1951	bpo	lp: dg 2535 804 lp: cetra FE 50 lp: tanaka AT 04 cd: refrain (japan) DR 92 0018 cd: elaborations (japan) ELA 903 tanaka, refrain and elaborations incorrectly dated 4 september 1951
vienna 8 march 1954	vpo	lp: emi XLP 30090/1C149 03584-03586 lp: french furtwängler society XPMX 2273 lp: private issue (japan) NA 96 cd: emi CHS 566 7702

iphigenie in aulis overture

frankfurt 15 december 1952	orchestra of hessischer rundfunk	lp: discocorp RR 419 lp: nippon columbia OZ 7512 lp: cetra FE 50 cd: refrain (japan) DR 92 0018 cd: emblem (usa) EF 4004 rehearsal performance; cetra incorrectly dated 16 december
vienna 22 february 1953	vpo	lp: private issue (japan) GMV 10S lp: tanaka AT 09-10 cd: refrain (japan) DR 92 0022 cd: theatre (japan) 400.3531 cd: german furtwängler society TMK 10670
vienna 8 march 1954	vpo	lp: emi XLP 30090/1C149 03584-03586 lp: french furtwängler society XPMX 2273 lp: private issue (japan) NA 96 cd: emi CHS 566 7702

orfeo ed euridice

mjlan 13 april 1951	la scala orchestra and chorus barbieri, güden, gabory	lp: discocorp RR 419 lp: estro armonico EA 022 lp: cetra LO 19/FE 46 lp: turnabout THS 65112-65113 cd: documents LV 933-934 FE 46 incorrectly states that part of orfeo is sung by simionato, who only took part in the performance of 7 april

GEORGE FRIDERIC HANDEL (1685-1759)

concerto grosso op 6 no 5

berlin 13 september 1939	bpo	cd: history 20.3090/20.3093 *cd: tahra FURT 1014-1015*
berlin 27 april 1954	bpo	lp: dg 2535 806 lp: private issue (japan) P 1001 cd: virtuoso 269.7392 issued on cd by dg in japan only

concerto grosso op 6 no 10

berlin 7-8 february 1944	bpo	lp: melodiya M10 46005 000 lp: french furtwängler society SWF 8601 lp: private issue (japan) W 22-23 cd: melodiya MEL 10 00721 cd: russian compact disc RCD 25012 cd: dante LYS 250 cd: dg 427 7772/427 7732
buenos aires 23 april 1950	teatro colon orchestra	lp: tanaka AT 03 cd: refrain (japan) DR 92 0032
berlin 20 june 1950	bpo	lp: dg 2535 806 lp: private issue (japan) P 1001 cd: virtuoso 269.7402 issued on cd by dg in japan only
caracas 20 march 1954	venezuela so	lp: furtwängler society FURT 101 cd: classical society CSCD 116 awaiting re-issue by french furtwängler society

FRANZ JOSEF HAYDN (1732-1809)

symphony no 88

stuttgart 22 october 1951	vpo	lp: french furtwängler society SWF 8501 lp: victor/jvc (japan) RCL 3337 cd: virtuoso 269.7332 cd: french furtwängler society SWF 931 cd: evangel (japan) FRL 1002

berlin
5 december
1951
	bpo	78: dg LVM 72 157-72 158
		lp: dg LPM 18 015/LPM 18 283/
		    LPM 18 725/LPM 18 858/KL 27-31/
		    88 007/478 146/2535 828/
		    2721 202/2730 005/2740 260
		lp: decca (usa) DX 119/OL 9767
		lp: heliodor (usa) H 25073
		cd: dg 415 6612/427 4042/
		    439 8322/447 4392

turin 3 march 1952	rai torino orchestra	lp: discocorp RR 399 lp: nippon columbia OS 7075 cd: as-disc AS 371 cd: historical performers HP 11 cd: music bridge (japan) also issued on cd in japan by seven seas

symphony no 94 "surprise"

stockholm 25 september 1950	vpo	lp: discocorp RR 399 lp: private issue (japan) GC 570234-570235 lp: nippon columbia OS 7075 cd: music bridge (japan) *cd: music and arts CD 802* <u>also issued on cd in japan by seven seas</u>

vienna
11-17
january
1951
	vpo	78: hmv DB 21506-21508
		45: victor WHMV 1018
		lp: hmv ALP 1011
		lp: hmv (france) FALP 188/FBLP 25034
		lp: hmv (italy) QALP 188
		lp: electrola E 90025/WALP 1011/
		    E 91075/WALP 562/STE 91075/
		    SME 91075/SMVP 8053
		lp: columbia (austria) VALP 505
		lp: victor LHMV 1018
		lp: unicorn WFS 11
		lp: emi 1C027 00906M
		cd: emi CHS 566 7702

symphony no 104 "london"

buenos aires 14 april 1950	teatro colon orchestra	lp: tanaka AT 03 cd: refrain (japan) DR 92 0032 cd: music bridge (japan)

PAUL HINDEMITH (1895-1963)

die harmonie der welt

berlin 8 december 1952	bpo	lp: discocorp RR 438 lp: nippon columbia OZ 7593 lp: german furtwängler society F670.027-F670.028 cd: music and arts CD 713
salzburg 30 august 1953	vpo	lp: cetra FE 22 cd: cetra CDE 1049 cd: emi CHS 565 3532 also issued on cd in japan by toshiba

concerto for orchestra

berlin 20 june 1950	bpo	lp: cetra FE 22 lp: nippon columbia OZ 7593 cd: cetra CDE 1049 cd: virtuoso 269.7322 cd: german furtwängler society MMS 9010 cd: music and arts CD 713

symphonic metamorphoses on themes of carl maria von weber

berlin 16 september 1947	bpo	lp: dg LPM 18 857/2535 164 cd: dante LYS 212 issued on cd by dg in japan only

KARL HOELLER (born 1907)

cello concerto no 2

berlin	bpo	lp: cetra FE 31
18 october	hoelscher	cd: originals SH 834
1949		

ARTHUR HONEGGER (1892-1955)

mouvement symphonique no 3

berlin	bpo	lp: cetra FE 15
10 february		cd: cetra CDE 1044
1952		cd: virtuoso 269.7322
		cd: german furtwängler society
		TMK 05294
		cd: music and arts CD 719

FRANZ LISZT (1811-1886)

les préludes

vienna	vpo	lp: hmv ALP 1220/XLP 30106
3 march		lp: hmv (france) FALP 363/FBLP 25024
1954		lp: hmv (italy) QALP 10088
		lp: electrola E 90097/WALP 1220/
		E 60661/WDLP 667/E 80801/
		WCLP 854/SME 80801/
		HZE 105/SHZE 105
		lp: emi F666.702/1C149 03584-03586/
		2C053 01193
		cd: palladio PD 4122
		cd: historical performers HP 14
		cd: emi CHS 566 7702

GUSTAV MAHLER (1860-1911)

lieder eines fahrenden gesellen

salzburg 19 august 1951	vpo fischer-dieskau	lp: cetra LO 510/FE 29 lp: rococo 2105 lp: discocorp IGI 382/RR 314 lp: nippon columbia OZ 7603 lp: german furtwängler society F667.497-F667.498M cd: priceless D 18355 cd: cetra CDE 1045 cd: virtuoso 269.7392 *cd: orfeo C336 931B* also issued on cd in japan by seven seas

london
24-25
june
1952
	philharmonia
	fischer-dieskau
		lp: hmv ALP 1270/XLP 30044
		lp: hmv (france) FALP 392/FALP 30250
		lp: electrola E 90106/WALP 1270/
		    SME 91387/SHZE 338
		lp: angel 35522
		lp: melodiya D 06441-06442
		lp: emi 1C063 00898/100 8981/
		    2C061 01208
		cd: emi CDC 747 6572

vienna 30 november 1952	vpo poell	lp: cetra FE 29

FELIX   MENDELSSOHN-BARTHOLDY   (1809-1847)

violin   concerto

turin 11 march 1952	rai torino orchestra de vito	lp: rococo 2027 lp: nippon columbia DXM 159/OW 7819 lp: discocorp RR 510 lp: cetra FE 35 cd: refrain (japan) MADR 204 <u>also issued on cd in japan by seven seas</u>

berlin
26 may
1952
	bpo
	menuhin
		45: victor WDM 1720
		lp: hmv ALP 1135
		lp: hmv (france) FALP 312/GHLP 1016
		lp: hmv (italy) QALP 10071
		lp: electrola E 90074/WALP 1135/
		    E 60546/WDLP 602/SME 91486/
		    SMVP 8040
		lp: victor LM 1720
		lp: angel (argentina) LPC 11582
		lp: emi 1C047 00907/2C051 03612
		cd: movimento musica 051.052
		cd: emi CDC 747 1192/CDH 769 7992/
		    CDM 566 9752

a midsummer night's dream, overture

berlin 1929	bpo	78: grammophon 66925-66926/ 69206-69207 78: brunswick 90137-90138 lp: dg 88 012/2535 821 cd: dante LYS 116 <u>cd: history 20.3090/20.3093</u> *cd: koch 3-7073-2*
berlin 30 september 1947	bpo	lp: cetra FE 35 cd: german furtwängler society TMK 08080 *cd: tahra FURT 1020* <u>also issued on cd in japan by seven seas</u>

the hebrides, overture

berlin   bpo   *cd: tahra FURT 1008-1011*
1930   unpublished grammophon 78rpm
                                  recording of rehearsal sequence

berlin   bpo   78: grammophon 95470
1930   78: brunswick 90401
                                  78: decca CA 8090
                                  lp: dg 88 012/2535 821
                                  cd: grammofono AB 78574
                                  cd: dante LYS 116
                                  cd: koch 3-7073-2

vienna   vpo   78: hmv DB 6941
15 february   78: victor 66-6024
1949   45: hmv 7R 102
                                  45: hmv (france) 7RF 102
                                  45: hmv (italy) 7RQ 102
                                  lp: hmv ALP 1526/XLP 30097
                                  lp: hmv (france) FALP 617
                                  lp: hmv (italy) QALP 10298
                                  lp: electrola E 60655/WDLP 662
                                  lp: emi 1C149 03584-03586M
                                  lp: french furtwängler society SWF 8001
                                  cd: emi CHS 566 7702

salzburg   vpo   lp: german furtwängler society
19 august   F667.497-F667.498
1951   lp: discocorp RR 314
                                  lp: cetra FE 35
                                  lp: nippon columbia OZ 7590
                                  cd: salzburg festival/orfeo SF 001
                                  also issued on cd in japan by seven seas

WOLFGANG AMADEUS MOZART (1756-1791)

symphony no 39

berlin 1942-1943	bpo	lp: dg LPM 18 725/LPM 18 856/ 88 007/KL 27-31/2535 828/ 2721 202/2730 005/2740 260 lp: eterna 720 158 cd: dante LYS 246 cd: dg 431 8732/439 8322 cd: history 20.3090/20.3091 *cd: music and arts CD 954*
berlin 7-8 february 1944	bpo	lp: melodiya M10 46005 000 lp: french furtwängler society SWF 8601 lp: private issue (japan) W 22-23 cd: melodiya MEL 10 00716 cd: russian compact disc RCD 25007 cd: dante LYS 117 cd: iron needle IN 1340 cd: dg 427 7762/427 7732
berlin october 1944	bpo	cd: french furtwängler society SWF 991 although it was anticipated that this recent edition would be a re-issue of one of the performances above, swf argues that it comes from the series of magnetophonkonzerte which also yielded the well-known bruckner symphony no 9

symphony no 40

vienna	vpo	cd: music and arts CD 258
2-3		cd: as-disc AS 112
june		cd: history 20.3090/20.3091
1944		*cd: tahra FURT 1014-1015*

incorrectly dated by music and arts
and as-disc as february 1949

vienna	vpo	78: hmv DB 6997-6999/
7-8		DB 9441-9443 auto
december		45: victor WHMV 1010
1948 and		lp: hmv ALP 1498/XLP 30104
17 february		lp: hmv (france) FALP 117/FALP 50033
1949		lp: hmv (italy) QALP 117
		lp: electrola E 90152/WALP 1498/
		E 91075/WALP 562/E 70361/
		STE 91075/SME 91075
		lp: victor LHMV 1010
		lp: emi 1C027 00906M
		cd: dante LYS 246
		cd: emi CDH 763 1932/*CHS 566 7702*

wiesbaden	bpo	lp: german furtwängler society
10 june		F666.156-F666.157M
1949		lp: discocorp RR 395
		lp: nippon columbia OZ 7598-7599
		lp: cetra FE 18
		cd: cetra CDE 1015/CDE 3009
		cd: virtuoso 269.7352
		cd: tahra FURT 1021-1022

also issued on cd in japan by seven seas

piano concerto no 20

lugano	bpo	lp: french furtwängler society
15 may	lefébure	XPMX 2273
1954		lp: unicorn WFS 11

lp: cetra LO 529/FE 18
lp: discocorp RR 395
cd: virtuoso 269.7352
cd: cetra CDE 1015/CDE 3009
cd: as-disc AS 372
cd: ermitage ERM 120
cd: emi CZS 569 4732
also issued in japan by toshiba
and seven seas

piano concerto no 22

vienna	vpo	lp: discocorp AUDAX 765
27 january	badura-skoda	lp: nippon columbia OW 7826/OZ 7602
1952		lp: french furtwängler society

SWF 8401-8402
cd: music and arts CD 895
also issued on lp and cd in japan by
seven seas; all other lp editions have
edits with sections from performances
probably not conducted by furtwängler

serenade for 13 wind

vienna	vpo members	78: hmv DB 6707-6711/
11 november-		DB 9226-9230 auto
3 december		lp: electrola E 91175/WALP 579
1947		lp: unicorn WFS 10

lp: emi 1C047 01244M
cd: dante LYS 250
cd: emi CDH 763 8182
cd: french furtwängler society SWF 991

eine kleine nachtmusik

berlin 1936-1937	bpo	78: grammophon 67156-67158/ 67182-67184 78: polydor (france) 566188-566190 78: decca X 211-213 45: dg EPL 30 576 lp: dg LPM 18 960/2535 827/2730 005 lp: melodiya D 030275-030276 lp: heliodor (usa) H 25079/HS 25079 cd: dante LYS 117 cd: dg 431 8732 cd: history 20.3090/20.3091 *cd: koch 3-7059-2*

vienna
1 april
1949
	vpo	78: hmv DB 6911-6912
		45: hmv 7R 122-123
		45: hmv (france) ERF 17013
		45: electrola E 50063/7ERW 5315
		45: victor 11-7965-7966/WHMV 1018
		lp: hmv ALP 1498/XLP 30104
		lp: hmv (france) FALP 117/FALP 30033
		lp: hmv (italy) QALP 117
		lp: electrola E 90152/WALP 1498/
		   E 60543/WDLP 601/E 80801/
		   SME 80801/WCLP 854/
		   HZE 105/SHZE 105
		lp: victor LHMV 1018
		lp: emi 1C149 03584-03586M
		cd: emi CDH 763 8182

eine kleine freimaurerkantate, arranged as austrian national
hymn

stockholm   vpo   lp: private issue (japan)
25 september   GC 570234-570235
1950   lp: tanaka AT 13-14

die entführung aus dem serail, overture

berlin   bpo   78: grammophon 35013
1933   78: brunswick 90402
                                 78: decca CA 8187
                                 45: dg EPL 30 172
                                 lp: dg LPM 18 960/2535 827
                                 lp: heliodor (usa) H 25079/HS 25079
                                 cd: dante LYS 117
                                 cd: dg 431 8732
                                 cd: koch 3-7059-2

le nozze di figaro

salzburg	vpo	lp: ed smith GMR 999
7 august	vienna	lp: discocorp IGI 343
1953	opera chorus	lp: cetra LO 8/FE 27
	schwarzkopf,	cd: rodolphe RPC 32527-32530
	seefried,	*cd: emi CHS 566 0802*
	güden,	<u>excerpts</u>
	kunz,	lp: melodram MEL 082
	schöffler	cd: melodram MEL 16501
	<u>sung in german</u>	<u>excerpts also on cd in japan by seven</u> <u>seas: GMR 999 appeared to have a</u> <u>different performance of porgi amor</u>

le nozze di figaro, overture

berlin	bpo	78: grammophon 35013
1933		78: brunswick 90402
		78: decca CA 8187
		45: dg EPL 30 172
		lp: dg LPM 18 960/2535 827
		lp: heliodor (usa) H 25079/HS 25079
		cd: symposium 1043
		cd: dante LYS 117
		cd: dg 431 8732
		<u>cd: history 20.3090/20.3093</u>
		cd: koch 3-7059-2

don giovanni

salzburg	vpo	lp: ed smith EJS 419
27 july	vienna	lp: olympic 9109
1950	opera chorus	lp: discocorp RR 407
	schwarzkopf,	lp: turnabout THS 65154-65156
	welitsch,	lp: melodram MEL 713
	seefried,	cd: victor/jvc (japan) R30C 1014-1016
	dermota,	cd: priceless D 16581
	kunz,	cd: laudis LCD 34001
	gobbi,	cd: emi CHS 566 5672
	greindl,	excerpts
	poell	lp: discoreale DR 10037
		lp: melodram MEL 082/MEL 088/ MEL 095
		cd: melodram MEL 16501/MEL 26511
		side 3 of olympic version derives from 1953 performance listed below

salzburg	vpo	cd: rodolphe RPC 32527-32530
27 july	vienna	cd: virtuoso 269.9052
1953	opera chorus	cd: gala GL 100.602
	schwarzkopf,	
	grümmer,	
	berger,	
	dermota,	
	edelmann,	
	siepi,	
	arié,	
	berry	

don giovanni/continued

salzburg	vpo	lp: morgan 5302
3 august	vienna	lp: discocorp MORG 003
1954	schwarzkopf,	lp: cetra LO 7
	grümmer,	lp: foyer FO 1017
	berger,	lp: nippon columbia OZ 7568-7571
	dermota,	lp: emi EX 29 06673
	edelmann,	cd: music and arts CD 003
	siepi,	cd: cetra CDE 1050
	ernster,	cd: arkadia CD 509/CDHP 509
	berry	*cd: emi CHS 763 8602*

excerpts
lp: gioielli della lirica GML 05
excerpts also on cd in japan by seven
seas; complete opera also issued in
japan by cetra and toshiba;
final scene of opera is missing
from this recording and replacement
spliced in from the 1953 version
listed above; CD 509/CDHP 509 is
incorrectly dated 1953 throughout

don giovanni/concluded

salzburg	vpo	unused soundtrack recording for
august	vienna	the paul czinner film (see below)
1954	opera chorus	this recording may not have been
	schwarzkopf,	completed, as schwarzkopf did not
	grümmer,	in the event participate in the film
	berger,	
	dermota,	
	edelmann,	
	siepi,	
	ernster,	
	berry	

salzburg	vpo	*vhs video: dg 072 4403*
august	vienna	final scene of the opera
1954	opera chorus	lp: private issue (japan) W 28-29
	della casa,	
	grümmer,	
	berger,	
	dermota,	
	edelmann,	
	siepi,	
	ernster,	
	berry	

die zauberflöte

salzburg 27 july 1949	vpo vienna opera chorus seefried, lipp, oravez, w.ludwig, schmitt-walter, greindl, schöffler	lp: ed smith EJS 572 lp: discocorp IGI 337 lp: nippon columbia OZ 7572-7574 cd: arlecchino ARL 78-80 cd: music and arts CD 882 excerpts cd: di stefano GDS 1201 also issued in japan by cetra
salzburg 6 august 1951	vpo vienna opera chorus seefried, lipp, oravez, dermota, kunz, greindl, schöffler	lp: cetra LO 9/FE 19 lp: foyer FO 1028 cd: foyer 3CF-2003 cd: priceless D 16603 cd: rodolphe RPC 32527-32530 cd: virtuoso 269.9192 cd: emi CHS 565 3562 excerpts cd: virtuoso 269.7352 cd: music and arts CD 882 cd: verona 28013 excerpts also on cd in japan by seven seas

die zauberflöte, excerpts (zum leiden bin ich auserkoren; der hölle rache)

vienna 3 february 1950	vpo lipp	lp: emi RLS 764/1C137 43187-43189M lp: french furtwängler society SWF 8601 lp: tanaka AT 13-14 cd: emi CHS 566 7702 unpublished hmv 78 rpm recordings

OTTO NICOLAI (1810-1849)

die lustigen weiber von windsor, overture

vienna	vpo	78: hmv DB 21502
18 january		45: victor WHMV 1020/EHA 9
1951		lp: hmv ALP 1526/XLP 30097
		lp: hmv (france) FALP 617
		lp: hmv (italy) QALP 10298
		lp: electrola E 60655/WALP 662/ SMVP 8016
		lp: victor LHMV 1020
		lp: emi 1C149 03584-03586M
		cd: emi CHS 764 2942/CDH 764 2982/ CHS 566 7702

ERNST PEPPING (1901-1981)

symphony no 2

berlin	bpo	lp: melodiya M10 049721 000
31 october-		lp: tanaka AT 13-14
3 november		cd: melodiya MEL 10 00725
1943		cd: arkadia CDWFE 365
		cd: grammofono AB 78510
		cd: russian compact disc RCD 25016

HANS PFITZNER (1869-1949)

symphony in c op 46

salzburg	vpo	lp: rococo 2109
7 august		lp: discocorp RR 437
1949		lp: cetra FE 26
		lp: nippon columbia OZ 7593
		cd: as-disc AS 370
		cd: dante LYS 212
		cd: theatre (japan) 400.3531
		cd: german furtwängler society TMK 10670

palestrina, three preludes

wiesbaden	bpo	lp: rococo 2034
10 june		lp: german furtwängler society F666.156-F666.157M
1949		lp: discocorp RR 477
		lp: cetra FE 26
		lp: nippon columbia OZ 7598-7599
		cd: as-disc AS 370
		cd: tahra FURT 1021-1022

MAURICE RAVEL (1875-1937)

rapsodie espagnole

stuttgart 22 october 1951	vpo	lp: cetra FE 15 lp: french furtwängler society SWF 8501 cd: cetra CDE 1044 cd: virtuoso 269.7332 cd: french furtwängler society SWF 931 cd: evangel (japan) FRL 1002 *cd: music and arts CD 719* <u>also issued on cd in japan by dg</u>
turin 3 march 1952	rai torino orchestra	lp: discocorp BWS 708/DIS 708 lp: nippon columbia OZ 7592

daphnis et chloé, second suite

berlin 20-22 march 1944	bpo	lp: melodiya M10 45949 008 lp: french furtwängler society SWF 8801-8803 <u>cd: dg 427 7832/427 7732</u> cd: classical collection CD3-CLC 4006 cd: melodiya MEL 10 00712 cd: russian compact disc RCD 25003 cd: dante LYS 124

valses nobles et sentimentales

hamburg 15 april 1953	bpo	lp: private issue (japan) GMV 10S *cd: tahra FURT 1014-1015* <u>rehearsal performance</u>

GIOACHINO ROSSINI (1792-1868)

✓ **il barbiere di siviglia, overture**

berlin	bpo	78: grammophon 35028
1935		78: brunswick 95057
		78: fonit 91028
		78: decca CA 8218
		lp: dg 88 021
		lp: melodiya D030275-030276
		cd: symposium 1043
		cd: dante LYS 116
		cd: music and arts CD 954
		cd: koch 3-7059-2

✓ **la gazza ladra, overture**

berlin	bpo	78: grammophon 95427
1930		78: brunswick 90188
		78: fonit 91021
		78: decca CA 8055
		lp: dg 88 021
		lp: tanaka AT 13-14
		cd: grammofono AB 78574
		cd: dante LYS 116
		cd: history 20.3090/20.3093
		cd: music and arts CD 954
		cd: koch 3-7059-2

FRANZ SCHUBERT (1797-1828)

symphony no 8 "unfinished"

stockholm 12 may 1943	vpo	lp: french furtwängler society SWF 8403-8404 lp: tanaka AT 05-06 cd: dante LYS 109 cd: french furtwängler society SWF 973 *cd: music and arts CD 802* <u>first movement only; also issued on cd in japan by seven seas</u>
✓ berlin 12 december 1944	bpo	*cd: tahra FURT 1008-1011* <u>first movement only</u>
berlin 24 october 1948	bpo	lp: nippon columbia DXM 157 lp: turnabout TV 34478 cd: priceless D 13272 cd: german furtwängler society TMK 12681 also issued on cd in japan by palette

vienna
19-21
january
1950
	vpo	78: hmv DB 21131-21133/
		    DB 9538-9540 auto
		45: victor WHMV 1020
		lp: hmv (france) FALP 317/
		    FALP 30043/FBLP 1005
		lp: electrola E 90153/WALP 1500/
		    E 60550/WDLP 603/SME 91486/
		    SMVP 8040
		lp: victor LHMV 1020
		lp: emi XLP 30104/1C047 00907/
		    2C051 03614
		cd: emi CDC 747 1202/CDH 763 1932/
		    CDM 565 9172/CMS 565 9152/
		    CHS 566 7702

symphony no 8/concluded

berlin december 1951	bpo	lp: period (usa) SPL 716 lp: everest SDBR 3252 lp: nippon columbia OS 7076 lp: french furtwängler society SWF 8403-8404 vhs video: teldec 4509 950383 laserdisc: teldec 4509 950386 <u>rehearsal of opening bars only</u>
berlin 10 february 1952	bpo	lp: dg 2535 804/2721 202 cd: virtuoso 269.7332 cd: dg 423 5722/439 8322
turin 11 march 1952	rai torino orchestra	lp: private issue (japan) W 19 lp: tanaka AT 05-06 cd: refrain (japan) DR 92 0023
berlin 15 september 1953	bpo	lp: paragon DSV 52101 lp: cetra FE 11 lp: victor/jvc (japan) RCL 3337 cd: curcio CON 03 cd: classical society CSCD 118 cd: music and arts CD 795 *cd: tahra FURT 1017* <u>also issued on cd in japan by seven seas</u>

paris
4 may
1954
	bpo	lp: cetra LO 519/FE 45
		lp: private issue (japan) TPR 1159
		lp: nippon columbia OZ 7512/
		    OW 7819/OW 7590
		lp: discocorp RR 394
		cd: french furtwängler society
		    SWF 942-943
		cd: elaborations (japan) ELA 901
		<u>also issued on cd in japan by seven seas</u>

<u>telefunken recording of the symphony scheduled with vpo on 17 october 1944, and noted in vpo archives, appears not to have taken place</u>

symphony no 9 "great"

✓ berlin 31 may- 1 june or 6-8 december 1942	bpo	lp: melodiya D 010033-0100034/ M10 10033 007 lp: nippon columbia DXM 109 lp: french furtwängler society SWF 7201 lp: turnabout TV 4364 cd: priceless D 13272 cd: bayer da capo 20.003 cd: dg 427 7812/427 7732 cd: classical collection CD3-CLC 4006 cd: melodiya MEL 10 00723 cd: russian compact disc RCD 25014 cd: palladio PD 4176 cd: dante LYS 114 *cd: music and arts CD 826* <u>also issued in japan by toshiba,</u> <u>palette and dg</u>
✓ stockholm 12 may 1943	vpo	lp: discocorp RR 405 lp: private issue (japan) JP 1190-1192 lp: french furtwängler society SWF 8403-8404 lp: nippon columbia OZ 7589 cd: french furtwängler society SWF 973 cd: dante LYS 109 cd: history 20.3090/20.3090 *cd: music and arts CD 802* <u>also issued on cd in japan by seven seas</u>
berlin 18 june 1950	bpo	lp: tanaka AT 05-06 cd: refrain (japan) DR 92 0023

berlin
december
1951
	bpo	78: dg LVM 72 153-72 156
		lp: dg LPM 18 015-18 016/LPM 18 347/
		    KL 27-31/88 006/2535 808/
		    2721 202/2730 005/2740 260
		lp: decca (usa) DX 119/DL 9746
		lp: eterna 820 068
		lp: heliodor (usa) H 25074/HS 25074
		cd: dg 415 6602/427 4052/
		    439 8322/447 4392
		<u>LPM 18 347 issued both without and</u>
		<u>with side break in slow movement</u>

symphony no 9/concluded

salzburg	vpo	lp: victor/jvc (japan) RCL 3336
30 august		cd: virtuoso 269.7362
1953		*cd: emi CHS 565 3532*
		also issued on cd in japan by toshiba;
		virtuoso incorrectly dated 1952

berlin	bpo	lp: cetra FE 12
15 september		lp: german furtwängler society
1953		F670.027-F670.028
		lp: longanesi GCL 43
		cd: arkadia CD 525/CDHP 525
		cd: foyer CDS 16005
		cd: emblem (usa) EF 4002
		cd: music and arts CD 795
		cd: tahra FURT 1008-1011/*FURT 1017*
		also issued on cd in japan by seven seas;
		foyer incorrectly dated 10 september
		1953

rosamunde overture

✓ berlin 1930	bpo	78: brunswick 90147 lp: private issue (japan) JP 1101-1102 lp: tanaka AT 05-06 lp: furtwängler society FURT 100 cd: symposium 1043 cd: palladio PD 4176 cd: dante LYS 114 cd: history 20.3090/20.3092 *cd: koch 3-7059-2* also issued on cd in japan by dg

vienna
3-17
january
1951
	vpo	lp: hmv (france) FALP 317/FALP 30043
		lp: electrola E 90153/WALP 1500/
		    E 70420/WBLP 558
		lp: emi XLP 30097/2C051 03614/
		    1C149 03584-03586M/F666.699
		cd: emi CDH 763 1932/CHS 566 7702

turin 11 march 1952	rai torino orchestra	lp: discocorp RR 405 lp: nippon columbia OZ 7590 lp: cetra FE 50
berlin 15 september 1953	bpo	lp: dg 2535 804 lp: cetra FE 11 cd: arkadia CD 525/CDHP 525 cd: virtuoso 269.7362 cd: dg 415 6602/427 4052 also issued on cd in japan by seven seas and dg

rosamunde, ballet music no 2

✓ berlin 1929	bpo	78: grammophon 66935/95458 78: brunswick 90050 78: decca CA 8098 78: polydor (japan) S 4041 45: dg EPL 30 164 lp: dg 88 021 cd: symposium 1043 cd: palladio PD 4176 cd: danye LYS 114 cd: history 20.3090/20.3092 *cd: koch 3-7059-2*

vienna
2 february
1950
	vpo	78: hmv DB 21192/DB 11530
		45: hmv 7R 121
		45: hmv (france) 7RF 145
		45: hmv (italy) 7RQ 3012
		45: electrola 7RW 122
		45: victor WHMV 1020
		lp: hmv (france) FALP 317/FALP 30043
		lp: electrola E 90153/WALP 1500/
		    E 70420/WBLP 558
		lp: victor LHMV 1020
		lp: emi XLP 30106/2C051 03614/
		    1C149 03584-03586M
		cd: emi CDH 763 1932/*CHS 566 7702*

buenos aires 5 may 1950	teatro colon orchestra	lp: tanaka AT 03 cd: refrain (japan) DR 92 0032

rosamunde, entr'acte no 3

berlin 1929	bpo	78: grammophon 95458 78: polydor (japan) S 4041 lp: tanaka AT 05-06 <u>grammophon catalogue number 95458</u> <u>also used for the 1930 recording</u> <u>listed below</u>
✓ berlin 1930	bpo	78: grammophon 95418/95458 78: brunswick 90162 78: decca CA 8098 78: polydor (japan) 45153 lp: dg 88 021 cd: symposium 1043 cd: palladip PD 4176 cd: dante LYS 114 cd: history 20.3090/20.3092 cd: koch 3-7059-2 <u>grammophon catalogue number 95458</u> <u>also used for the 1929 recording</u> <u>listed above</u>
vienna 2-3 june 1944	vpo	cd: tahra FURT 1014-1015

vienna
2 february
1950
	vpo	78: hmv DB 21192/DB 11530
		45: hmv 7R 121
		45: hmv (france) 7RF 145
		45: hmv (italy) 7RQ 3012
		45: electrola 7RW 122
		45: victor WHMV 1020
		lp: hmv (france) FALP 317/FALP 30043
		lp: electrola E 90153/WALP 1500/
		    E 70420/WBLP 558
		lp: victor LHMV 1020
		lp: emi XLP 30106/2C051 03614/
		    1C149 03584-03586M
		cd: emi CDH 763 1932/CHS 566 7702

buenos aires 5 may 1950	teatro colon orchestra	lp: tanaka AT 03 cd: refrain (japan) DR 92 0032

HEINZ SCHUBERT (1908-1945)

hymnisches konzert for soloists, organ and orchestra

berlin	bpo	lp: melodiya M10 049721 000
6-8	berger,	cd: melodiya MEL 10 00725
december	w.ludwig,	cd: grammofono AB 78510
1942	heitmann	cd: arkadia CDWFE 365
		cd: russian compact disc RCD 25016

ROBERT SCHUMANN (1810-1856)

symphony no 1 "spring"

munich 29 october 1951	vpo	lp: mrf records MRF 45/MRF 64 lp: decca ECM 684/592.110/417 2871 lp: nippon columbia DXM 170 cd: decca 417 2872 cd: virtuoso 269.7402 cd: arlecchino ARL 151-152 also issued in japan by decca and seven seas

symphony no 4

berlin
14 may
1953
	bpo	78: dg LVM 72 361-72 363
		lp: dg LP 16 063/LPE 17 170/
		    LPM 18 858/KL 27-31/88 008/
		    478 146/2535 805/2721 202/
		    2730 005/2740 260
		lp: decca (usa) DL 9767
		lp: heliodor (usa) H 25073/HS 25073
		lp: longanesi GCL 15
		cd: arlecchino ARL 151-152
		cd: dg 415 6612/427 4042/
		    439 8322/457 7222
		excerpts
		45: dg EPL 30 253
		lp: dg LPEM 19 078/004 279

lucerne 26 august 1953	lucerne festival orchestra	cd: french furtwängler society SWF 961-962 cd: elaborations (japan) ELA 904-905 cd: music and arts CD 1018

piano concerto

berlin	bpo	lp: melodiya M10 36605-36606
1-3	gieseking	lp: everest SDBR 8434
march		lp: discocorp IGI 348
1942		lp: french furtwängler society SWF 7701
		lp: nippon columbia OZ 7596
		cd: melodiya MEL 10 00719
		cd: russian compact disc RCD 25010
		cd: dg 427 7792/427 7732
		cd: dante LYS 196
		cd: arlecchino ARL 151-152
		also issued on cd in japan by dg

cello concerto

berlin	bpo	lp: melodiya M10 42555-42558
25-28	de machula	lp: discocorp RR 538
october		lp: french furtwängler society
1942		SWF 8201-8202
		lp: nippon columbia OZ 7596
		cd: melodiya MEL 10 00721
		cd: russian compact disc RCD 25012
		cd: dg 427 7792/427 7732
		cd: dante LYS 196
		cd: arlecchino ARL 151-152
		also issued on cd in japan by dg

berlin	bpo	cd: venezia (japan) V 1002
13-16	fournier	cd: dante LYS 196
november		*cd: tahra FURT 1008-1011*
1943		third movement only

manfred overture

berlin	bpo	lp: dg 2535 805
18 december		cd: dg 415 6612/427 4042
1949		cd: virtuoso 269.7402
		cd: arlecchino ARL 151-152

vienna	vpo	78: hmv DB 9787-9789
24 january		45: victor WHMV 1023
1951		lp: hmv BLP 1009/XLP 30097
		lp: hmv (france) FBLP 1046
		lp: hmv (italy) QBLP 5006
		lp: electrola E 70023/WBLP 1009/
		E 70362/WBLP 546/E 60661/
		WDLP 667
		lp: columbia (austria) VBLP 802
		lp: victor WHMV 1023
		lp: emi 1C047 01415M
		cd: emi CHS 764 2942/CDH 764 2982/
		CHS 566 7702

JEAN SIBELIUS (1865-1957)

violin concerto

berlin	bpo	lp: unicorn UNI 107
7-8	kulenkampff	lp: nippon columbia DXM 112
february		lp: melodiya M10 45909 004
1943		lp: french furtwängler society SWF 8604
		cd: melodiya MEL 10 00718
		cd: russian compact disc RCD 25009
		cd: music and arts CD 799
		<u>also issued in japan by toshiba</u>

en saga

berlin	bpo	lp: melodiya M10 45909 004
7-8		lp: french furtwängler society SWF 8604
february		cd: melodiya MEL 10 00718
1943		cd: russian compact disc RCD 25009
		cd: dg 427 7832/427 7732
		cd: grammofono AB 78558
		cd: music and arts CD 799
		<u>also issued on cd in japan by dg</u>

stockholm	vpo	lp: private issue (japan)
25 september		GC 570234-570235
1950		lp: discocorp RR 403/RR 507
		cd: theatre (japan) 400.3531
		cd: music and arts CD 799
		<u>also issued on cd in japan by seven seas</u>

BEDRICH SMETANA (1824-1884)

the moldau/ma vlast

vienna	vpo	78: hmv DB 9787-9789
24 january		45: hmv (france) 7ERF 153/ERF 17023
1951		45: electrola E 41130/7EGW 8596
		45: victor WHMV 1023
		lp: hmv BLP 1009/XLP 30106
		lp: hmv (france) FBLP 1046/FBLP 25024
		lp: hmv (italy) QBLP 5006/QALP 10298
		lp: electrola E 70023/WBLP 1009/
		E 60543/WDLP 601/E 80801/
		WCLP 854/SME 80801/
		HZE 105/SHZE 105
		lp: columbia (austria) VBLP 802
		lp: victor LHMV 1023
		lp: emi 1C149 03584-03586M/
		2C053 01193/F666.702
		cd: palladio PD 4122
		cd: historical performers HP 14
		cd: emi CHS 764 2942/CDH 2982/
		CDH 565 1972

JOHANN AND JOSEF STRAUSS

pizzicato polka

vienna	vpo	78: hmv DB 21173
2-3		45: hmv 7R 134/7ER 5001
february		45: hmv (france) 7RF 148/7ERF 131
1950		45: hmv (italy) 7RQ 3032/7ERQ 110
		45: electrola E 50033/7RW 101/
		7ERW 5001
		lp: emi XLP 30106/1C149 03584-03586
		cd: emi CHS 566 7702
		2 different takes of the 78rpm recording,
		one with standard triangle part and one
		without, seem to have circulated

JOHANN STRAUSS (1825-1899)

die fledermaus, overture

✓ berlin 1937	bpo	78: grammophon 67121 78: fonit 91091 78: polydor (france) 566194 78: polydor (japan) S 4038 lp: dg 88 021 lp: melodiya D 030275-030276 lp: tanaka AT 09-10 cd: preiser 90090 cd: history 20.3090/20.3093 *cd: koch 3-7073-2*

kaiserwalzer

stockholm 12 may 1943	vpo	lp: french furtwängler society SWF 8403-8404 cd: french furtwängler society SWF 973 *cd: music and arts CD 802* recording incomplete
vienna 24 january 1950	vpo	78: hmv DB 21174 45: hmv (france) 7RF 104 45: hmv (italy) 7RO 104 lp: hmv ALP 1526/XLP 30106 lp: hmv (france) FALP 617 lp: electrola SMVP 8016 lp: french furtwängler society SWF 8001 cd: dg 435 3352 *cd: emi CHS 566 7702*
berlin 1952	bpo	vhs video: teldec 4509 957103 extract only filmed at berlin presseball

RICHARD STRAUSS (1864-1949)

sinfonia domestica

berlin	bpo	lp: melodiya M10 40961-40962
9-12		lp: french furtwängler society SWF 7902
january		lp: discocorp IGI 364
1944		lp: arabesque AR 8082
		lp: cetra FE 41
		cd: arabesque Z 6082
		cd: as-disc AS 331-332
		cd: melodiya MEL 10 00717
		cd: dg 427 7822/427 7732
		cd: dante LYS 203
		cd: russian compact disc RCD 25008
		cd: magic talent MT 48090
		cd: arlecchino ARL 111-112
		also issued in japan by toshiba

metamorphosen for 23 solo strings

berlin	bpo	lp: dg LPM 18 857/2535 816/2548 719
27 october		cd: dante LYS 212
1947		cd: arlecchino ARL 111-112
		cd: music and arts CD 719
		also issued in japan by nippon
		gramophone and dg

don juan

berlin 15-17 february 1942	bpo	lp: melodiya M10 41233-41234 lp: french furtwängler society SWF 7906 lp: discocorp RR 476 cd: dg 427 7822/427 7732 cd: melodiya MEL 10 00717 cd: russian compact disc RCD 25008 cd: history 20.3090/20.3093 *cd: music and arts CD 829*
stockholm 25 november 1942	stockholm po	lp: orfeus (sweden) 1-73-2 lp: nippon columbia OZ 7512 lp: french furtwängler society SWF 8403-8404 *cd: music and arts CD 814*
berlin 16 september 1947	bpo	lp: dg LPM 18 960/2535 816/ 2548 719/2721 202 cd: dg 439 8372 cd: arlecchino ARL 111-112

don juan/concluded

stockholm 25 september 1950	vpo	lp: private issue (japan) GC 570234-570235 lp: discocorp RR 460 cd: *music and arts CD 802* also issued on cd in japan by seven seas
rome 1 may 1951	bpo	lp: cetra FE 41

vienna
2-3
march
1954
	vpo	lp: hmv ALP 1208/HQM 1137
		lp: hmv (france) FBLP 25082
		lp: hmv (italy) QALP 10085
		lp: electrola E 90093/WALP 1208/
		    E 70429/WBLP 561/HZEL 71
		lp: victor LHMV 19
		lp: angel 60094
		lp: emi 1C049 01155M/10 11551/
		    F666.702
		cd: emi CHS 764 2942/CDH 764 2982/
		    CHS 565 3532/*CDH 565 1972*

caracas 21 march 1954	venezuela so	lp: furtwängler society FURT 101 cd: furtwängler society FURT 102 awaiting re-issue by french furtwängler society
berlin 27 april 1954	bpo	lp: german furtwängler society F668.164-F668.165M cd: nuova era 013.6317 cd: virtuoso 269.7302 cd: evangel (japan) FRL 1003 also issued on cd in japan by palette and seven seas; virtuoso incorrectly dated 1953

till eulenspiegels lustige streiche

berlin 1930	bpo	lp: french furtwängler society SWF 7906 lp: dg 2740 260 lp: tanaka AT 13-14 <u>rehearsal extract for grammophon</u> <u>78 rpm recording: issued on cd in</u> <u>japan by dg</u>
berlin 1930	bpo	78: grammophon 95410-95411 78: fonit 91024-91025 78: decca CA 8053-8054 lp: rococo 2014 lp: private issue (japan) JP 1101-1102 lp: dg 2740 260 cd: arlecchino ARL 111-112 <u>cd: history 20.3090/20.3093</u> <u>*cd: koch 3-7073-2*</u> <u>also issued on cd in japan by dg</u>
berlin 13-16 november 1943	bpo	45: dg EPL 30 589 45: eterna 520 439 lp: dg LPM 18 960/2535 816/ 2548 719/2721 202 lp: royale 1259/1370 lp: gramophone (usa) 2097 <u>cd: dg 427 7832/427 7732/439 8372</u> <u>*cd: music and arts CD 829*</u> <u>royale and gramophone editions did</u> <u>not identify conductor: LPM 18 960</u> <u>incorrectly dated 1947: 2548 719</u> <u>incorrectly dated 1931</u>

till eulenspiegels lustige streiche/concluded

berlin december 1951	bpo	lp: period SPL 176 lp: everest SDBR 3252 lp: nippon columbia OS 7076 *vhs video: teldec 4509 957103* film version also contains sequences of ballet
berlin 14 april 1953	bpo	lp: german furtwängler society F666.624-F666.625 lp: private issue (japan) WFJ 2-3 cd: nuova era 013.6317 cd: virtuoso 269.7302 cd: evangel (japan) FRL 1003 also issued on cd in japan by seven seas
vienna 3 march 1954	vpo	lp: hmv ALP 1208/HQM 1137 lp: hmv (france) FBLP 25082 lp: hmv (italy) QALP 10085 lp: electrola E 90093/WALP 1208/ E 70429/WBLP 561/HZEL 71 lp: victor LHMV 19 lp: angel 60094 lp: emi 1C049 01155M/10 11551/ F666.702 *cd: emi CDH 565 1972*
turin 14 may 1954	bpo	lp: tanaka AT 13-14
lugano 15 may 1954	bpo	lp: cetra LO 529/FE 41 cd: refrain (japan) DR 92 0031 *cd: tahra FURT 1008-1011* (labelled 1944)

tod und verklärung

hamburg 9 june 1947	philharmonisches staatsorchester	lp: discocorp RR 511 lp: cetra FE 41 lp: french furtwängler society SWF 8602 cd: nuova era 013.6317 cd: virtuoso 269.7302 cd: french furtwängler society SWF 921-922 cd: originals SH 834 cd: arlecchino ARL 111-112 cd: evangel (japan) FRL 1003 *cd: music and arts CD 829* also issued on cd in japan by seven seas

vienna 21-24 january 1950	vpo	78: hmv DB 21169-21171/
		    DB 9592-9594 auto
		45: victor WHMV 1023
		lp: hmv (france) FALP 546
		lp: hmv (italy) QALP 10216
		lp: electrola HZEL 71
		lp: victor LHMV 1023
		lp: angel 60094
		lp: emi HQM 1137/10 11551/
		    1C049 01155M
		cd: emi CDH 565 1972

turin 3 march 1952	rai torino orchestra	cd: cetra CDE 1045

4 letzte lieder

london 22 may 1950	philharmonia flagstad	lp: ed smith EJS 432 lp: cetra LO 501/FE 41 lp: rococo 5380 lp: turnabout THS 65116/TV 34830 cd: melodram CDM 25009 cd: arlecchino ARL 111-112 cd: simax PSC 1823 *cd: eklipse EKRCD 15* some issues incorrectly dated and orchestra incorrectly described; all editions derive from a poorly edited acetate recording of the final rehearsal performance, the BBC broadcast of the actual premiere not having been traced; in her later performances of the songs with other conductors or pianists, flagstad omitted the first song "frühling"

lieder with orchestra: **waldseligkeit:** **liebeshymnus:** **verführung: winterliebe**

berlin 15-17 february 1942	bpo anders	lp: melodiya M10 41233-41234 lp: french furtwängler society SWF 7906 lp: discocorp IGI 382 lp: arabesque AR 8082 lp: nippon columbia OZ 7603 lp: cetra FE 41 cd: priceless D 18355 cd: arabesque Z 6082 cd: melodiya MEL 10 00723 cd: russian compact disc RCD 25014 cd: dante LYS 203 cd: music and arts CD 829 cd: tahra FURT 1034-1039/ TAH 201-202/*FURT 1038-1039*

IGOR STRAVINSKY (1882-1971)

le baiser de la fée

berlin	bpo	lp: discocorp BWS 708/DIS 708
18 may		lp: cetra FE 14
1953		lp: german furtwängler society
		F668.164-F668.165M
		lp: nippon columbia OZ 7592
		cd: cetra CDE 1043
		cd: virtuoso 269.7392
		cd: music and arts CD 713

symphony in 3 movements

salzburg	vpo	lp: cetra FE 14
15 august		cd: varese sarabande VCD 47259
1950		cd: cetra CDE 1043
		cd: virtuoso 269.7322

PIOTR TCHAIKOVSKY (1840-1893)

symphony no 4

vienna	vpo	45: victor WHMV 1005
8-10		lp: hmv ALP 1025/ENC 109
january		lp: hmv (france) FALP 120
1951		lp: electrola E 90030/WALP 1025
		lp: columbia (austria) VALP 515
		lp: victor LHMV 1005/LVT 1018
		lp: melodiya D 078793-078794
		lp: unicorn WFS 7
		cd: palladio PD 4124
		cd: historical performers HP 8
		cd: emi CHS 764 8552

hmv 78rpm catalogue numbers DB 21376-21381 were allocated for this recording, but it was never issued in 78rpm format; furtwängler had originally proposed recording the work with london philharmonic for decca in march 1948, but the schedule was changed to brahms symphony no 2 on that occasion

symphony no 5

turin	rai torino	lp: discocorp DIS 3702
6 june	orchestra	lp: olympic OL 8137
1952		lp: nippon columbia OZ 7591
		cd: as-disc AS 371
		cd: historical performers HP 11
		cd: music and arts CD 712

furtwängler makes a cut in the final movement of the symphony, as also done by mengelberg, sargent and others

> **symphony no 6 "pathétique"**

✓ berlin   bpo   78: hmv DB 4609-4614/
october-   DB 8600-8605 auto
november   78: victor M 553/AM 553/DM 553
1938   lp: hmv (france) COLH 21/TRX 6140
                                 lp: electrola E 91079
                                 lp: world records H 107
                                 lp: emi RLS 768/F669.711-F669.715
                                 lp: melodiya D 020049-020050
                                 cd: novello NVLCD 904
                                 cd: claremont GSE 78.5051
                                 cd: palladio PD 4122
                                 cd: historical performers HP 14
                                 cd: grammofono AB 78558
                                 cd: history 20.3090/20.3091
                                 cd: music and arts CD 954
                                 cd: emi CHS 764 8552/CDF 300 0122
                                 cd: biddulph WHL 006-007/*WHL 007*

cairo   bpo   lp: dg 2535 165
19-22   lp: longanesi GCL 23
april   issued on cd by dg in japan only
1951

waltz/serenade for strings

vienna	vpo	78: hmv DB 21173
2 february		45: hmv 7R 134/7ER 5001
1950		45: hmv (france) 7RF 148/7ERF 131
		45: hmv (italy) 7RQ 3032/7ERQ 110
		45: electrola E 50033/7ERW 5001/
		7RW 101
		lp: hmv ALP 1526
		lp: hmv (france) FALP 617
		lp: electrola SMVP 8016
		lp: unicorn WFS 7
		lp: emi 1C149 03584-03586M
		cd: emi CHS 764 8552

finale/serenade for strings

vienna	vpo	78: hmv DB 21172
2 february		78: hmv (australia) ED 1227
1950		45: hmv 7R 140/7ER 5001
		45: hmv (france) 7RF 146/7ERF 131
		45: hmv (italy) 7RQ 3002/7ERQ 110
		45: electrola E 50033/7ERW 5001/
		7RW 123
		45: victor EHA 9
		lp: hmv ALP 1526
		lp: hmv (france) FALP 617
		lp: electrola SMVP 8016
		lp: unicorn WFS 7
		lp: emi 1C149 03584-03586M
		cd: emi CHS 764 8552

GIUSEPPE VERDI (1813-1901)

otello

salzburg	vpo	lp: mrf records MRF 45
7 august	vienna	lp: discocorp IGI 342
1951	opera chorus	lp: cetra LO 6/FE 28
	martinis,	lp: turnabout THS 65120-65122
	wagner,	lp: foyer FO 1018
	vinay,	cd: foyer 2CF-2002
	dermota,	cd: arkadia CDWFE 303/CDWFE 353
	schöffler	cd: rodolphe RPC 32561-32562
		cd: virtuoso 269.7382
		cd: emi CHS 565 7512
		also issued on lp in japan by cetra

RICHARD WAGNER (1813-1883)

der fliegende holländer, overture

vienna	vpo	78: hmv DB 6975-6976/
30 march-		DB 9727-9728 auto
4 april		78: hmv (australia) ED 1233-1234
1949		lp: hmv (france) FALP 289/FALP 30039
		lp: electrola E 90023/WALP 534/
		E 91074/WALP 561
		lp: columbia (austria) VALP 538
		lp: unicorn WFS 2-3
		lp: angel 6024
		lp: melodiya D 0132137-0132138
		lp: emi 29 12343/1C149 01197-01198M
		cd: historical performers HP 4
		cd: emi CZS 252 3282/*CHS 764 9352*
turin	rai torino	lp: cetra FE 47
6 june	orchestra	cd: cetra CDE 1012/CDAR 2032
1952		cd: classical collection CD3-CLC 4006
		cd: music and arts CD 712/*CD 794*

götterdämmerung

milan 4 april 1950	la scala orchestra and chorus flagstad, h.konetzni, höngen, lorenz, herrmann, weber, pernerstorfer	lp: ed smith EJS 538 lp: discocorp RR 420 lp: murray hill 940.477 lp: everest S 476 lp: cetra CFE 101/FE 40 cd: cetra CDC 28 cd: arkadia CDWFE 301/CDWFE 351/ CDWFE 364 cd: virtuoso 269.9112/269.9082 cd: *music and arts CD 914* excerpts lp: ed smith EJS 318 lp: acanta 40.23520 cd: cetra CDC 16 cd: acanta 44.1055 cd: grammofono AB 78610 cd: dante LYS 115 cd: iron needle IN 1364-1365 CDWFE 364 incorrectly dated 2 april 1950; AB 78610, LYS 115 and IN 1364-1365 incorrectly described as berlin 1940
rome 20-27 november 1953	rai roma orchestra and chorus mödl, jurinac, klose, suthaus, poell, greindl, pernerstorfer	lp: mrf records MRF 34 lp: emi RLS 702/EX 29 06703/ 1C147 02288-02292M cd: arkadia CDWFE 359 cd: emi CZS 767 1362/*CZS 767 1232* excerpts lp: angel 60200 act one performed on 20 november, act two on 24 november and act three on 27 november (concert performances)

götterdämmerung, act three

rome	rai roma	lp: ed smith EJS 318
✓ 31 may	orchestra	lp: cetra FE 20
1952	and chorus	*cd: music and arts CD 866*
	flagstad,	<u>excerpts</u>
	h.konetzni,	cd: cetra CDE 1012/CDAR 2032
	suthaus	cd: classical collection CD3-CLC 4006
	greindl,	<u>ed smith incorrectly described as</u>
	herrmann	<u>milan 1950</u>

cd: tahra FURT 1092

götterdämmerung, excerpts (zu neuen taten; altgewohntes geräusch...to end act 1; heil dir gunther...to end act 2; her den ring!...to end of opera)

london	lpo	lp: ed smith EJS 431
1 june	covent garden	lp: private issue (japan) JPL 1020-1022
1937	chorus	lp: discocorp RR 429
	flagstad,	cd: eklipse EKR 62
	nezadal,	cd: dante LYS 219-221
	thorborg,	*cd: music and arts CD 1035*
	melchior,	<u>her den ring! only</u>
	janssen,	lp: acanta 40.23520
	weber	cd: acanta 44.1055
		cd: grammofono AB 78610
		cd: iron needle IN 1364-1365
		<u>all excerpts are taken from hmv 78rpm</u>
		<u>test pressings; the excerpts also issued</u>
		<u>on cd in japan by palette</u>

götterdämmerung, excerpts (heil dir gunther!; welches unholds list...to end of opera)

london	lpo	lp: ed smith EJS 342
7 june	covent garden	cd: eklipse EKR 62
1938	leider,	cd: dante LYS 219-221
	stosch,	*cd: pearl GEMMCD 9331*
	melchior,	<u>heil dir gunther only</u>
	janssen,	lp: acanta 40.23502
	schirp	<u>ed smith incorrectly dated 6 july 1938</u>

götterdämmerung,   excerpt (starke scheite schichtet mir dort!)

london   philharmonia   78: hmv DB 6792-6794/
26 march   flagstad   DB 9323-9325 auto
1948   45: victor WHMV 1024
                                     lp: hmv (france) FALP 119/FALP 194
                                     lp: victor LHMV 1024
                                     lp: french furtwängler society SWF 7803
                                     lp: emi 1C147 01491-01492M/
                                          2C051 03855/EX 29 12273
                                     cd: emi CMS 565 2122/*CDH 763 0302*
                                     catalogue number FALP 194 was also
                                     used for 1952 recording (see below)

london   philharmonia   lp: hmv ALP 1016/HQM 1057
23 june   flagstad   lp: hmv (france) FALP 194/FALP 30295
1952   lp: hmv (italy) QALP 10079
                                 lp: electrola E 90026/WALP 1016/
                                      E 80954/WCLP 953
                                 lp: victor LHMV 1072
                                 lp: emi 1C047 01149M
                                 lp: angel 60003
                                 lp: melodiya D 033213-033214
                                 cd: emi CHS 764 9352
                                 catalogue number FALP 194 was also
                                 used for 1948 recording (see above)

additional versions of immolation scene included in the complete recordings
and extracts from götterdämmerung listed previously

götterdämmerung,   siegfried's funeral march

berlin 1933	bpo	78: grammophon 67054 78: brunswick 90251 78: fonit 91026 78: decca CA 8173 lp: dg 88 021/2700 703/2721 113 lp: melodiya D 033213-033214 cd: symposium 1043 cd: history 20.3090/20.3092 *cd: koch 3-7073-2*
berlin 19 december 1949	bpo	lp: dg 2535 826 cd: dg 415 6632/427 4062 *cd: music and arts CD 794*

götterdämmerung, siegfried's rhine journey

vienna 23 february 1949	vpo	78: hmv DB 6949-6950 lp: hmv (france) FALP 110/ FALP 194/COLH 307 lp: electrola SME 91399 lp: victor LHMV 1049 lp: french furtwängler society SWF 7803 lp: emi 2C051 03855 cd: testament SBT 1141 also issued on cd in japan by toshiba; catalogue number FALP 194 also used for 1954 recording (see below)
turin 6 june 1952	rai torino orchestra	lp: cetra FE 47 cd: cetra CDE 1012/CDAR 2032 cd: classical collection CD3-CLC 4006
vienna 8 march 1954	vpo	lp: hmv ALP 1016/XLP 30082 lp: hmv (france) FALP 194/FALP 30295 lp: hmv (italy) QALP 10079 lp: electrola E 90026/WALP 1016 lp: angel 60003 lp: melodiya D 033213-033214 lp: emi F666.701/29 12342/ 1C149 01197-01199M cd: emi CZS 252 3282/CHS 764 9352 29 12343 and 1C149 01197-01199M incorrectly dated february 1949; catalogue number FALP 194 also used for 1949 recording (see above)

additional versions of rhine journey included in the complete recordings of
götterdämmerung listed previously

siegfried's funeral march/concluded

vienna 31 january 1950	vpo	78: hmv DB 6946 45: hmv 7R 151 45: hmv (france) 7RF 149 45: hmv (italy) 7RQ 3011 45: electrola 7RW 124 45: victor EHB 2 lp: hmv (france) FALP 194 lp: victor LHMV 1049 lp: french furtwängler society SWF 7803 lp: emi 2C051 03855 *cd: testament SBT 1141* <u>also issued on cd in japan by toshiba</u> <u>shinseido; catalogue number FALP 194</u> <u>also used for 1954 recording (see below)</u>

vienna
2 march
1954
	vpo	lp: hmv ALP 1016/XLP 30082
		lp: hmv (france) FALP 194/
		    FALP 30295/FBLP 25057
		lp: hmv (italy) QALP 10079
		lp: electrola E 90026/WALP 1016
		lp: angel 60003
		lp: french furtwängler society SWF 8001
		lp: emi F666.701/29 12343/
		    1C149 01197-01199M
		cd: emi CZS 252 3582/*CHS 764 9352*
		<u>SWF 8001 incorrectly dated february</u>
		<u>1949 (see section on unpublished</u>
		<u>recordings); catalogue number FALP 194</u>
		<u>also used for 1950 recording (see above)</u>

<u>additional versions of funeral march included in the complete recordings</u>
<u>of götterdämmerung listed previously</u>

lohengrin, excerpts from act three (prelude; treulich geführt; das süsse lied verhallt; heil könig heinrich!; in fernem land; mein lieber schwan...to end of opera)

bayreuth	bayreuth	lp: ed smith EJS 399
19 july	festival	lp: french furtwängler society SWF 7801
1936	orchestra	lp: cetra FE 25
	and chorus	lp: acanta 40.23502/40.23520
	müller,	cd: fonoteam CD 74807
	klose,	cd: acanta 44.1055
	völker,	cd: grammofono AB 78515
	manowarda	cd: iron needle IN 1364-1365
		IN 1364-1365 incorrectly dated 1931;
		40.23502 omits mein lieber schwan;
		CD 74807 omits prelude, treulich
		geführt and das süsse lied verhallt

cd: tahra FURT 1092

lohengrin,   prelude

✓ berlin   bpo   78: grammophon 95408
  1930   78: brunswick 90231
                                               78: fonit 91030
                                               78: decca CA 8089
                                               lp: dg 88 021
                                               lp: top classic TC 9054
                                               cd: history 20.3090/20.3092
                                               cd: koch 3-7073-2

  lucerne   lucerne   *cd: testament SBT 1141*
  30 august   festival   unpublished hmv 78rpm recording
  1947   orchestra

  lucerne   lucerne   lp: french furtwängler society SWF 7801
  29 august   festival   lp: tanaka AT 04/AT 09-10
  1949   orchestra   *cd: music and arts CD 1018*
                                               unpublished hmv 78rpm recording;
                                               SWF 7801 and AT 09-10 incorrectly
                                               dated 1947; CD 1018 incorrectly
                                               dated 15 september 1949

  vienna   vpo   lp: hmv ALP 1220/XLP 30082
  4 march   lp: hmv (france) FALP 362/FALP 30213
  1954   lp: hmv (italy) QALP 10088
                                               lp: electrola E 90097/WALP 1220/
                                                    E 91074/WALP 561
                                               lp: angel 6024
                                               lp: melodiya D 032137-032138
                                               lp: emi 1C149 01197-01199M/
                                                    29 12343
                                               cd: historical performers HP 4
                                               cd: emi CZS 252 3282/*CHS 764 9352*

die meistersinger von nürnberg

bayreuth	bayreuth	lp: ed smith UORC 266
15-24	festival	lp: estro armonico EA 008
july	orchestra	lp: foyer FO 1043
1943	and chorus	lp: emi 1C181 01797-01801M
	müller,	cd: laudis LCD 44008
	kallab,	cd: dante LYS 026-027
	lorenz,	cd: grammofono AB 78602-78605
	zimmermann,	excerpts
	prohaska,	lp: emi 1C181 30669-30678M
	fuchs,	lp: acanta 40.23502
	greindl	cd: acanta 44.1055
		cd: history 20.3090/20.3092
		cd: music and arts CD 794
		estro armonico incorrectly dated 1944; all issues have act 1 scene 1 and act 3 quintet missing; also issued on cd in japan by toshiba

die meistersinger von nürnberg, excerpts (overture; da zu dir der
heiland kam; wann dann die flur vom frost befreit; fanget an!;
jerum! jerum!; den tag seh' ich erscheinen; zu hilfe! zu hilfe!;
act 3 prelude; selig wie die sonne; jetzt all am fleck!; silentium!;
morgenlich leuchtend; im drang der schlimmen jahr')

vienna	vpo	*cd: koch 3-1470-2*
25 november	vienna	<u>fanget an!, morgenlich leuchtend and</u>
1937	opera chorus	<u>im drang der schlimmen jahr' only</u>
	reining,	lp: teletheater 762.8691-762.8692
	szantho,	
	lorenz,	
	zimmermann,	
	kamann,	
	alsen,	
	wiedemann	

die meistersinger von nürnberg, excerpts (overture; da zu dir der
heiland kam; halt meister, nicht so geeilt!; was duftet doch der
flieder/guten abend meister; jerum! jerum!; wollt mich beim
wahne fangen; so lang as beckmesser lebt; ist das erlaubt, so spät
zur nacht?; act 3 prelude; wahn, wahn, überall wahn!/grüss gott,
mein junker!; doch lasst dem ruh'/mein freund, in holder
jugendzeit; o sachs mein freund!/da streicht die lene schon ums
haus/ein kind ward hier geboren; selig wie die sonne; wach auf!;
sein töchterlein, sein höchstes gut!; das lied, fürwahr, ist nicht
von mir; verachtet mir die meister nicht/ehrt eure deutschen
meister!)

nürnberg	vpo	lp: ed smith UORC 224
5 september	vienna	lp: private issue (japan) JP 1143-1144
1938	opera and	*cd: koch 3-1452-2*
	nürnberg	<u>halt meister, nicht so geeilt!</u>
	opera choruses	lp: acanta 40.23520
	lemnitz,	cd: acanta 44.1055
	berglund,	<u>was duftet doch der flieder and</u>
	laholm,	<u>guten abend meister</u>
	zimmermann,	lp: acanta 40.23520
	bockelmann,	cd: acanta 44.1055
	fuchs,	cd: grammofono AB 78610
	manowarda	cd: iron needle IN 1364-1365
		<u>guest performance by vienna staatsoper;</u>
		<u>excerpts also on cd in japan by palette</u>

die meistersinger von nürnberg, overture

berlin	bpo	lp: private issue (japan) W 22-23
26 february		lp: tanaka AT 09-10
1942		lp: french furtwängler society
		SWF 8801-8803
		cd: tahra FURT 1034-1039/
		FURT 1036-1037
		vhs video: bel canto society BCS 0052
		<u>performed for workers' concert</u>
		<u>at aeg factory</u>

vienna	vpo	78: hmv DB 6942-6943
1-4		lp: hmv (france) FALP 289/FALP 546/
april		FALP 30039/FALP 30213
1949		lp: hmv (italy) QALP 10216
		lp: electrola E 90023/WALP 534/
		E 80801/WCLP 854/E 91074/
		WALP 561/SME 80801/E 83388/
		WCLP 820/HZE 105/SHZE 105
		lp: columbia (austria) VALP 538
		lp: victor LHMV 1049
		lp: unicorn WFS 2-3
		lp: angel 6024
		lp: emi 1C149 01197-01199M/
		29 12343
		cd: historical performers HP 4
		cd: emi CZS 252 3282/*CHS 764 9352*
		<u>opening bars only</u>
		lp: electrola E 83387-83388

berlin	bpo	lp: dg 2535 113/2721 113/
19 december		2721 202/2740 260
1949		cd: dg 415 6632/427 4062/439 8372

berlin	bpo	lp: period SPL 716
december		vhs video: teldec 4509 950383
1951		laserdisc: teldec 4509 950386
		<u>opening bars only recorded</u>

die meistersinger von nürnberg, act 3 prelude

vienna	vpo	lp: private issue (japan) JP 1114
1 february		lp: unicorn WFS 2-3
1950		lp: emi 1C149 01197-01199M/
		29 12343
		cd: historical performers HP 4
		cd: emi CHS 764 9352
		<u>unpublished hmv 78rpm recording</u>

die meistersinger von nürnberg, dance of the apprentices

vienna	vpo	78: hmv DB 6943
4 april		45: hmv 7R 141/7P 206
1949		45: hmv (france) 7RF 203
		45: hmv (italy) 7RQ 3004
		45: electrola 7RW 125
		45: victor EHA 17
		lp: victor LHMV 1049
		lp: unicorn WFS 2-3
		lp: emi 1C149 01197-01199M/
		29 12343
		cd: emi CZS 252 3282/*CHS 764 9352*

<u>additional versions of meistersinger overture, act 3 prelude and dance of
the apprentices included in the complete recording (and extracts) listed
previously</u>

parsifal, prelude

✓ berlin   bpo
15 march
1938

78: hmv DB 3445-3446/
      DB 8494-8496 auto
78: victor M 514/AM 514/DM 514
lp: hmv (france) COLH 307
lp: electrola SME 91399/
      SMVP 8055-8056
lp: unicorn WFS 2-3
lp: angel 6024
lp: top classic TC 9054
lp: emi 1C147 29229-29230/29 12343/
      1C149 01197-01199M
lp: acanta 40.23520
lp: discocorp RR 229
cd: acanta 43.121/44.1055
cd: music and arts CD 954
cd: history 20.3090/20.3092
cd: magic talent MT 48090
cd: grammofono AB 78515
cd: dante LYS 115
cd: iron needle IN 1364-1365
cd: biddulph WHL 006-007/*WHL 006*
cd: emi CHS 764 9352
acanta, discocorp, grammofono and iron
needle issues incorrectly described as
berlin staatskapelle 1940

parsifal,   karfreitagszauber

✓berlin
15 march
1938
	bpo	78: hmv DB 3446-3447/
		    DB 8494-8496 auto
		78: victor M 514/AM 514/DM 514
		lp: hmv (france) COLH 307
		lp: electrola SME 91399/
		    SMVP 8055-8056
		lp: unicorn WFS 2-3
		lp: angel 6024
		lp: top classic TC 9054
		lp: emi 1C147 29229-29230/29 12343/
		    1C149 01197-01199M
		cd: music and arts CD 954
		cd: history 20.3090/20.3092
		cd: dante LYS 115
		cd: biddulph WHL 006-007/*WHL 006*
		cd: emi CHS 764 9352
		TC 9054 has side 2 of the 78rpm
		recording missing and side 3 given
		twice

alexandria 25 april 1951	bpo	lp: dg 2535 826/2721 202/2740 260 cd: dg 415 6632/427 4062/439 8372 *cd: music and arts CD 794*

das rheingold

milan 4 march 1950	la scala orchestra wegener, weth-falke, höngen, markwort, frantz, pernerstorfer, weber, emmerich	lp: ed smith UORC 128 lp: discocorp RR 420 lp: murray hill 940 477 lp: everest S 473 lp: cetra CFE 101/FE 37 cd: cetra CDC 26 cd: arkadia CDWFE 301/CDWFE 351 cd: virtuoso 269.7282/269.9082 cd: music and arts CD 914 excerpts cd: cetra CDC 16
rome 26 october 1953	rai roma orchestra grümmer, malaniuk, siewert, patzak, frantz, neidlinger, frick, greindl	lp: mrf records MRF 14 lp: emi RLS 702/RLS 703/29 06703/ 1C147 02275-02277M cd: arkadia CDWFE 359 cd: emi CZS 767 1242/CZS 767 1232 excerpts lp: angel 60200

siegfried

milan	la scala	lp: ed smith UORC 123
22 march	orchestra	lp: discocorp RR 420
1950	flagstad,	lp: murray hill 940 477
	moor,	lp: everest S 475
	höngen,	lp: cetra CFE 101/FE 39
	svanholm,	cd: cetra CDC 27
	markwort,	cd: arkadia CDWFE 301/CDWFE 351
	herrmann,	cd: virtuoso 269.9082/269.9092
	weber,	cd: music and arts CD 914
	pernerstorfer	excerpts
		lp: acanta 40.23502
		cd: acanta 44.1055
		cd: cetra CDC 16
		cd: dante LYS 115
		LYS 115 incorrectly described as
		berlin staatskapelle 1940

rome	rai roma	lp: mrf records MRF 23
10-17	orchestra	lp: emi RLS 702/29 06703/
november	mödl,	1C147 02283-02288M
1953	streich,	cd: arkadia CDWFE 359
	klose,	cd: emi CZS 767 1312/CZS 767 1232
	suthaus,	excerpts
	patzak,	lp: angel 60200
	frantz,	act one performed on 10 november,
	greindl,	act two on 13 november and act three
	pernerstorfer	on 17 november (concert performances)

siegfried, excerpt (selige öde auf sonniger höh'..to end of opera)

milan	la scala	cd: arkadia CDWFE 364
26 march	orchestra	this excerpt is confirmed by henry
1950	flagstad,	fogel not to be from the 22 march
	svanholm	performance listed above

siegfried idyll

vienna	vpo	78: hmv DB 6916-6917
16-17		lp: hmv (france) FALP 110/FALP 546
february		lp: hmv (italy) QALP 10216
1949		lp: victor LHMV 1049
		lp: unicorn WFS 2-3
		lp: angel 6024
		lp: emi 1C149 01197-01199M/
		29 12343
		cd: emi CZS 252 3282
		cd: testament SBT 1141
turin	rai torino	lp: cetra FE 47
6 june	orchestra	cd: cetra CDE 1012/CDAR 2032
1952		cd: classical collection CD3-CLC 4006
		cd: music and arts CD 712

tannhäuser, excerpts (dich teure halle; gar viel und schön;
vernehmt durch mich, was gottes wille ist; dir, hohe liebe, töne/
dir, göttin der liebe; ein engel stieg aus lichtem äther/erbarm'
dich mein; als du in kühnem sange)

vienna	vpo	dich teure halle
13 october	vienna	lp: ed smith UORC 242
1935	opera chorus	lp: teletheater 643.333
	bathy,	*cd: koch 3-1470-2*
	pistor,	gar viel und schön
	maikl,	lp: teletheater 643.333
	hofmann,	vernehmt durch mich, was gottes wille
	sved,	lp: ed smith UORC 242
	markhoff,	dir hohe liebe/dir göttin der liebe
	wernigk,	lp: ed smith UORC 242
	ettl	lp: acanta 40.23520
		cd: acanta 44.1055
		ein engel stieg/erbarm' dich mein
		lp: ed smith UORC 242
		als du in kühnem sange
		lp: ed smith UORC 242
		lp: teletheater 643.333

tannhäuser, excerpt (wohl wusst' ich hier/o du mein holder
abendstern)

vienna	vpo	lp: ed smith UORC 242
18 october	sved	lp: teletheater 643.333
1935		

tannhäuser, excerpts (dir töne lob!; dich teure halle; zu deinen
füssen/o stehet auf!; seht mich die jungfrau/ich fleh' für ihn;
zum heil den sündigen zu führen/erbarm' dich mein)

vienna	vpo	*cd: koch 3-1470-2*
9 january	vienna	dir töne lob only
1936	opera chorus	lp: teletheater 643.333
	müller,	
	lorenz	

tannhäuser, overture

vienna 17-22 february 1949	vpo	*cd: testament SBT 1141* <u>unpublished hmv 78rpm recording</u>
rome 1 may 1951	bpo	lp: discocorp RR 413 lp: dg 2535 826/2740 260 cd: dg 415 6632/427 4062 *cd: music and arts CD 794*

tannhäuser overture/concluded

| vienna
2-3
december
1952 | vpo | 45: hmv (france) 7ERF 154/ERF 17024
lp: hmv ALP 1220/XLP 30082
lp: hmv (france) FALP 289/FALP 362/
    FALP 30039/FALP 30215/
    FBLP 25057
lp: hmv (italy) QALP 10088
lp: electrola E 90023/WALP 1220/
    E 90097/WALP 534/
    E 91074/WALP 561
lp: columbia (austria) VALP 538
lp: angel 6024
lp: melodiya D 032137-032138
lp: emi 1C149 01197-01199M/
    29 12343
lp: french furtwängler society SWF 8001
lp: acanta 40.23520
lp: discocorp RR 229
cd: acanta 43.121/44.1055
cd: historical performers HP 4
cd: magic talent MT 48090
cd: dante LYS 115
cd: grammofono AB 78515
cd: iron needle IN 1364-1365
cd: emi CZS 252 3282/CHS 764 9352
SWF 8001 and 29 12343 incorrectly
dated february 1949; discocorp,
acanta, grammofono, dante, magic
talent and iron needle incorrectly
described as berlin staatskapelle 1940 |
| caracas
21 march
1954 | venezuela so | lp: tanaka AT 09-10
cd: furtwängler society FURT 102
awaiting re-issue by french
furtwängler society |

148

tristan und isolde

london
10-22
june
1952

philharmonia
covent garden
chorus
flagstad,
thebom,
suthaus,
schock,
e.evans,
fischer-dieskau
greindl

lp: hmv ALP 1030-1035/RLS 684/
    HQM 1001-1005
lp: hmv (france) FALP 221-226/
    FALP 30331-30335
lp: electrola E 90032-90037/
    WALP 1030-1035/E 91170-91174/
    WALP 574-578
lp: columbia (austria) VALP 521-526
lp: victor LM 6700
lp: angel 3588
lp: emi 1C147 00899-00903M/
    10 08993/EX 29 06843
cd: emi CDS 747 3228/*CDS 556 2542*
excerpts
78: hmv DB 21586
45: hmv 7ER 5036
45: hmv (italy) 7ERQ 123
45: electrola E 50042/7ERW 5036
lp: hmv HQM 1235
lp: hmv (france) OVC 2015C
lp: electrola E 91074/WALP 561/
    E 80712-80713/WCLP 746-747/
    SME 80712-80713
lp: victor LHMV 1072/LM 1829
lp: angel 60145
cd: historical performers HP 4
cd: emi CZS 252 3282/CDM 565 9172/
    CMS 565 9152

tristan und isolde, acts 2 and 3

berlin	staatskapelle	lp: french furtwängler society
3 october	schlüter,	SWF 8205-8207
1947	klose,	lp: cetra FE 43
	suthaus,	cd: cetra CDE 1046
	rehm,	cd: french furtwängler society
	witting,	SWF 981-982
	prohaska,	cd: dante LYS 194-195
	frick	cd: radio years RY 103-104
		excerpts
		lp: cetra FE 25
		lp: acanta 40.23520
		cd: acanta 43.121/44.1055
		cd: fonoteam CD 74807
		excerpts also on cd in japan by palette;
		all editions have standard cut in the
		act 2 liebesnacht

tristan und isolde, act 3

vienna	vpo	cd: koch 3-1461-2
2 january	a.konetzni,	
1943	klose,	
	lorenz,	
	monthy,	
	gallos,	
	schöffler,	
	alsen	

tristan und isolde, excerpts (elend im sterben lag/das schwert, ich liess es fallen; so reihte sie die mutter/ans land ihn zu begleiten; müht euch die?/dass du nicht dir's entfallen lässt)

bayreuth 18 august 1931	bayreuth festival orchestra larsen-todsen, helm, pistor, bockelmann	lp: danacord DACO 131-133

tristan und isolde, excerpts (hörst du sie noch?; frau minne kenntest du nicht?; sink hernieder, nacht der liebe; selbst dann bin ich der welt/einsam wachend; so stürben wir; wohin nun tristan scheidet)

vienna 25 december 1941	vpo a.konetzni, klose, lorenz	lp: ed smith UORC 267 <u>hörst du sie noch?</u> cd: koch 3-1461-2 <u>frau minne kenntest du nicht?</u> cd: koch 3-1461-2 <u>sink hernieder, nacht der liebe</u> cd: koch 3-1456-2 <u>einsam wachend</u> lp: ed smith EJS 399 lp: acanta HB 22.863 cd: radio years RY 76 cd: koch 3-1456-2 <u>so stürben wir</u> cd: koch 3-1456-2 <u>wohin nun tristan scheidet</u> cd: koch 3-1461-2 <u>acanta and radio years issues incorrectly described as berlin 1942</u>

tristan und isolde, excerpts (westwärts schweift der blick;
auf jeder stelle, wo ich steh'/herr morolt zog zum meere her;
auf das tau! anker los!/wohl kenn' ich irlands königin; tristan!
isolde! trauteste holde!; isolde! tristan! geliebte!; sink hernieder,
nacht der liebe; einsam wachend; lausch' geliebter! lass mich
sterben!; so stürben wir; als für ein fremdes land)

vienna	vpo	cd: koch 3-1461-2
2 january	vienna	
1943	opera chorus	
	a.konetzni,	
	klose,	
	lorenz,	
	franter,	
	monthy,	
	schöffler	

tristan und isolde,   prelude and liebestod

berlin   bpo   78: grammophon 95438-95439
1930   78: brunswick 90201-90202
                                     78: fonit 91028-91029
                                     78: decca CA 8039 and 8156
                                     lp: dg 88 021
                                     cd: koch 3-7073-2
                                     liebestod only
                                     45: dg EPL 30 540
                                     prelude and liebestod also issued
                                     on cd in japan by dg

berlin   bpo   78: hmv DB 3419-3420
11 february   78: victor M 653/DM 653
1938   78: columbia (japan) JS 114
                                     lp: hmv (france) COLH 307
                                     lp: electrola SME 91399
                                     lp: unicorn WFS 2-3
                                     lp: melodiya D 03367-03368
                                     lp: angel 6024
                                     lp: top classic TC 9054
                                     lp: emi 1C149 01197-01199M/
                                         F666.701/2C061 00932
                                     lp: bayreuth festival 1976
                                     cd: dante LYS 115
                                     cd: music and arts CD 954
                                     cd: biddulph WHL 006-007/*WHL 006*
                                     cd: emi CHS 764 9352
                                     prelude only
                                     lp: acanta HB 22.863/40.23520
                                     lp: emi RLS 7711
                                     cd: acanta 43.121
                                     cd: iron needle IN 1364-1365
                                     cd: grammofono AB 78610
                                     prelude only also issued on cd in japan
                                     by palette; all editions of prelude only
                                     except emi are incorrectly described
                                     as bayreuth 1931

prelude and liebestod/concluded

berlin 8-10 november 1942	bpo	lp: melodiya M10 45949 008 lp: french furtwängler society 　　SWF 8801-8803 cd: melodiya MEL 10 00721 cd: music and arts CD 730 cd: russian compact disc RCD 25012 cd: tahra FURT 1004-1007/ 　　FURT 1034-1039/FURT 1036-1037 also issued on cd in japan by seven seas
stockholm 25 november 1942	stockholm po	lp: discocorp RR 505 cd: bis BISCD 424B cd: grammofono AB 78515 cd: history 20.3090/20.3092 cd: music and arts CD 794 liebestod only lp: acanta 40.23520 cd: acanta 44.1055 cd: iron needle IN 1364-1365 prelude and liebestod also issued on cd in japan by seven seas
turin 11 march 1952	rai torino orchestra	lp: cetra LAR 46/FE 43 cd: cetra CDE 1012/CDAR 2032/ 　　ARCD 2054 cd: classical collection CD3-CLC 4006 LAR 46 and ARCD 2054 incorrectly dated 11 march 1953
berlin 27 april 1954	bpo	lp: cetra FE 25 lp: german furtwängler society 　　F666.164-F666.165M lp: discocorp RR 229 cd: dg 415 6632/427 4062
turin 14 may 1954	bpo	lp: tanaka AT 09-10 cd: refrain (japan) DR 92 0031

die walküre

milan 9 march 1950	la scala orchestra flagstad, h.konetzni, höngen, treptow, frantz, weber	lp: ed smith EJS 534 lp: discocorp RR 420 lp: murray hill 940.477 lp: everest S 474 lp: cetra LO 86/CFE 101/FE 38 cd: cetra CDC 15 cd: arkadia CDWFE 301/CDWFE 351 cd: virtuoso 269.9082/269.9102 *cd: music and arts CD 914* excerpts lp: ed smith EJS 327 cd: cetra CDC 16
rome 29 october- 6 november 1953	rai roma orchestra mödl, h.konetzni, cavelti, windgassen, frantz, frick	lp: mrf records MRF 41 lp: emi RLS 702/29 06703/ 1C147 02278-02282M cd: arkadia CDWFE 359 cd: emi CZS 767 1272/*CZS 767 1232* excerpts lp: angel 60200 act one performed on 29 october, act two on 3 november and act three on 6 november (concert performances)

vienna
28 september-
6 october
1954
	vpo
	mödl,
	rysanek,
	klose,
	suthaus,
	frantz,
	frick
		lp: hmv ALP 1257-1261/
		  HQM 1019-1023
		lp: hmv (france) FALP 383-387
		lp: hmv (italy) QALP 10098-10102
		lp: electrola E 90100-90104/
		  WALP 1257-1261/SME 90100-90104
		lp: victor LHMV 900
		lp: angel 6012
		cd: emi CHS 763 0452
		excerpts
		lp: electrola E 80039/WCLP 601/
		  SME 80039
		lp: eterna 820 510
		lp: emi 1C063 00830

die walküre, act one

rome	rai roma	lp: cetra FE 47
15 january	orchestra	cd: *music and arts CD 866*
1952	h.konetzni,	
	treptow,	
	rohr	

die walküre, act three

london	lpo	lp: ed smith EJS 450
26 may	flagstad,	lp: private issue (japan) JPL 1020-1022
1937	müller,	lp: discocorp RR 417
	bockelmann	lp: acanta 40.23520
		cd: acanta 44.1055
		cd: myto MCD 91443
		cd: grammofono AB 78512
		cd: dante LYS 217-218
		cd: *music and arts CD 1035*
		<u>excerpts</u>
		cd: acanta 43.121
		<u>unpublished hmv 78 rpm recordings;</u>
		<u>excerpts also on cd in japan by palette</u>

die walküre, excerpts (prelude; wes herd dies auch sei; labung
biet' ich; weither, traun; auf den leichen lag sie tot; was gleisst
dort hell?; höre mich an/eine waffe lass' mich dir weisen; du bist
der lenz; ein minnetraum; nun zäume dein ross/hojotoho!;
verweile, süssestes weib!; wo bist du, siegmund?; nicht fahr' ich
nach walhall; walkürenritt; fort denn eile!/o hehrstes wunder!;
du zeugtest ein edles geschlecht; loge hör'!; wer meines speeres
spitze fürchtet)

vienna	vpo	cd: dante LYS 217-218
13 february	a.konetzni,	cd: *koch 3-1470-2*
1936	müller,	<u>labung biet' ich</u>
	hadrabova,	lp: ed smith EJS 451/EJS 543
	völker,	<u>ed smith incorrectly dated</u>
	grossmann,	<u>december 1937</u>
	jerger	

die walküre, excerpt (hojotoho!)

london   lpo   lp: ed smith EJS 170/UORC 234
1 june   leider
1938

die walküre, walkürenritt

vienna   vpo   78: hmv DB 6950
31 march   45: hmv 7R 141/7P 206
1949   45: hmv (france) 7RF 203
                              45: hmv (italy) 7RQ 3004
                              45: electrola 7RW 125
                              45: victor EHA 17
                              lp: hmv (france) FBLP 25057
                              lp: victor LHMV 1049
                              lp: unicorn WFS 2-3
                              lp: angel 6024
                              lp: emi 1C149 01197-01199M/
                                  29 12343
                              cd: emi CZS 252 3282/*CHS 764 9352*
                              CZS 252 3282 incorrectly dated 1954

CARL MARIA VON WEBER (1786-1826)

aufforderung zum tanz, arranged by berlioz

berlin 1932	bpo	78: grammophon 67056 78: brunswick 90313 lp: dg 88 021/2535 821 lp: melodiya D 030275-030276 cd: dante LYS 116 *cd: koch 3-7073-2*

euryanthe, overture

vienna 6 march 1954	vpo	lp: victor LHMV 19 lp: emi XLP 30090/F666.699/ 1C149 03584-03586M cd: palladio PD 4124 cd: historical performers HP 8 *cd: emi CHS 566 7702*
paris 4 may 1954	bpo	lp: dg 2535 805 lp: cetra LO 519/FE 45 cd: french furtwängler society SWF 942-943 <u>also issued on cd in japan by dg</u>
turin 14 may 1954	bpo	lp: discocorp RR 413 lp: rococo 2106 lp: paragon DSV 52101 lp: nippon columbia OZ 7590 lp: cetra FE 50 cd: as-disc AS 373

der freischütz

salzburg	vpo	lp: discocorp IGS 008-010/IGI 338
26 july	vienna	lp: cetra LO 21/FE 24
1954	opera chorus	lp: turnabout THS 65148-65150
	grümmer,	lp: robin hood RHR 522
	streich,	lp: nippon columbia OZ 7575-7577
	hopf,	cd: rodolphe RPC 32519-32520
	edelmann,	cd: nuova era 013.6324-013.6326
	böhme,	cd: arkadia CDWFE 302/CDWFE 352
	poell	cd: virtuoso 269.7222
		cd: gala 100.510

overture
cd: foyer CDS 16007
cd: german furtwängler society
    TMK 10670
virtuoso edition omits spoken dialogue;
some issues incorrectly described as a
stereophonic recording

der freischütz,   overture

berlin   bpo   78: grammophon 66466
1926   lp: private issue (japan) JP 1101-1102
                                        lp: discocorp RR 431
                                        cd: symposium 1043
                                        cd: dante LYS 116
                                        cd: koch 3-7059-2

berlin   bpo   78: grammophon 67108-67109
1935   78: brunswick 95030-95031
                                        78: decca CA 8262-8263
                                        78: polydor (france) 566177-566178
                                        lp: rococo 2014
                                        lp: private issue (japan) NA 121-122
                                        lp: dg 2535 821
                                        cd: dante LYS 116
                                        cd: history 20.3090/20.3093
                                        cd: koch 3-7073-2
                                        cd: dg 459 0012/459 0652

berlin   bpo   lp: melodiya M10 41233-41234
20-22   lp: french furtwängler society
march   SWF 8203-8204
1944   lp: tanaka AT 09-10
                                        cd: dg 427 7812/427 7732
                                        cd: melodiya MEL 10 00712
                                        cd: russian compact disc RCD 25003
                                        cd: music and arts CD 826

berlin   bpo   lp: cetra FE 50
7 december   issued on cd only in japan by seven seas
1952

der freischütz overture/concluded

berlin	bpo	lp: german furtwängler society
8 december		F670.027-F670.028
1952		lp: tanaka AT 04
		cd: elaborations (japan) ELA 903
		cd: music and arts CD 795

vienna	vpo	lp: victor LHMV 19
5-6		lp: emi 1C149 03584-03586M/
march		XLP 30090
1954		cd: palladio PD 4124
		cd: historical performers HP 8
		cd: emi CHS 566 7702

der freischütz, act 3 prelude

berlin   bpo   78: grammophon 67109/95411
1935   78: brunswick 95031
                                  78: decca CA 8263
                                  78: polydor (france) 566178
                                  78: polydor (japan) S 4040
                                  lp: rococo 2014
                                  lp: private issue (japan) NA 121-122
                                  lp: dg 2535 821
                                  cd: dante LYS 116
                                  cd: koch 3-7073-2

oberon,   overture

vienna   vpo   78: hmv DB 21104
1 february   78: hmv (australia) ED 1246
1950   45: hmv (france) 7RF 258
                                  45: hmv (italy) 7RQ 258
                                  lp: hmv ALP 1526/XLP 30090
                                  lp: hmv (france) FALP 617
                                  lp: hmv (italy) QALP 10298
                                  lp: electrola E 60655/WDLP 662/
                                      SMVP 8016
                                  lp: melodiya M10 41233-41234
                                  lp: emi 1C149 03584-03586M/
                                      F666.699
                                  cd: palladio PD 4124
                                  cd: historical performers HP 8
                                  cd: emi CHS 566 7702

HUGO WOLF (1860-1903)

lieder: 1.im frühling; 2.elfenlied; 3.lebewohl; 4.schlafendes jesus-
kind; 5.phänomen; 6.die spröde; 7.die bekehrte; 8.anakreons grab;
9.blumengruss; 10.epiphanias; 11.wie lange schon; 12.was soll der
zorn?; 13.nein junger herr!; 14.mein liebster hat zu tische;
15.bedeckt mich mit blumen; 16.herr, was trägt der boden hier?;
17.in dem schatten meiner locken; 18.mögen alle bösen zungen;
19.wie glänzt der helle mond; 20.wiegenlied im sommer;
21.nachtzauber; 22.die zigeunerin

salzburg	schwarzkopf	complete recital
12 august	furtwängler,	lp: cetra FE 30
1953	piano	lp: emi 143 5491
		cd: cetra CDC 21
		cd: virtuoso 269.7312
		nos. 2-7, 9, 10, 12, 16 and 19-21
		lp: emi ALP 2114/1C063 01915M
		lp: angel 60179
		nos. 1-10
		cd: virtuoso 269.7152
		nos. 1-10 and 15-18
		cd: priceless D 18355
		nos. 1, 8, 15, 17, 18 and 22
		lp: discocorp IGI 382
		lp: nippon columbia OZ 7603
		nos. 1, 8, 11, 13-15, 17, 18 and 22
		lp: melodram MEL 088
		lp: discocorp RR 208
		complete recital also issued in japan
		by toshiba and seven seas

MISCELLANEOUS

du gamla du fria,   arrangement of swedish national hymn

stockholm	vpo	lp: private issue (japan)
25 september		GC 570234-570235
1950		lp: tanaka AT 13-14
		cd: theatre (japan) 400.3531

UNPUBLISHED FURTWÄNGLER RECORDINGS
known to have been stored in radio archives or in private hands, but in
many cases probably now irretrievably lost (particularly pre-war items)

beethoven/symphony no 3 "eroica"
salzburg   vpo   private archive berlin
31 august
1950

beethoven/symphony no 4
munich   munich po   private archive munich
26-29
january
1949

beethoven/symphony no 8/second and third movements
berlin   bpo   german radio archives
20 december
1932

beethoven/symphony no 9 "choral"
milan   la scala   rai milano or private archive
28 may   orchestra
1949   and chorus
                  cecil,
                  simionato
                  prandelli,
                  siepi

beethoven/symphony no 9 "choral"/second movement
berlin   bpo   german radio archives
16 june
1930

beethoven/symphony no 9 "choral"/excerpts
berlin   bpo   german radio archives
18 april   kittel choir
1932   ginster,
                  dierolf,
                  rosvaenge,
                  bockelmann

beethoven/symphony no 9 "choral"/concluding bars

berlin	bpo	newsreel picture only
19 april	kittel choir	sound dubbed in from the 22-24
1942	berger,	march 1942 performance
	höngen,	
	rosvaenge,	
	watzke	

salzburg	vpo	newsreel footage
31 august	vienna	used in several tv documentaries
1951	opera chorus	about furtwängler
	seefried,	
	wagner,	
	dermota,	
	greindl	

beethoven/piano concerto no 4

berlin	bpo	private archive vienna
2-4	kempff	possibly recorded by hermann may
november		
1941		

beethoven/grosse fuge

munich	bpo	private archive munich
7 may		
1952		

beethoven/coriolan overture

london	vpo	bbc studio recording
1 october		concert broadcast on 25 december 1949
1949		

beethoven/egmont overture

berlin	bpo	german radio archives
15 september		
1933		

beethoven/fidelio/gott! welch dunkel hier!

vienna	vpo	private archive vienna
7 january	lorenz	possibly recorded by hermann may
1942		

berlioz/marche hongroise from la damnation de faust
cairo or   bpo   cairo radio archive
alexandria
19-25
april
1951

brahms/symphony no 3
cairo or   bpo   cairo radio archive
alexandria   tape of this performance is
20-25   in circulation
april
1951

brahms/symphony no 3/final movement
berlin   bpo   german radio archives
15 march
1932

brahms/symphony no 4
frankfurt   vpo   private archive munich
21 october
1951

brahms/violin concerto/rehearsal extract
salzburg   vpo   newsreel footage
13 august   menuhin   used in several tv documentaries
1947   about furtwängler

brahms/haydn variations
london   vpo   bbc studio recording
1 october   concert broadcast on 25 december 1949
1949

furtwängler/symphony no 2
hamburg   bpo   private archive berlin
15 january
1953

handel/concerto grosso op 6 no 5
munich   munich po   private archive munich
8-10
january
1950

haydn/die schöpfung

lucerne	lucerne	swiss radio archive
27-28	festival	tapes almost certainly erased
august	orchestra	
1949	and chorus	
	seefried,	
	w.ludwig,	
	christoff	

hindemith/die harmonie der welt

berlin	bpo	sender freies berlin
7 december		
1952		

hindemith/concerto for orchestra

cairo	bpo	cairo radio archive
20 april		
1951		

mendelssohn/hebrides overture

vienna	vpo	unpublished hmv/emi takes
7 december		
1948		

mozart/concerto for 2 pianos

vienna	vpo	private archive vienna
8 february	bella,	recording published by discocorp,
1949	badura-skoda	nippon columbia, french furtwängler
		society and music and arts, supposedly
		of this performance, does not seem to
		be conducted by furtwängler; this is
		not to deny that a genuine recording
		exists

mozart sinfonia concertante for violin and viola/third movement
berlin   bpo   german radio archives
27 october   goldberg,
1932   hindemith

mozart don giovanni
salzburg   vpo   unused soundtrack recording
august   vienna   for paul czinner film of the opera
1954   opera chorus <u>recording may not have been</u>
       schwarzkopf, <u>completed (see main discography)</u>
       grümmer,
       berger,
       dermota,
       edelmann,
       siepi,
       ernster,
       berry

reger/fugue from mozart variations
berlin   bpo   german radio archives
27 october
1932

schubert symphony no 8 "unfinished"
london   vpo   bbc studio recording
1 october   <u>concert broadcast on 25 december 1949</u>
1949

copenhagen vpo   danish radio archive
1 october
1950

vienna   vpo   private archive vienna
30 may
1954

j.strauss/kaiserwalzer
london   vpo   bbc studio concert
1 october   <u>concert broadcast on 25 december 1949</u>
1949

strauss/till eulenspiegel/rehearsal extract

berlin	staatskapelle	newsreel footage
2 june		<u>used in several tv documentaries</u>
1947		<u>about furtwängler</u>

tchaikovsky/symphony no 5/extract from second movement

berlin	bpo	german radio archives
6 february		
1933		

wagner/götterdämmerung funeral march

vienna	vpo	unpublished hmv/emi takes
23 february		
1949		

wagner/das rheingold

london	lpo	unpublished hmv test pressings
24 may	wray,	
1937	thorborg,	
	furmedge,	
	fuchs,	
	bockelmann,	
	weber,	
	easton	

wagner/siegfried/extracts

london	lpo	unpublished hmv test pressings
28 may	flagstad,	
1937	andreva,	
	furmedge,	
	melchior,	
	zimmermann,	
	bockelmann,	
	fuchs,	
	easton	

wagner/tristan und isolde/liebestrank; hörst du sie noch?; sink hernieder

bayreuth	bayreuth	german radio archives
23 july	festival	
1931	orchestra	
	larsen-todsen.	
	helm,	
	melchior,	
	manowarda	

wagner/tristan und isolde prelude

bayreuth	bayreuth	german radio archives
18 august	festival	
1931	orchestra	

wagner/die walküre/des frech frevelnden paars

london	lpo	private acetate
1 june	thorborg,	
1938	kamann	

weber/der freischütz overture

cairo	bpo	cairo radio archive
20-22		
april		
1951		

PUBLISHED RECORDINGS INCORRECTLY ATTRIBUTED TO WILHELM FURTWÄNGLER

it will be noted that certain unscrupulous producers of pirate cds continue to publish certain of the recordings listed below, in spite of the fact the performances have been known for a considerable time not to be genuine furtwängler versions

beethoven/symphony no 2
berlin   bpo   lp: olympic OL 8120
1929   lp: eurodisc XFK 28631
this was identified as the 1929 grammophon recording by erich kleiber and the berlin staatskapelle

beethoven/symphony no 8
berlin   bpo   lp: mrf records MRF 50/MRF 64
april   lp: bjr records BJR 118
1953   cd: palette (japan) PAL 1026
this was identified as probably the 1957-1958 hmv recording by andré cluytens and the berlin philharmonic

beethoven/coriolan overture
hamburg   bpo   cd: rodolphe RPC 32522-32524
june   this was identified as a recording by
1949   hermann scherchen

brahms/symphony no 1
vienna   vpo   lp: nippon columbia DXM 163
1942   although copies of this lp have not been sighted, it probably contained the 1944 electrola recording by böhm and the vienna philharmonic

d'albert/tiefland overture
july   bayreuth or   lp: melodiya M10 46683 000
1944   munich   lp: private issue (japan) W 22-23
                 orchestra   cd: melodiya MEL 10 00724
cd: palladio PD 4204
cd: russian compact disc RCD 25015
also issued on cd by iron needle; furtwängler never conducted this opera by d'albert, which in fact does not have an overture!

dvorak/symphony no 9 "from the new world"
berlin   bpo   lp: relief (switzerland) REL 813
november   cd: relief (switzerland) CR 1813
1941   cd: philips (japan) 30CD-3036
                        cd: as-disc AS 111
research by ernst lumpe revealed this to be a reichsrundfunk recording by oswald kabasta and the munich philharmonic

glazunov/stenka razin
vienna   vpo   lp: melodiya M10 46683 000
february   lp: private issue (japan) W 22-23
1945   cd: melodiya MEL 10 00710
                        cd: palladio PD 4204
                        cd: russian compact disc RCD 25001
                        cd: history 20.3090/20.3091
also issued on cd by iron needle; furtwängler never conducted this work

grieg/piano concerto
1944   bpo   lp: melodiya M10 36605-36606
            gieseking   lp: everest SDBR 8434
                        lp: discocorp IGI 348
                        cd: melodiya MEL 10 00711
                        cd: grammofono AB 78538
                        cd: russian compact disc RCD 25002
                        cd: history 20.3090/20.3094
also issued on cd by iron needle; orchestra and soloist are as stated, but the conductor was robert heger

haydn/symphony no 104 "london"
berlin   bpo   lp: melodiya M10 37145-37146
1944   lp: discocorp RR 441
                        cd: dg 427 7762/427 7732
                        cd: melodiya MEL 10 00713
                        cd: dante LYS 246
                        cd: russian compact disc RCD 25004
research by ernst lumpe revealed this to be a recording by alfons dressel and the munich radio orchestra

mozart/symphony no 40/final movement

berlin	bpo	lp: period SPL 716
december		lp: everest SDBR 3252
1951		lp: nippon columbia OZ 7076

this was taken from the soundtrack of
the film botschafter der musik, where
the conductor is clearly seen to be
bruno walter

mozart/concerto for 2 pianos

vienna	vpo	lp: discocorp AUDAX 765
8 february	badura-skoda,	lp: nippon columbia OZ 7602
1949	bella	lp: french furtwängler society
		SWF 8401-8402

cd: music and arts CD 895
it is felt by various researchers that
the genuine recording of this
performance remains unpublished
and that the version issued on the
above labels does not bear the
characteristics of furtwängler's
conducting

schubert/symphony no 2

| undated | vpo | lp: nippon columbia DXM 165 |

this symphony was not in furtwängler's
repertoire

schubert/symphony no 3

| undated | vpo | lp: nippon columbia DXM 165 |

this symphony was not in furtwängler's
repertoire

tchaikovsky/symphony no 6 "pathétique"

münster	vpo	cd: palette (japan) PAL 1071
13 october		
1951		

although furtwängler conducted the
work on this date, this recording bears
no resemblance to his interpretation

wagner/parsifal/closing scene

bayreuth	bayreuth	lp: discocorp RR 379
1937	festival	
	orchestra	
	and chorus	
	lorenz,	
	janssen	

this is either a 1933 performance at
bayreuth conducted by richard strauss
or one elsewhere conducted by fritz
reiner

wagner/der ring des nibelungen/extracts

bayreuth	bayreuth	die walküre/ein schwert verhiess mir
july-	festival	lp: bayreuth festival 1976
august	orchestra	götterdämmerung/scenes from acts 2 & 3
1937	and chorus	lp: french furtwängler society SWF 7802
	leider,	lp: discocorp RR 540
	heidersbach,	cd: dante LYS 219-221
	lorenz,	this comprises furtwängler performances
	prohaska,	from london (1937) and milan (1950)
	hofmann	and leider's commercial recording of
		the immolation scene conducted by
		leo blech

WILHELM FURTWÄNGLER THE COMPOSER

furtwängler's own performances of his second symphony and symphonic concerto, included of course in the main discography, are now supplemented by a growing number of other recorded performances of both those works as well as a considerable selection from his remaining output

symphonic allegro/1908

kosice	slovak state po	cd: marco polo 8.223645
12 february	a.walter	
1993		

symphonic largo/1908

kosice	slovak state po	cd: marco polo 8.223645
31 august	a.walter	
1993		

symphony no 1/1941

kosice	slovak state po	cd: marco polo 8.223295
3-8	a.walter	
may		
1993		

symphony no 2/1948

berlin 11 may 1982	bpo barenboim	unpublished radio broadcast <u>only the scherzo movement was performed at this concert during the bpo centenary year</u>
tokyo 2 july 1984	osaka po asahina	cd: victor/jvc (japan) VDC 5007-5008 <u>also issued on lp by victor/jvc</u>
london 23-24 january 1992	bbc so a.walter	cd: marco polo 8.223436
jena 6 november 1997	jena po ehwald	unpublished radio broadcast

<u>unpublished radio broadcasts of early performances of the symphony by
joseph keilberth and eugen jochum may also survive</u>

symphony no 3/1954

bamberg 1956	bamberg so keilberth	unpublished radio broadcast also unpublished video recording of closing bars
berlin 30 november 1979	bpo maazel	unpublished radio broadcast concert to mark 25th anniversary of furtwängler's death
munich 7 january 1980	bayerisches staatsorchester sawallisch	lp: french furtwängler society SWF 8603 cd: orfeo C406 961B
vienna 27 january 1986	austrian ro menuhin	unpublished radio broadcast furtwängler centenary concert
brussels december 1987	belgian ro a.walter	cd: marco polo 8.223105
marl 12 june 1993	philharmonia hungarica g.a.albrecht	unpublished private recording
weimar 28 november 1998	staatskapelle weimar g.a.albrecht	unpublished radio broadcast

keilberth, maazel and sawallisch conduct the incomplete 3-movement
version of the symphony

symphonic concerto for piano and orchestra

munich 27 june 1963	bavarian ro then-bergh kubelik	cd: tahra TAH 197
turin 23 august 1963	rai torino bella argento	unpublished radio broadcast
beromünster 1964	beromünster ro barenboim mehta	unpublished radio broadcast
los angeles 1967	los angeles po barenboim mehta	lp: penzance PR 13
vienna 17 january 1986	austrian ro badura-skoda zagrosek	unpublished radio broadcast furtwängler centenary concert
kosice 2-4 july 1990	slovak state po lively a.walter	cd: marco polo 8.223333

a version of the concerto with the bavarian ro and soloist homero francesch
is also reported to be stored in bavarian radio archives

overture in e flat

| kosice 30 june 1993 | slovak state po a.walter | cd: marco polo 8.223645 |

te deum for soloists, chorus and orchestra

| berlin 12 march 1967 | bpo chemin-petit philharmonic choir mathis, wagner, jelden, dooley | unpublished radio broadcast and unpublished video recording |

| vienna 27 january 1986 | austrian ro menuhin orf chorus fontana, hintermeier, moser, helm | unpublished radio broadcast furtwängler centenary concert |

| frankfurt an der oder 22-25 june 1993 | frankfurt po a.walter frankfurt singakademie unnamed soloists | cd: marco polo 8.223546 |

| berlin 29 november 1994 | rundfunk- sinfonie- orchester m.fischer-dieskau latvian state choir schäfer, schreckenbach, lang, kraus | unpublished radio broadcast |

schwindet ihr dunklen wölbungen, for chorus and orchestra

frankfurt an der oder 22-25 june 1993	frankfurt po a.walter frankfurt singakademie	cd: marco polo 8.223546

religiöser hymnus for tenor, soprano, chorus and orchestra

frankfurt an der oder 22-25 june 1993	frankfurt po a.walter frankfurt singakademie unnamed soloists	cd: marco polo 8.223546

piano quintet

heidelberg c.1975	elyséen string quartet bellik	lp: da camera magna SM 92814-92815 cd: bayer 100269
paris 17-20 may 1993	sine nomine string quartet kerdoncuff	cd: timpani 1C-1018
jena 9 november 1997	brandis, nahmer, rohde, boettcher, zichner	unpublished private recording

violin sonata no 1

stuttgart 28 january 1986	lessing, bergemann	unpublished radio broadcast
amsterdam 16 november 1994	kang, kerdoncuff	unpublished radio broadcast
paris december 1994	kang, kerdoncuff	cd: timpani 1C-1029
details uncertain	unger, webersinke	cd: ricophon 400.5342
jena 29 november 1998	süssmuth, krahnert	unpublished private recording

violin sonata no 2

heidelberg december 1971	müller-nisho, dennemarck	lp: da camera magna SM 93314 cd: bayer 100268
paris 9-10 june 1989	galpérine, kerdoncuff	cd: timpani 1C-1001
jena 8 november 1997	süssmuth, krahnert	unpublished private recording

piano sonata

usa 1985	rivard	cassette tape: symposium 1009 limited edition for furtwängler society members

theme and variations for piano

usa 1985	rivard	cassette tape: symposium 1009 limited edition for furtwängler society members

2 fugues for piano

usa 1985	rivard	cassette tape: symposium 1009 limited edition for furtwängler society members

2 fantasias for piano

usa 1985	rivard	cassette tape: symposium 1009 limited edition for furtwängler society members

11 lieder: der traurige jäger; der schatzgräber; geduld; auf dem see; du sendest, freund, mir lieder; erinnerung i; das vaterland; möwenflug; lied; erinnerung ii; der soldat

brussels 7-8 october 1993	pikal, a.walter	cd: marco polo 8.223546

FURTWÄNGLER EDITION

Furtwängler
SYMPHONY No. 2 IN E MINOR

SINFONIE ORCHESTER
DES HESSISCHEN RUNDFUNKS

417 287-1

CÉSAR FRANCK: Symphony
SCHUMANN: Symphony No. 1

WIENER PHILHARMONIKER
WILHELM FURTWÄNGLER

Introduction to the concert register

The long period of research which has elapsed since my previous compilation of Wilhelm Furtwängler's concert and opera performances (which appeared in The Furtwängler Sound, 3rd edition 1990) has enabled me to fill many gaps. I have been helped by other reference works which have appeared in the meantime, such as "Klangbilder: Porträt der Staatskapelle Berlin" by Georg Quander (Propyläen Verlag 1995) with its precise details of Furtwängler's concerts at the head of that orchestra; the occasional publications from Société Wilhelm Furtwängler with information on concerts in particular countries (France, Switzerland, Italy); and the 1997 Concert Listing of René Trémine. As far as the last book is concerned, I have corrected a number of errors (and many spelling mistakes) without, I hope, creating too many new ones of my own !

The central pillars of Furtwängler's performing activity, as I see them, can be summarised as follows:-

1.Early years, mainly Lübeck and Mannheim
2.Early Berlin (Staatskapelle and Philharmonic), Vienna (Ton-künstler, described throughout this listing by their present-day name of Vienna Symphony) and Frankfurt and Leipzig years
3.Pre-war operatic activity in Berlin, Vienna, Paris, London and Bayreuth
4.Central Berlin Philharmonic years 1930-1954, interrupted between 1945-1947
5.Post-war guest conducting with leading concert orchestras and operatic institutions in Salzburg, Milan, Berlin and Vienna
Added to these are Furtwängler's activities outside Europe (USA 1925-1927, Egypt 1951 and South America 1948, 1950 and 1954).

Furtwängler's style of programme building mirrors an outlook rooted in the period before classical music was generally available by means of gramophone recordings. In other words, the purpose of the symphony concert in the early years of the twentieth century was comparable to that of a museum or art gallery, making accessible the considered masterworks of musical literature. A standard programme of overture, concerto and symphony was only a guide for Furtwängler: that order might be reversed, or the concerto perhaps placed in the second half of the programme. On extended tours with his Berlin and Vienna orchestras, he was not content to repeat night after night an identical programme: there would be endless permutations of a selected repertoire, as well as a generous helping of encore pieces (these are included as part of the listing where known, although in some cases the concert reviews did not mention the encores). The more than generous inclusion of new works in Furtwängler's concert programmes will become evident, and contradicts the assertion that he neglected new music.

Various attempts have been made over the years to draw up statistics on Wilhelm Furtwängler's repertoire. Every reader can now perform this task for himself, with the concert listing now claiming to be at least 95 per cent complete. In 1941 Friedrich Herzfeld published his book "Wilhelm Furtwängler: Weg und Wesen" (Goldmann-Verlag Leipzig), from which one was able to see how many times Furtwängler had conducted the most popular items in his repertoire. It is therefore interesting to update Herzfeld's figures to include the remaining 14 years of the conductor's career after 1940. Performances of the works for commercial recording sessions are not included, but I have rounded up the figures to allow for the small number of concerts where programme content is not known. The results are :-

A final note concerning this concert listing: because of their variegated nature, I have not included in the list the series of popular concerts which Furtwängler inherited when he took up his post in Lübeck. As can be seen from Trémine's catalogue, those programmes included a variety of lighter repertoire, some of which might be considered "classical" and some not.

Work	Number of public performances
Beethoven 5	240
Beethoven 7	175
Brahms 1	170
Strauss Till Eulenspiegel	165
Wagner Meistersinger overture	145

Runners-up for this Top Five are Beethoven 3 and Strauss Tod und Verklärung

munich 19 february 1906
kaim-orchester
beethoven weihe des hauses overture
furtwängler adagio in b minor
bruckner symphony 9
first public concert

zürich 10 october 1906
ballet performance
blättermann tanzbilder

zürich 31 october 1906
ibsen das fest auf solhaug
furtwängler conducted pfitzner's
incidental music to this stage play

zürich 23 december 1906
rübezahl
furtwängler conducted incidental
music to this stage play on the
above date and 9 further occasions

zürich 3 february 1907
lehar die lustige witwe
also 8 further performances

munich 1907-1910
furtwängler worked at munich hofoper
during this period as repetiteur only

strassburg 27 september 1910
donizetti l'elisir d'amore

strassburg 18 october 1910
maillart das glöckchen des eremiten
also 4 further performances

strassburg 27 december 1910
flotow martha
also 2 further performances

strassburg 1 january 1911
messager die kleinen michus
also 2 further performances

strassburg 4 march 1911
suppé die flotten burschen
also 1 further performance

strassburg 11 march 1911
verdi rigoletto

lübeck 5 april 1911
lübeck orchestra
volkmann
weber der freischütz overture
beethoven symphony 5 excerpts
wagner lohengrin prelude
smetana moldau
liszt hungarian rhapsody 2
sibelius valse triste
maillart glöckchen des eremiten ov.
fantasy on gounod's faust
volkmann cello concerto
j.strauss wiener blut
this was furtwängler's audition
concert for the lübeck position

lübeck 21 october 1911
lübeck orchestra
friedberg
beethoven programme
symphony 7, piano concerto 5 and
leonore 3 overture

lübeck 18 november 1911
lübeck orchestra
senius-euler
liszt dante symphony
berlioz carnaval romain overture
berlioz romeo and juliet love scene
arias and songs by handel, wagner,
liszt and weingartner, some of which
accompanied by furtwängler on the
piano

lübeck 22 november 1911
lübeck orchestra and chorus
schmidt, stronck-kappel,
arlberg, hells
mendelssohn elijah

strassburg 6 december 1911
strassburg orchestra and chorus
schuster, altmann-kuntz,
batteux, gless
furtwängler te deum

lübeck 16 december 1911
lübeck orchestra
carreno
mendelssohn hebrides overture
tchaikovsky piano concerto 1
tchaikovsky symphony 5

190

lübeck 13 january 1912
lübeck orchestra
bach brandenburg concerto 4
mozart symphony 40
beethoven symphony 3

lübeck 29 january 1912
furtwängler provided piano
accompaniment to karl erb for 2 of
the liszt petrarch sonnets
<u>concert conducted by siegfried wagner</u>

lübeck 10 february 1912
lübeck orchestra
culp
berlioz corsaire overture
debussy prélude à l'après-midi
brahms symphony 4
lieder by beethoven and schubert,
accompanied by furtwängler at the
piano

lübeck 24 february 1912
lübeck orchestra and chorus
beer-waldbrunn sinfonia
beethoven elegischer gesang
wolf feuerreiter & morgenhymnus
wagner tristan prelude & liebestod
wagner meistersinger overture

lübeck 23 march 1912
lübeck orchestra
kase
schumann manfred overture
schubert symphony 9
arias by marschner and pfitzner

lübeck 4 and 5 april 1912
lübeck orchestra and chorus
stretten, beckershaus,
wörmsbacher, rothenbücher
bach cantata 161
mozart requiem

lübeck 20 april 1912
lübeck orchestra
flesch
schillings oedipus rex prelude
brahms violin concerto
beethoven symphony 5

<u>in addition to the above subscription</u>
<u>concerts in lübeck, furtwängler also</u>
<u>conducted many "popular" concerts</u>
<u>there, comprising overtures, suites,</u>
<u>and a variety of other shorter works</u>
<u>of serious and light nature: these</u>
<u>continued in subsequent lübeck seasons</u>

lübeck 12 october 1912
lübeck orchestra
marteau, szanto, nowack
beethoven symphony 4
mozart violin concerto 5
vivaldi concerto for 3 violins
strauss till eulenspiegel

lübeck 19 october 1912
<u>chamber concert</u>
in which furtwängler partnered
hofmeier in brahms sonata for 2
pianos in f minor

lübeck 9 november 1912
lübeck orchestra
freund
bruckner symphony 7
mahler kindertotenlieder
wagner fliegende holländer overture

lübeck 16 november 1912
<u>chamber concert</u>
in which furtwängler partnered
szanto and corbach in beethoven
piano trios and franck violin sonata

lübeck 20 november 1912
lübeck orchestra and chorus
lammen-lauprechts, ladiges,
schreiber, tödten
schumann paradies und die peri

lübeck 7 december 1912
lübeck orchestra
schnitzer
reger romantische suite
grieg piano concerto
beethoven symphony 6

lübeck 4 january 1913
lübeck orchestra
szanto, ulrich, furtwängler
bach brandenburg concerto 5
schubert symphony 8
brahms symphony 1

vienna 26 january 1913
konzertvereins-orchester
szell, ritter
beethoven leonore 2 overture
beethoven piano concerto 3
wolf lieder
strauss till eulenspiegel
furtwängler's vienna debut

lübeck 1 february 1913
lübeck orchestra and chorus
erb
haydn symphony 103
beethoven florestan's aria/fidelio
liszt psalm 13
boethe tragic overture

lübeck 1 march 1913
lübeck orchestra
braunfels
schumann genoveva overture
dukas l'apprenti sorcier
braunfels piano concerto
beethoven symphony 8

lübeck 29 march 1913
lübeck orchestra and chorus
köhnen
tchaikovsky symphony 6
brahms alto rhapsody
beethoven egmont overture
lieder by schubert, schumann & brahms

lübeck 18 april 1913
chamber concert
in which furtwängler accompanied
szanto in violin sonatas by brahms
and saint-saens and küller in lieder
by schubert, brahms and wolf

lübeck 26 april 1913
lübeck orchestra and chorus
ohlhoff, küller,
fischer, van eweyk
wagner parsifal prelude and
      karfreitagszauber
beethoven symphony 9

lübeck 11 october 1913
lübeck orchestra
ripper
strauss sinfonia domestica
liszt piano concerto 1
weber oberon overture
brahms hungarian dance

lübeck 8 november 1913
lübeck orchestra
bosetti
reger böcklin-suite
tchaikovsky symphony 4
arias and songs by mozart, wolf
      and pfitzner

lübeck stadttheater 20 november 1913
wagner die meistersinger von nürnberg
furtwängler's first stage performance
of a wagner music drama

lübeck 6 december 1913
lübeck orchestra
gérardy
grammann aventiure sinfonie
saint-saens cello concerto 1
haydn symphony 100

lübeck 3 january 1914
lübeck orchestra
szanto
mozart symphony 39
bach violin concerto 2
beethoven symphony 5

lübeck 31 january 1914
lübeck orchestra and chorus
tödten
beethoven coriolan overture
brahms gesang der parzen
liszt faust symphony

lübeck 28 february 1914
lübeck orchestra
berber
hausegger wieland der schmied
beethoven violin concerto
schumann symphony 1

hamburg 13 march 1914
stadttheater orchestra
droucker
brahms programme
tragic overture, piano concerto 2
and symphony 1

lübeck 28 march 1914
lübeck orchestra
durigo
bruckner symphony 8
arias and songs by mozart & schubert

lübeck 7, 14 and 20 april 1914
beethoven violin sonata cycle
furtwängler accompanied szanto

lübeck 8 april 1914
lübeck orchestra and chorus
nicolai ein' feste burg
mozart ave verum corpus
wagner parsifal karfeitagszauber

lübeck 9 and 10 april 1914
lübeck orchestra and chorus
schmidt, fischer-maresski, hardoff
bach saint matthew passion

lübeck 25 april 1914
lübeck orchestra
lamond
gluck alceste overture
brahms piano concerto 2
beethoven symphony 7

munich 3 july 1914
konzertvereins-orchester
berlioz corsaire overture
schubert symphony 8
beethoven symphony 5

lübeck 10 october 1914
lübeck orchestra
wagner kaisermarsch & siegfried idyll
beethoven symphony 5

lübeck 14 october 1914
lübeck orchestra
szanto
mendelssohn heimkehr aus der fremde
beethoven violin concerto
wagner siegfried's rhine journey

lübeck 7 november 1914
lübeck orchestra
szanto
brahms symphony 3
brahms violin concerto
strauss tod und verklärung

hamburg 15 and 16 november 1914
stadttheater-orchester
kwast-hodapp
beethoven programme
leonore 3 overture, piano concerto 1
and symphony 7

lübeck 5 december 1914
lübeck orchestra
fromm
weber der freischütz overture
schumann piano concerto
bruckner symphony 4

lübeck 2 january 1915
lübeck orchestra
szanto, poppeck, furtwängler
bach brandenburg concerto 5
mozart symphony 38
beethoven symphony 3

lübeck 30 january 1915
lübeck orchestra
szanto, corbach, furtwängler
wagner faust overture
beethoven triple concerto
mendelssohn symphony 3

lübeck 27 february 1915
lübeck orchestra
mysz-gmeiner
goldmark sakuntala overture
beethoven symphony 6
lieder by mahler and wolf

lübeck 13 march 1915
lübeck orchestra
szanto
reger patriotic overture
dvorak violin concerto
schubert symphony 9

lübeck stadttheater 23 march 1915
beethoven fidelio

lübeck 1 and 2 april 1915
lübeck orchestra and chorus
bach saint matthew passion

lübeck 10 april 1915
lübeck orchestra
bach suite 2
beethoven symphony 8
brahms symphony 1

lübeck stadttheater 16 april 1915
nicolai die lustigen weiber
von windsor

lübeck 28 april 1915
lübeck orchestra
szanto
bach suite 2
beethoven violin concerto
weber der freischütz overture
liszt hungarian rhapsody no 4
wagner meistersinger overture

mannheim opera 7 september 1915
beethoven fidelio

mannheim opera 12 & 21 september 1915
marschner hans heiling

mannheim opera 3 october 1915
wagner der fliegende holländer

mannheim opera 10 october 1915
weber der freischütz

mannheim 19 october 1915
mannheim orchestra
haydn symphony 100
beethoven symphony 5

mannheim opera 1 november 1915
beethoven fidelio

mannheim opera 7 november 1915
wagner die walküre

mannheim 16 november 1915
mannheim orchestra
flesch
vivaldi concerto
mozart violin concerto
bruckner symphony 4

mannheim opera 28 november and
2 december 1915
schillings mona lisa

mannheim opera 5 december 1915
weber der freischütz

mannheim 7 december 1915
mannheim orchestra
reger
bach piano concerto in d minor
rest of concert conducted by reger

mannheim opera 9 & 17 december 1915
schillings mona lisa

mannheim opera 12 december 1915
wagner siegfried

mannheim opera 19 december 1915
götterdämmerung

mannheim opera 1 january 1916
wagner die walküre

mannheim 11 january 1916
mannheim orchestra
hoehn
graener abendmusik
schumann piano concerto
brahms symphony 1

mannheim opera 20 january 1916
nicolai die lustigen weiber
von windsor

mannheim opera 23 january 1916
wagner tristan und isolde

mannheim opera 27 january 1916
wagner der fliegende holländer

mannheim 1 february 1916
mannheim orchestra
havemann
mendelssohn hebrides overture
dvorak violin concerto
berlioz symphonie fantastique

mannheim opera 3 & 25 february 1916
schillings mona lisa

mannheim opera 8 february 1916
nicolai die lustigen weiber
von windsor

mannheim opera 20 february 1916
mozart don giovanni

mannheim 22 february 1916
mannheim orchestra
schnabel
schumann genoveva overture
brahms piano concerto 1
beethoven symphony 3

mannheim opera 2 march 1916
nicolai die lustigen weiber
von windsor

mannheim opera 7 march 1916
mozart don giovanni

mannheim opera 9 march 1916
schillings mona lisa

mannheim opera 11-19 march 1916
first complete ring cycle
11 march
wagner das rheingold
12 march
wagner die walküre
15 march
wagner siegfried
19 march
wagner götterdämmerung

mannheim 28 march 1916
mannheim orchestra
bach brandenburg concerto 3
strauss tod und verklärung
strauss eine alpensinfonie

mannheim opera 14 april 1916
wagner der fliegende holländer

mannheim opera 23 april 1916
wagner parsifal

mannheim opera 2 and 5 may 1916
klenuau sulamith
klenau klein idas blumen

mannheim opera 24 may 1916
pfitzner der arme heinrich

mannheim opera 28 may 1916
wagner tristan und isolde

mannheim opera 1 june 1916
wagner parsifal

mannheim opera 4 june 1916
wagner die walküre

mannheim opera 16 june 1916
pfitzner der arme heinrich

mannheim opera 18 june 1916
beethoven fidelio

mannheim opera 22 june 1916
wagner der fliegende holländer

mannheim opera 26 june 1916
nicolai die lustigen weiber
von windsor

mannheim opera 1 september 1916
wagner der fliegende holländer

mannheim opera 3 & 21 september 1916
bizet carmen

mannheim opera 17 september 1916
wagner die walküre

mannheim opera 1 october 1916
wagner tannhäuser

mannheim 10 october 1916
mannheim orchestra
gerhardt
mozart symphony 40
schubert die allmacht
schubert symphony 9

mannheim opera 13 october 1916
nicolai die lustigen weiber
von windsor

mannheim opera 14 & 29 october 1916
weber der freischütz

mannheim opera 17 october 1916
bizet carmen

mannheim opera 24 october 1916
wagner der fliegende holländer

mannheim opera 25 october 1916
mozart die entführung aus dem serail

mannheim opera 26 october 1916
j.strauss die fledermaus

mannheim 31 october 1916
mannheim orchestra
busch
reger romantische suite
brahms violin concerto
liszt tasso

mannheim opera 7 november 1916
mozart die entführung aus dem serail

mannheim 12 november 1916 am
mannheim orchestra

mannheim opera 12 november 1916 pm
verdi aida

mannheim opera 14 november 1916
weber der freischütz

mannheim 21 november 1916
mannheim orchestra
metzger, lippmann
mahler das lied von der erde
beethoven symphony 6

mannheim opera 26 november 1916
wagner die walküre

mannheim opera 3 december 1916
bizet carmen

mannheim opera 6, 15 & 21
december 1916
klenau klein idas blumen

mannheim 12 december 1916
mannheim orchestra
schapira
klenau dante-sinfonie
wolf italian serenade
liszt hungarian fantasia
strauss burleske
strauss till eulenspiegel

mannheim opera 17 december 1916
verdi aida

mannheim opera 19 december 1916
strauss ariadne auf naxos

mannheim opera 31 december 1916
j.strauss die fledermaus

mannheim opera 3 & 16 january 1917
strauss ariadne auf naxos

mannheim 9 january 1917
mannheim orchestra
onegin
haydn symphony 94
mozart parto parto/clemenza di tito
schumann symphony 4

mannheim opera 14 & 27 february 1917
strauss salome

mannheim 17 january 1917
mannheim orchestra
beethoven symphony 4
rest of concert conducted by strauss

mannheim opera 18 february 1917
wagner tannhäuser

mannheim opera 4 march 1917
wagner siegfried

mannheim 6 march 1917
mannheim orchestra
birkigt
hausegger wieland der schmied
bruch scottish fantasy
brahms symphony 4

mannheim opera 14 march 1917
strauss salome

mannheim 20 march 1917
mannheim orchestra
pauer
beethoven programme
coriolan overture, piano concert 4
and symphony 3

mannheim opera 23 march 1917
bizet carmen

mannheim opera 24 march 1917
j.strauss die fledermaus

mannheim opera 1 & 11 april 1917
beethoven fidelio

mannheim opera 4 april 1917
weber der freischütz

mannheim opera 8 april 1917
wagner parsifal

mannheim opera 13 april 1917
wagner das rheingold

mannheim opera 15 april 1917
wagner die walküre

mannheim opera 24 and 27 april 1917
mozart die zauberflöte

mannheim opera 29 april 1917
wagner siegfried

mannheim opera 2 and 23 may 1917
mozart die zauberflöte

mannheim opera 4 and 30 may 1917
beethoven fidelio

mannheim opera 6 may 1917
weber der freischütz

mannheim opera 12 may 1917
j.strauss die fledermaus

mannheim opera 17 and 28 may 1917
wagner parsifal

mannheim opera 27 may 1917
wagner tannhäuser

mannheim opera 3 and 17 june 1917
mozart die zauberflöte

mannheim opera 7 june 1917
verdi aida

mannheim opera 20 and 27 june 1917
korngold violanta
korngold der ring des polykrates

mannheim opera 24 june 1917
wagner tristan und isolde

mannheim opera 29 june 1917
wagner das rheingold

mannheim opera 1 july 1917
wagner die walküre

mannheim opera 4 july 1917
korngold violanta
korngold der ring des polykrates

mannheim opera 15 july 1917
wagner götterdämmerung

mannheim opera 2 september 1917
mozart die zauberflöte

baden-baden 13-21 september 1917
complete ring cycle in guest
performance by mannheim opera
13 september
wagner das rheingold
15 september
wagner die walküre
18 september
wagner siegfried
21 september
wagner götterdämmerung

mannheim opera 28 september-
7 october 1917
complete ring cycle
28 september
wagner das rheingold
30 september
wagner die walküre
4 october
wagner siegfried
7 october
wagner götterdämmerung

mannheim 2 october 1917
mannheim orchestra
wagner meistersinger overture
president hindenburg's 70th birthday
commemoration

mannheim 12 october 1917
mannheim orchestra
charity concert
works by j.strauss, beethoven,
schubert, brahms and liszt

mannheim 14 october 1917
mannheim orchestra
weber jubel overture
event for national war bond day

mannheim 16 october 1917
mannheim orchestra
berber
reger mozart variations
bach violin concerto 2
beethoven symphony 7

mannheim opera 19 october 1917
wagner der fliegende holländer

mannheim opera 2, 9, 15 and 28
november 1917
sekles shéhérazade

mannheim 6 november 1917
mannheim orchestra
bruhn
bruckner symphony 8
braunfels chinese songs
schubert lieder

mannheim opera 14 november 1917
nicolai die lustigen weiber
von windsor

mannheim 17 november 1917
mannheim orchestra
gyarfas
hubay czardas
goldmark violin concerto
liszt mazeppa
smetana moldau
strauss tod und verklärung

mannheim opera 18 november 1917
weber der freischütz

mannheim opera 25 november 1917
bizet carmen

mannheim 27 november 1917
mannheim orchestra
schapira, müller
tchaikovsky piano concerto 1
strauss don quixote
baussern symphony 4
(conducted by the composer)

mannheim opera 7 december 1917
mozart die zauberflöte

mannheim 8 december 1917
pfitzner concert
furtwängler provided piano
accompaniments

mannheim 11 december 1917
mannheim orchestra
busch
brahms symphony 4
beethoven violin concerto
sekles die temperamente
(conducted by the composer)

berlin 14 december 1917
bpo
knothe, feinhals
wagner tannhäuser overture
wagner scenes from tannhäuser,
        parsifal, meistersinger and
        die walküre
strauss don juan
strauss 3 songs with orchestra
strauss kunrad's scene from feuersnot
furtwängler's berlin debut

mannheim opera 21 december 1917
strauss ariadne auf naxos

mannheim opera 1 & 20 january 1918
wagner tristan und isolde

mannheim opera 6 january 1918
mozart die zauberflöte

mannheim 7 january 1918
mannheim orchestra
birkigt, fühler, furtwängler
bach brandenburg concerto 5
schubert symphony 8
beethoven symphony 5

berlin 25 january 1918
bpo
pauer
beethoven leonore 3 overture
schumann piano concerto
bruckner symphony 4

mannheim 29 january 1918
mannheim orchestra
fischer
szell variations on an original theme
brahms piano concerto 2
tchaikovsky symphony 4

mannheim opera 12 february 1918
sekles shéhérazade

mannheim opera 15 february 1918
wagner das rheingold

mannheim opera 17 february 1918
wagner die walküre

mannheim 19 february 1918
mannheim orchestra
stegemann
liszt dante symphony
pfitzner herr oluf
mahler lieder eines fahrenden gesellen
wagner meistersinger overture

mannheim opera 22 february 1918
nicolai die lustigen weiber
von windsor

mannheim opera 24 february 1918
wagner siegfried

berlin 8 march 1918
bpo
fischer
beethoven coriolan overture
beethoven piano concerto 5
brahms symphony 1

mannheim opera 10 march 1918
bizet carmen

mannheim 12 march 1918
mannheim orchestra
rehberg
beethoven symphony 1
mozart piano concerto 9
schubert symphony 9

mannheim opera 13 march 1918
wagner der fliegende holländer

mannheim opera 17 march 1918
weber der freischütz

mannheim opera 31 march 1918
wagner parsifal

mannheim opera 4 & 11 april 1918
klenau kjartan und gudrun

mannheim opera 7 april 1918
wagner tristan und isolde

mannheim 12 april 1918
mannheim orchestra
fischer
beethoven piano concerto 5
bruckner symphony 8

mannheim opera 28 april 1918
wagner siegfried

mannheim opera 5 may 1918
klenau kjartan und gudrun

mannheim opera 7 may 1918
mozart die zauberflöte

mannheim opera 16 may 1918
pfitzner der arme heinrich

mannheim opera 23 may 1918
rossini il barbiere di siviglia

mannheim opera 28 may 1918
mozart die entführung aus dem serail

mannheim opera 30 may 1918
bizet carmen

mannheim opera 2 june 1918
weber der freischütz

mannheim opera 23 june 1918
wagner die walküre

mannheim opera 25 june 1918
mozart die zauberflöte

mannheim opera 27 june 1918
klenau kjartan und gudrun

mannheim opera 30 june 1918
beethoven fidelio

mannheim opera 2 july 1918
pfitzner der arme heinrich

mannheim opera 7 july 1918
weber der freischütz

mannheim opera 6 & 17 september 1918
rossini il barbiere di siviglia

mannheim opera 15 september 1918
wagner tristan und isolde

mannheim opera 22 september 1918
beethoven fidelio

mannheim opera 29 september 1918
wagner die meistersinger von nürnberg

ludwigshafen 3 october 1918
mannheim orchestra
reinhardt
berlioz corsaire overture
weber aria from der freischütz
schubert symphony 8
mahler 3 lieder
beethoven symphony 5

mannheim opera 4 october 1918
mozart die entführung aus dem serail

mannheim opera 6 october 1918
wagner die meistersinger von nürnberg

mannheim 7 october 1918
pfitzner concert
furtwängler provided piano
accompaniments

mannheim opera 9 october 1918
weber der freischütz

mannheim 15 october 1918
mannheim orchestra
bernstein
bruckner symphony 9
mozart violin concerto
strauss don juan

berlin 1 november 1918
bpo
friedberg
berlioz corsaire overture
schubert symphony 8
beethoven piano concerto 4
beethoven symphony 5

mannheim 5 november 1918
mannheim orchestra
kwast-hodapp
reger beethoven variations
beethoven piano concerto 3
brahms symphony 1

mannheim opera 6 november 1918
rossini il barbiere di siviglia

frankfurt 15 november 1918
frankfurt opera orchestra
kreutzer
strauss don juan
rachmaninov piano concerto 2
brahms symphony 1

frankfurt 17 november 1918
frankfurt opera orchestra
kreutzer
weber der freischütz overture
grieg piano concerto
schubert symphony 9

mannheim opera 21 november 1918
wagner der fliegende holländer

vienna 30 november 1918
vso
duhan
strauss don juan
mahler lieder eines fahrenden gesellen
bruckner symphony 4

mannheim 10 december 1918
mannheim orchestra
onegin
tiessen liebeslied und rondo
arias by gluck and berlioz
schumann symphony 1

mannheim opera 12 december 1918
wagner der fliegende holländer

mannheim opera 15 december 1918
wagner tristan und isolde

mannheim opera 17 & 29 december 1918
pfitzner christelflein

mannheim opera 19 december 1918
beethoven fidelio

mannheim opera 22 december 1918
rossini il barbiere di siviglia

mannheim opera 25 december 1918
bizet carmen

mannheim opera 5 january 1919
sekles herr dandolo

mannheim 7 january 1919
mannheim orchestra
birkigt, müller
bach suite 2
brahms double concerto
beethoven symphony 6

mannheim opera 8 january 1919
wagner der fliegende holländer

mannheim opera 11, 18 and 26
january 1919
pfitzner christelflein

frankfurt 17 january 1919
frankfurt opera orchestra
ziegler, bottermund
berlioz benvenuto cellini overture
dvorak cello concerto
liszt faust symphony

munich 22 january 1919
konzertvereins-orchester
beethoven leonore 2 overture
bruckner symphony 4

mannheim 28 january 1919
mannheim orchestra
müller, kreutzer
schreker prelude to a drama
rachmaninov piano concerto 2
mahler symphony 4

mannheim opera 2 february 1919
bizet carmen

mannheim 8 february 1919
mannheim orchestra
koppel
wagner faust overture
liszt hungarian fantasia
schumann piano concerto
wagner tannhäuser overture

mannheim opera 14 february 1919
sekles herr dandolo

mannheim opera 16 february 1919
mozart die zauberflöte

mannheim 18 february 1919
mannheim orchestra
grümmer
mozart symphony 38
d'albert cello concerto
schoenberg verklärte nacht
weber oberon overture

frankfurt 21 february 1919
frankfurt opera orchestra
klinger
beethoven leonore 3 overture
spohr violin concerto 8
schoenberg verklärte nacht
strauss till eulenspiegel

mannheim 27 february 1919
lieder recital
furtwängler accompanied lindberg in
a performance of schubert winterreise

mannheim opera 28 february 1919
weber der freischütz

mannheim 5 march 1919
mannheim orchestra
kämpfert
reisch symphony in e
tchaikovsky francesca da rimini
songs and arias by berlioz,
wolf and schillings

vienna 22 march 1919
vso
beethoven leonore 2 overture
strauss till eulenspiegel
brahms symphony 1

mannheim 1 april 1919
mannheim orchestra and chorus
müller, lippe,
lippmann, fenten
handel concerto grosso no 10
beethoven symphony 9

mannheim opera 3 april 1919
beethoven fidelio

munich 9 april 1919
konzertvereins-orchester
weber der freischütz overture
strauss don juan
schubert symphony 9

mannheim opera 16 and 22 april 1919
gluck orfeo ed euridice

mannheim opera 21 april 1919
wagner die meistersinger von nürnberg

vienna 29 april 1919
vso and chorus
kiurina, kittel, maikl, mayr
beethoven symphony 9

mannheim opera 11 may 1919
beethoven fidelio

mannheim opera 13 may 1919
weber der freischütz

mannheim opera 15 may 1919
gluck orfeo ed euridice

mannheim opera 25 may 1919
bizet carmen

darmstadt 2 june 1919
landestheater-orchester
spiwakovski
berlioz benvenuto cellini overture
tchaikovsky piano concerto 1
tchaikovsky symphony 5

mannheim opera 6 june 1919
gluck orfeo ed euridice

mannheim opera 9 june 1919
wagner parsifal

mannheim opera 15 june 1919
verdi aida

mannheim opera 19 june 1919
verdi otello

mannheim opera 29 june 1919
wagner die walküre

mannheim opera 2 july 1919
mozart le nozze di figaro

mannheim opera 8 july 1919
mozart die entführung aus dem serail

mannheim opera 9 july 1919
verdi otello

mannheim opera 13 july 1919
beethoven fidelio

mannheim opera 4 september 1919
wagner der fliegende holländer

mannheim opera 5 september 1919
rossini il barbiere di siviglia

mannheim opera 7 september 1919
bizet carmen

mannheim 10 and 18 september 1919
egmont
furtwängler conducted beethoven's
incidental music to this performance
of goethe's play

mannheim opera 11 september 1919
beethoven fidelio

mannheim opera 19 september 1919
mozart le nozze di figaro

mannheim opera 23 september 1919
weber der freischütz

mannheim opera 2 october 1919
gluck orfeo ed euridice

mannheim opera 5 and 29 october 1919
tchaikovsky iolanta
weber abu hassan

mannheim 7 october 1919
mannheim orchestra
stückgold
haydn symphony 88
bruckner symphony 7
songs and arias by mozart and strauss

mannheim opera 8 and 24 october 1919
mozart le nozze di figaro

vienna 16 october 1919
vso
beethoven programme
coriolan overture and symphonies 6 & 5

mannheim opera 26 october 1919
wagner tristan und isolde

mannheim 28 october 1919
mannheim orchestra
schnabel
weber der freischütz overture
mozart piano concerto 23
strauss sinfonia domestica

vienna 4 november 1919
vso
wüllner
beethoven programme
egmont incidental music & symphony 5

vienna 6 november 1919
vso
schapira
weber der freischütz overture
rachmaninov piano concerto 2
strauss sinfonia domestica

vienna 27 november 1919
tonkünstler-orchester
rubinstein
berlioz benvenuto cellini overture
beethoven violin concerto
schubert symphony 9

vienna 29 november 1919
vso and chorus
kittel
mahler symphony 3

mannheim 9 december 1919
mannheim orchestra
kwast-hodapp
g.schumann ringen um ein ideal
beethoven piano concerto 4
bruckner symphony 5

mannheim opera 10 december 1919
mozart die entführung aus dem serail

frankfurt 12 december 1919
frankfurt opera orchestra
d'albert
beethoven piano concerto 5
bruckner symphony 5

mannheim opera 14 december 1919
beethoven fidelio

mannheim opera 16 december 1919
tchaikovsky iolanta
weber abu hassan

mannheim opera 19 december 1919
wagner siegfried

mannheim opera 21 december 1919
mozart le nozze di figaro

mannheim opera 23 & 29 december 1919
pfitzner christelflein

mannheim opera 28 december 1919
wagner tristan und isolde

vienna 8 january 1920
vso
fischer
schumann symphony 4
brahms piano concerto 2
beethoven leonore 3 overture

mannheim opera 11 january 1920
wagner der fliegende holländer

vienna 12 january 1920
vso
fischer
mozart piano concerto 22
brahms piano concerto 1

mannheim 13 january 1920
mannheim orchestra and chorus
lippmann, birgikt
hausegger symphonic variations
brahms violin concerto
liszt faust symphony

mannheim opera 22 january 1920
wagner die walküre

mannheim opera 25 january 1920
weber der freischütz

mannheim 27 january 1920
mannheim orchestra
reinhardt
reger mozart variations
wagner wesendonk-lieder
brahms symphony 4
furtwängler accompanied wesendonk-
lieder at the piano

vienna 5 february 1920
vso
gallos
berlioz corsaire overture
schoenberg verklärte nacht
liszt faust symphony

berlin 13 february 1920
bpo
fischer
bruckner symphony 8
brahms piano concerto 2

mannheim opera 20 february 1920
pfitzner christelflein

mannheim 2 march 1920
mannheim orchestra
dvorak husitska overture
schoenverg pelleas uns melisande
tchaikovsky symphony 5

mannheim 23 march 1920
mannheim orchestra and chorus
müller, lippe, lippmann, fenten
beethoven symphony 9

mannheim opera 28 march 1920
pfitzner palestrina

berlin 2 april 1920
staatskapelle
wagner parsifal prelude
bach suite 3
beethoven symphony 3

berlin 3 april 1920
staatskapelle and chorus
hansa, branzell, mann, armster
handel concerto grosso 10
beethoven symphony 9

mannheim opera 5 april 1920
pfitzner palestrina

vienna 10 april 1920
vso and chorus
kittel
mahler symphony 3

vienna 17 april 1920
vso
beethoven leonore 2 overture
bruckner symphony 9

vienna 22 april 1920
vso
schoenberg verklärte nacht
tchaikovsky symphony 5

vienna 28 and 29 april 1920
vso and chorus
foerstel, kittel, maikl, mayr
beethoven symphony 9

berlin 4 may 1920
staatskapelle
schumann symphony 4
kaun symphony 3
beethoven leonore 3 overture

mannheim opera 7 and 24 may 1920
pfitzner palestrina

mannheim opera 9 may 1920
bizet carmen

mannheim opera 11 may 1920
gluck orfeo ed euridice

mannheim opera 19 may 1920
mozart die entführung aus dem serail

mannheim opera 20 may 1920
verdi aida

mannheim opera 26 may 1920
wagner der fliegende holländer

mannheim opera 2 and 19 june 1920
pfitzner palestrina

vienna 8 june 1920
vso and chorus
kittel
mahler symphony 3

vienna 10 june 1920
vso and chorus
foerstel, kittel, maikl, mayr
beethoven symphony 9

mannheim opera 30 june 1920
mozart die entführung aus dem serail

frankfurt 24 & 26 september 1920
frankfurt opera orchestra
lange, naumann, furtwängler
bach brandenburg concerto 5
strauss bürger als edelmann
brahms symphony 1

berlin 1 october 1920
staatskapelle
de vries, zeiler, furtwängler
beethoven leonore 2 overture
bach brandenburg concerto 5
brahms symphony 1

stockholm 7 october 1920
stockholm po
beethoven leonore 3 overture
handel concerto grosso 10
brahms symphony 1

stockholm 10 october 1920
stockholm po
weber der freischütz overture
schubert rosamunde entr'actes
schubert symphony 9

stockholm 14 october 1920
stockholm po
schumann symphony 4
strauss don juan
wagner tannhäuser overture

stockholm 17 october 1920
stockholm po
berwald symphony 2
beethoven symphony 5

frankfurt 22 october 1920
frankfurt opera orchestra
flesch
handel concerto in f
mozart violin concerto 5
bruckner symphony 7

berlin 27 october 1920
staatskapelle
mozart symphony 38
bruckner symphony 7

vienna 3 and 4 november 1920
vso
schoenberg pelleas und melisande
brahms symphony 1

frankfurt 12 november 1920
frankfurt opera orchestra & chorus
kwast-hodapp
beethoven programme
grosse fuge, choral fantasy and
symphony 5

berlin 19 november 1920
staatskapelle and chorus
bettendorf, arndt-ober
handel concerto grosso 10
mahler symphony 2

vienna 24 and 25 november 1920
vso
busch
mozart violin concerto
bruckner symphony 7

vienna 1 and 2 december 1920
vso and chorus
schmidt
beethoven programme
choral fantasy and symphony 3

berlin 8 december 1920
staatskapelle
fischer
beethoven programme
grosse fuge, piano concerto 4 and
symphony 5

stockholm 12 december 1920
stockholm po
wolfstal, wilhelmi
mozart sinfonia concertante k364
tchaikovsky symphony 5

stockholm 16 december 1920
stockholm po and chorus
holmgren, kalmodin-lindgren,
ralf, johanson
beethoven symphony 9

stockholm 19 december 1920
stockholm po
press
beethoven programme
leonore 1 overture, violin concerto
and symphony 7

stockholm 26 december 1920
stockholm po
weber oberon overture
hallen toteninsel
berlioz damnation de faust excerpts
wagner tristan prelude
wagner tannhäuser bacchanale
wagner meistersinger overture

stockholm 30 december 1920
stockholm po and chorus
ralf
rangström divertimento elegiaco
liszt faust symphony

stockholm 2 january 1921
stockholm po
wilhelmi
haydn symphony 100
lindberg fran de stora skagorne
n.berg violin concerto
beethoven egmont overture

stockholm 6 january 1921
stockholm po
wolfstal, achatz, furtwängler
bach brandenburg concerto 5
bruckner symphony 4

berlin 12 january 1921
staatskapelle
strauss bürger als edelmann
schubert symphony 9

berlin 17 january 1921
bpo
erb
beethoven egmont overture
beethoven gott welch dunkel/fidelio
liszt faust symphony

frankfurt 21 january 1921
frankfurt opera orchestra
erb
schoenberg pelleas und melisande
weber durch die wälder/der freischütz
schubert symphony 9
programme also included schubert
lieder accompanied at the piano by
furtwängler

frankfurt 23 january 1921
frankfurt opera orchestra
schoenberg pelleas und melisande
schubert symphony 9

munich 26 january 1921
konzertvereins-orchester
reichel, stammann, furtwängler
bach brandenburg concerto 5
schumann symphony 4
berlioz benvenuto cellini overture

vienna 2 and 3 february 1921
vso
berlioz carnaval romain overture
strauss bürger als edelmann suite
beethoven symphony 7

berlin 9 february 1921
staatskapelle
premyslav
weber der freischütz overture
schillings violin concerto
beethoven symphony 7

frankfurt 16 february 1921
chamber concert in which furtwängler
accompanied h. lange and w.lange
brahms violin sonata 2
beethoven archduke trio

frankfurt 18 and 20 february 1921
frankfurt opera orchestra
petri
berlioz le corsaire overture
franck symphonic variations
liszt totentanz
tchaikovsky symphony 5

berlin 25 february 1921
staatskapelle
schumann genoveva overture
schoenberg verklärte nacht
tchaikovsky symphony 5

lübeck 28 february 1921
lübeck orchestra
weber der freischütz overture
bruckner symphony 4

frankfurt 4 and 6 march 1921
frankfurt opera orchestra
erdmann symphony in one movement
schumann symphony 4
wagner fliegende holländer overture

berlin 11 march 1921
staatskapelle
dvorak husitska overture
haussegger aufklänge
beethoven symphony 6

vienna 16 and 17 march 1921
vso and chorus
lefler, kittel
mahler symphony 2

frankfurt 1 april 1921
frankfurt opera orchestra
ivogün
mendelssohn hebrides overture
mozart martern aller arten/entführung
braunfels fantastic impressions
strauss grossmächtige prinzessin/
    ariadne auf naxos
strauss till eulenspiegel

berlin 6 april 1921
staatskapelle
haydn symphony 88
büttner symphony 4
strauss till eulenspiegel
büttner work conducted by composer

berlin 9 april 1921
staatskapelle
johann strauss evening
furtwängler participated together
with other conductors

berlin 11 april 1921
bpo
foldesy
mendelssohn hebrides overture
haydn cello concerto
bruckner symphony 4

frankfurt 15 and 17 april 1921
frankfurt opera orchestra & chorus
müller, ohms, enehjelm, fenten
beethoven symphony 9

vienna 20 and 21 april 1921
vso
braunfels fantastic impressions
schubert symphony 8
weber oberon overture

vienna 25 and 26 april 1921
vso and chorus
leuer, kittel, maikl, mayr
beethoven symphony 9

vienna 28 and 29 april 1921
vso
duhan
handel concerto grosso
korngold sursum corda
pfitzner herr oluf
strauss till eulenspiegel

berlin 4 may 1921
staatskapelle and chorus
hansa, arndt-ober, ludwig, schöpflin
beethoven symphony 9

berlin 9 may 1921
bpo
jadlowker
strauss don juan
brahms symphony 4
arias by mozart and tchaikovsky

wiesbaden opera 13 may 1921
beethoven fidelio

wiesbaden 7 june 1921
wiesbaden opera orchestra
busch, grümmer
brahms festival
haydn variations, double concerto
and symphony 1

wiesbaden 9 june 1921
wiesbaden opera orchestra
onegin, fischer
brahms festival
alto rhapsody, piano concerto 2
and symphony 4

mannheim opera 19 june 1921
beethoven fidelio

mannheim opera 21 june 1921
wagner tristan und isolde

leipzig 30 august 1921
gewandhaus-orchester
lambrino
weber der freischütz overture
schumann symphony 4
liszt piano concerto 1
strauss till eulenspiegel
liszt hungarian fantasy
first appearance in leipzig

vienna 29 and 30 september 1921
vso
beethoven leonore 2 overture
brahms haydn variations
mahler symphony 1

berlin 5 october 1921
staatskapelle
weber euryanthe overture
braunfels variations
beethoven symphony 3

berlin 10 october 1921
bpo
onegin
weber oberon overture
schumann symphony 4
brahms alto rhapsody & lieder
liszt mazeppa

frankfurt 14 october 1921
frankfurt opera orchestra
busch
bruckner symphony 8
brahms violin concerto

hannover 17 october 1921
hannover opera orchestra
beethoven leonore 3 overture
bruckner symphony 8

hamburg 23 and 24 october 1921
philharmonisches staatsorchester
siloti
bruckner symphony 8
schubert-liszt wanderer fantasy
wagner fliegende holländer overture
concert originally intended as trial
concert for post of generalmusik-
direktor

berlin 31 october 1921
bpo
sauer
beethoven leonore 2 overture
liszt piano concerto 2
mahler symphony 1

berlin 4 november 1921
staatskapelle
handel concerto grosso 11
bruckner symphony 8

vienna 10 and 11 november 1921
vso
handel concerto grosso 11
bruckner symphony 8

vienna 17 and 18 november 1921
vso
moodie
hausegger aufklänge
glazunov violin concerto
brahms symphony 2

vienna 30 november and
1 december 1921
vso and chorus
foerstl, bauer-pilecka, gallos
beethoven missa solemnis

berlin 4 december 1921
staatskapelle
furtwängler shared this programme
with conductors blech and schillings

berlin 7 december 1921
staatskapelle
haydn symphony 94
reznicek variations
beethoven symphony 7

berlin 12 december 1921
bpo
fischer
handel concerto grosso 10
beethoven piano concerto 1
brahms symphony 1

vienna 16 and 17 december 1921
vso and chorus
foerstl, kittel, maikl, roessl
beethoven missa solemnis

vienna 5 and 6 january 1922
vso
serkin
schumann symphony 1
reger piano concerto
wagner fliegende holländer overture

mannheim 10 january 1922
mannheim opera orchestra
beethoven leonore 3 overture
schumann symphony 4
strauss sinfonia domestica

frankfurt 13 january 1922
frankfurt opera orchestra
fischer
sekles passacaglia and fugue
brahms piano concerto 2
strauss sinfonia domestica

berlin 20 january 1922
staatskapelle
schumann symphony 1
strauss sinfonia domestica

leipzig 26 january 1922
gewandhaus-orchester
beethoven coriolan overture
beethoven funeral march/eroica
memorial for death of nikisch

berlin 30 january 1922
bpo
erdmann
beethoven symphony 1
rachmaninov piano concerto 2
berlioz symphonie fantastique

berlin 3 february 1922
staatskapelle
mozart maurerische trauermusik
braunfels fantastic impressions
mendelssohn symphony 3
memorial for death of nikisch

berlin 6 february 1922
bpo
beethoven symphony 3
memorial for death of nikisch;
furtwängler also accompanied raatz-
brockmann at the piano in brahms
4 ernste gesänge; other artists
also participated in the concert

vienna 16 and 17 february 1922
vso
beethoven symphony 1
berlioz symphonie fantastique

berlin 22 february 1922
staatskapelle
haydn symphony 100
schubert symphony 8
busoni sarabande & cortège/dr faust
liszt hungaria

vienna 28 february and 1 march 1922
vso
singverein
kiurina, rutschka, gallos, mayr
pfitzner von deutscher seele

munich 4 march 1922
konzertvereins-orchester
beethoven symphony 1
brahms symphony 4

mannheim 7 march 1922
mannheim opera orchestra
beethoven symphony 1
brahms symphony 4

berlin 13 march 1922
bpo
kittel choir
leonard, demlow, walter,
raatz-brockmann
beethoven symphony 9

berlin 17 march 1922
staatskapelle
koch romantic suite
reger mozart variations
beethoven symphony 8

vienna 21 and 22 march 1922
vso
mozart mauerische trauermusik
haydn symphony 94
beethoven symphony 5

vienna 25 and 26 march 1922
vpo
singverein
brahms programme for 25th anniversary
of composer's death
naydn variations, schicksalslied
and symphony 4
furtwängler's first concert with vpo

vienna 31 march and 1 april 1922
vso and choir
foerstel, kittel, maikl, mayr
beethoven symphony 9

rome 16 april 1922
santa cecilia orchestra
beethoven leonore 3 overture
beethoven symphony 5
malipiero pause del silencio
wagner tannhäuser overture

rome 19 april 1922
santa cecilia orchestra
beethoven symphony 3
strauss don juan
weber der freischütz overture

roma 23 april 1922
santa cecilia orchestra
brahms symphony 1
beethoven leonore 3 overture
reznicek theme and variations
wagner fliegende holländer overture

berlin 28 april 1922
staatskapelle
prill, saal
mozart symphony 40
mozart flute and harp concerto
beethoven symphony 5

berlin 29 april 1922
staatskapelle
beethoven programme
egmont overture, symphony 1 and
symphony 3

mannheim opera 10 may 1922
wagner die walküre

berlin 24 may 1922
bpo
leisner
brahms programme
haydn variations, alto rhapsody
and symphony 4

hamburg
concerts for 5th brahms festival
28 may 1922
bpo
busch
violin concerto
(other artists participated in concert)
29 may 1922
bpo
onegin, fischer
alto rhapsody, piano concerto 1 and
symphony 2
30 may 1922
bpo
haydn variations and symphony 1
(spengel conducted schicksalslied)

vienna 28 and 29 september 1922
vso
brahms symphony 3
beethoven symphony 7

berlin 8 and 9 october 1922
bpo
pembauer
bruckner symphony 7
franck symphonic variations
liszt totentanz
wagner meistersinger overture

leipzig 12 october 1922
gewandhaus-orchester
beethoven leonore 3 overture
bruckner symphony 7

leipzig 19 october 1922
gewandhaus-orchester
mysz-gmeiner
scriabin poème de l'extase
mahler kindertotenlieder
brahms symphony 2

berlin 22 and 23 october 1922
bpo
friedberg
scriabin poème de l'extase
schumann piano concerto
brahms symphony 2

leipzig 26 october 1922
gewandhaus-orchester
schumann
trapp symphony 2 premiere
beethoven symphony 5
arias by mozart

leipzig 2 november 1922
gewandhaus-orchester
busch
handel concerto grosso 5
bach violin concerto 2
reger mozart variations
busch violin concerto
strauss til! eulenspiegel

berlin 5 and 6 november 1922
bpo
kipnis
reger beethoven variations
beethoven symphony 7
vocal works by mozart & mussorgsky

leipzig 9 november 1922
gewandhaus-orchester
erb
mendelssohn hebrides overture
handel aria from acis and galatea
liszt faust symphony

vienna 14 and 15 november 1922
vso and chorus
foerstel, duhan
brahms ein deutsches requiem

vienna 18 and 19 november 1922
vso
schubert programme
symphony 8 and symphony 9

berlin 26 and 27 november 1922
bpo
erb
handel concerto grosso 5
handel aria from acis and galatea
liszt faust symphony

leipzig 30 november 1922
gewandhaus-orchester
gieseking
boccherini symphony op 16 no 3
marx piano concerto
schubert symphony 9

copenhagen 4 december 1922
philharmonic orchestra
beethoven leonore 3 overture
beethoven symphony 7
wagner siegfried idyll
wagner tannhäuser overture

leipzig 7 december 1922
gewandhaus-orchester
eden
weber der freischütz overture
strauss aria from ariadne auf naxos
schoenberg 5 pieces op 16
(premiere of revised version)
wagner siegfried idyll
wagner fliegende holländer overture

berlin 10 and 11 december 1922
bpo
schmüller
weber beherrscher der geister overture
glazunov violin concerto
schoenberg 5 pieces op 16
schubert symphony 9

vienna 15 and 16 december 1922
vso and chorus
foerstel, duhan
brahms ein deutsches requiem

leipzig 1 january 1923
gewandhaus-orchester
kipnis
haydn symphony 101
brahms symphony 1
songs by haydn and schubert

leipzig 11 january 1923
gewandhaus-orchester
mozart serenade 10
hindemith kammermusik 1
tchaikovsky symphony 5

berlin 14 and 15 january 1923
bpo
engell
haydn symphony 104
beethoven symphony 3
vocal works by handel and mahler

leipzig 18 january 1923
gewandhaus-orchester
kolessa
atterberg symphony 5
chopin piano concerto 2
beethoven symphony 1

leipzig 25 january 1923
gewandhaus-orchester
bokor
respighi fontane di roma
volkmann cello concerto
brahms symphony 4

berlin 28 and 29 january 1923
bpo
flesch
trapp symphony 2
beethoven violin concerto
strauss till eulenspiegel

leipzig 1 february 1923
gewandhaus-orchester
flesch
graener waldmusik premiere
beethoven violin concerto
mendelssohn symphony 3

vienna 6 and 7 february 1923
vso and chorus
hüni-mihacsek, kittel, gallos,
mayr, tausche
handel saul

vienna 9 and 10 february 1923
vso
kolessa
reger beethoven variations
mendelssohn symphony 3
liszt piano concerto 2
wagner tannhäuser overture

leipzig 15 february 1923
gewandhaus-orchester
borowsky
pfitzner käthchen von heilbronn ov.
schumann symphony 4
liszt totentanz
liszt tasso

berlin 18 and 19 february 1923
bpo
feuermann
pfitzner käthchen von heilbronn ov.
haydn cello concerto
brahms symphony 4

leipzig 1 march 1923
gewandhaus-orchester
moodie
sibelius en saga
schubert symphony 8
mendelssohn violin concerto
weber oberon overture

berlin 4 and 5 march 1923
bpo
van den berg
sibelius en saga
brahms violin concerto
tchaikovsky symphony 5

leipzig 6 march 1923
gewandhaus-orchester
merrem-nikisch
weber der freischütz overture
mozart deh vieni/le nozze di figaro
schubert symphony 8
wagner meistersinger overture
also lieder by schumann

leipzig 15 march 1923
gewandhaus-orchester
lampe, wollgandt,
o.fischer, furtwängler
beethoven leonore 2 overture
bach brandenburg concerto 5
mozart piano concerto 20
reger mozart variations

berlin 18 and 19 march 1923
bpo
van den berg, harzer, furtwängler
beethoven leonore 2 overture
bach brandenburg concerto 5
beethoven symphony 5

leipzig 22 march 1923
gewandhaus-orchester and chorus
hansen-schultheiss, adam,
graf, raatz-brockmann
beethoven symphony 9

berlin 26 march 1923
bpo
kittel choir
leonard, werner-jensen,
jadlowker, drissen
beethoven symphony 9

vienna 4 and 6 april 1923
tonkünstler-orchester
handel concerto grosso
haydn symphony 101
tchaikovsky symphony 5

vienna 7 and 8 april 1923
vso and chorus
kiurina-leuer, leisner,
gallos, mayr
mozart requiem

amsterdam 12 april 1923
concertgebouw orchestra
weber der freischütz overture
schumann symphony 4
tchaikovsky symphony 5

leipzig 19 april 1923
gewandhaus-orchester
handel concerto grosso 5
reger mozart variations
brahms symphony 1

bern 25 april 1923
gewandhaus-orchester
wagner meistersinger overture
reger mozart variations
beethoven symphony 7

bern 26 april 1923
gewandhaus-orchester
strauss don juan
schubert symphony 8
brahms symphony 1

zürich 27 april 1923
gewandhaus-orchester
strauss don juan
schubert symphony 8
brahms symphony 1

zürich 28 april 1923
gewandhaus-orchester
schumann symphony 4
tchaikovsky symphony 5

basel 29 april 1923
gewandhaus-orchester
wagner meistersinger overture
reger mozart variations
brahms symphony 1

milan 19 june 1923
la scala orchestra
beethoven symphony 7
wagner meistersinger overture
strauss tod und verklärung
santoliquido aquarelli

milan 23 june 1923
la scala orchestra
schumann symphony 4
reger mozart variations
beethoven egmont overture
wagner feuerzauber/die walküre
marinuzzi elegy for orchestra

vienna 27 and 28 september 1923
tonkünstler-orchester
strauss tod und verklärung
bruckner symphony 4

vienna 2 and 3 october 1924
vso
singverein
merz-tunner, willer, gallos, mayr
pfitzner von deutscher seele

leipzig 11 october 1923
gewandhaus-orchester
anday
haydn symphony 93
mahler lieder eines fahrenden gesellen
strauss sinfonia domestica

berlin 14 and 15 october 1923
bpo
guttmann
beethoven symphony 1
mahler lieder eines fahrenden gesellen
strauss sinfonia domestica

leipzig 18 october 1923
gewandhaus-orchester
szigeti
sekles gesichte
brahms violin concerto
beethoven symphony 3

leipzig 25 october 1923
gewandhaus-orchester
kwast-hodapp
bach brandenburg concerto 3
schubert symphony 8
pfitzner piano concerto
berlioz benvenuto cellini overture

berlin 28 and 29 october 1923
bpo
gieseking
bach brandenburg concerto 3
schubert symphony 8
pfitzner piano concerto
berlioz benvenuto cellini overture

leipzig 1 november 1923
gewandhaus-orchester
fischer
brahms haydn variations
stravinsky le sacre du printemps
beethoven piano concerto 5

leipzig 8 november 1923
gewandhaus-orchester
wollgandt, klengel
mendelssohn sommernachtstraum overture
brahms double concerto
tchaikovsky symphony 4

berlin 11 and 12 november 1923
bpo
szigeti
sekles gesichte
mozart violin concerto 4
corelli la follia
brahms symphony 1

prague 14 november 1923
bpo

vienna 20 and 21 november 1923
vso
singverein
kiurina, kindermann, formacher,
schmedes, manowarda
handel samson

berlin 25 and 26 november 1923
bpo
schnabel
cimarosa matrimonio segreto overture
mozart piano concerto 20
bruckner symphony 4

leipzig 29 november 1923
gewandhaus-orchester
leonard
respighi antiche arie e danze
beethoven symphony 8
works by bach and schubert

leipzig 30 november 1923
gewandhaus-orchester
beethoven programme
symphonies 3 and 8

halle 2 december 1923
gewandhaus-orchester
beethoven programme
symphonies 3 and 8

leipzig 6 december 1923
gewandhaus-orchester and chorus
bodky
beethoven programme
egmont overture, choral fantasy
and symphony 2

berlin 9 and 10 december 1923
bpo
kittel choir
kwast-hodapp
beethoven programme
leonore 3 overture, choral fantasy
and symphony 7

vienna 13 and 14 december 1923
vso
strauss don juan
schumann symphony 4
beethoven symphony 8

vienna 16 and 17 december 1923
vso
singverein
haydn die schöpfung

vienna 18 and 19 december 1923
vso
singverein
kiurina, rutschka, maikl, mayr
beethoven symphony 9

leipzig 1 january 1924
gewandhaus-orchester
eden
pfitzner alte weisen
bruckner symphony 4
also organ solo played by ramin

berlin 6 and 7 january 1924
bpo
fischer
handel concerto grosso 10
stravinsky le sacre du printemps
brahms piano concerto 2

leipzig 10 january 1924
gewandhaus-orchester
senatra
straesser symphony 4
zandonai violin concerto
beethoven symphony 7

magdeburg 12 january 1924
bpo

leipzig 13 january 1924
gewandhaus-orchester
beethoven symphony 2
brahms symphony 1

leipzig 17 january 1924
gewandhaus-orchester
rehkemper
schumann symphony 1
wolf 3 lieder
pfitzner herr oluf
strauss ein heldenleben

berlin 20 and 21 january 1924
bpo
rehkemper
schumann symphony 1
strauss 2 lieder
pfitzner herr oluf
strauss ein heldenleben

london 24 january 1924
philharmonic society orchestra
handel concerto grosso 10
strauss don juan
brahms symphony 1
furtwängler's british début; concert
also included vaughan williams
conducting his own on wenlock edge

liverpool 29 january 1924
liverpool po
moiseiwitsch
mendelssohn hebrides overture
tcherepnin piano concerto 1
brahms symphony 1
wagner fliegende holländer overture

london 4 february 1924
lso
weber der freischütz overture
beethoven symphony 5
strauss ein heldenleben
wagner meistersinger overture

leipzig 7 february 1924
gewandhaus-orchester
korngold much ado about nothing, suite
brahms symphony 3

berlin 10 and 11 february 1924
bpo
leisner
brahms programme
haydn variations, alto rhapsody
and symphony 3
also zigeunerlieder accompanied by
furtwängler at the piano

leipzig 14 february 1924
gewandhaus-orchester and chorus
adam, ramin
handel organ concerto 2
mahler symphony 3

london 16 february 1924
lso
weber oberon overture
schumann symphony 4
tchaikovsky symphony 5

vienna 24 february 1924
vpo
singverein
anday
mahler symphony 3

vienna 26 and 27 february 1924
vso
singverein
leonard, erler-schnaudt, erb,
rehkemper
bach saint matthew passion

berlin 2 and 3 march 1924
bpo and choirs
ellger
mahler symphony 3

leipzig 4 march 1924
gewandhaus-orchester
lind
beethoven egmont overture
mozart martern aller arten/entführung
beethoven symphony 7

leipzig 6 march 1924
gewandhaus-orchester
wollgandt, bassermann
kempff symphony 2 premiere
bach double violin concerto
beethoven symphony 5

leipzig 7 march 1924
gewandhaus-orchester
bruckner symphony 4
ramin played organ solos by bach
and handel

leipzig 13 march 1924
gewandhaus-orchester
furtwängler
haydn symphony 94
bach piano concerto in f minor
reger hiller variations

berlin 16 and 17 march 1924
bpo
furtwängler
haydn symphony 94
bach piano concerto in f minor
beethoven symphony 5

leipzig 20 march 1924
gewandhaus-orchester and chorus
hansem-schultess, adam, topitz,
raatz-brockmann
beethoven symphony 9

berlin 23 and 24 march 1924
bpo
kittel choir
leonard, ellger, madsen, nissen
beethoven symphony 9

mannheim opera 30 march 1924
bizet carmen

mannheim opera 5 april 1924
wagner die meistersinger von nürnberg

mannheim 7 april 1924
mannheim orchestra
furtwängler
haydn symphony 94
bach piano concerto in f minor
beethoven symphony 5

stettin 27 april 1954
bpo
haydn symphony 94
bruckner symphony 4
wagner meistersinger overture

lübeck 28 april 1924
bpo
beethoven leonore 3 overture
strauss don juan
bruckner symphony 4
wagner meistersinger overture

kiel 29 april 1924
bpo
haydn symphony 94
brahms symphony 4
strauss till eulenspiegel

hamburg 30 april 1924
bpo
haydn symphony 94
brahms symphony 4
strauss till eulenspiegel
wagner meistersinger overture

cologne 1 may 1924
bpo
beethoven leonore 3 overture
bruckner symphony 4
strauss don juan
wagner meistersinger overture

düsseldorf 2 may 1924
bpo
brahms symphony 4
beethoven symphony 7

krefeld 3 may 1924
bpo
weber der freischütz overture
beethoven symphony 5
strauss till eulenspiegel
wagner meistersinger overture

munich 5 may 1924
bpo
weber der freischütz overture
bruckner symphony 4
wagner meistersinger overture

munich 6 may 1924
bpo
haydn symphony 94
bach brandenburg concerto 5
beethoven symphony 5

st gallen 7 may 1924
bpo
kolessa
beethoven leonore 3 overture
schumann piano concerto
bruckner symphony 4
wagner meistersinger overture

bern 8 may 1924
bpo
haydn symphony 94
beethoven symphony 5
strauss till eulenspiegel

lausanne 9 may 1924
bpo
weber der freischütz overture
beethoven symphony 7
wagner tristan prelude and liebestod
wagner tannhäuser overture

geneva 10 may 1924
bpo
beethoven leonore 3 overture
beethoven symphony 5
strauss don juan
wagner meistersinger overture
wagner tristan prelude and liebestod

neuchâtel 11 may 1924
bpo
beethoven leonore 3 overture
beethoven symphony 7
strauss don juan
wagner tannhäuser overture

basel 12 may 1924
bpo
haydn symphony 94
strauss till eulenspiegel
brahms symphony 4

zürich 13 may 1924
bpo
furtwängler
haydn symphony 94
bach piano concerto in f minor
beethoven symphony 5

bern 14 may 1924
bpo
kolessa
weber der freischütz overture
mozart piano concerto 27
bruckner symphony 4

freiburg 15 may 1924
bpo
haydn symphony 94
beethoven symphony 5
strauss till eulenspiegel
wagner tannhäuser overture

karlsruhe 16 may 1924
bpo
bruckner symphony 4
strauss don juan
wagner meistersinger overture

stuttgart 17 may 1924
bpo
beethoven coriolan overture
bruckner symphony 4
strauss till eulenspiegel

mannheim opera 22 may 1924
wagner tristan und isolde

mannheim opera 25 may 1924
mozart die entführung aus dem serail

munich residenztheater 11 august 1924
mozart die entführung aus dem serail
ivogün/schumann/erb/seydel/bender

munich residenztheater 16 august 1924
mozart le nozze di figaro
ivogün/schumann/merz/brodersen/
sterneck

munich prinregententheater
21 august 1924
wagner tristan und isolde
englerth/willer/wolf/bender/brodersen

munich prinzregententheater
28 august 1924
wagner die meistersinger von nürnberg
merz/schreiber/krauss/bender

mannheim 30 september 1924
mannheim orchestra
haydn symphony 88
beethoven symphony 3

berlin 5 and 6 october 1924
bpo
leonard
busoni geharnischte suite
strauss 3 hölderlin hymns
beethoven symphony 3

magdeburg 8 october 1924
bpo

leipzig 9 october 1924
gewandhaus-orchester
davisson, klengel
klengel concerto for violin & cello
bruckner symphony 5

leipzig 16 october 1924
gewandhaus-orchester
leonard
strauss programme
festive prelude, 3 hölderlin hymns
and alpensinfonie

berlin 19 and 20 october 1924
bpo
moodie
haydn symphony 88
pfitzner violin concerto
brahms symphony 4

leipzig 23 october 1924
gewandhaus-orchester
pauer
trapp symphony 3 premiere
beethoven piano concerto 4
beethoven leonore 3 overture

leipzig 30 october 1924
gewandhaus-orchester
m.nikisch
bruckner symphony 9
tchaikovsky piano concerto 1
smetana bartered bride overture

berlin 2 and 3 november 1924
bpo
schnabel
Beethoven prometheus overture
mozart piano concerto 23
bruckner symphony 5

leipzig 6 november 1924
gewandhaus-orchester
mayr
j.c.bach sinfonia 2
graener divertimento premiere
strauss tod und verklärung
vocal works by haydn and wolf

leipzig 13 november 1924
gewandhaus-orchester
busch
braunfels don juan premiere
dvorak violin concerto
tchaikovsky symphony 6

berlin 16 and 17 november 1924
bpo
ivogün
braunfels don juan
tchaikovsky symphony 6
vocal works by mozart and handel

london 20 november 1924
philharmonic society orchestra
goodson
smetana bartered bride overture
strauss tod und verklärung
brahms piano concerto 1
beethoven symphony 7

leipzig 27 november 1924
gewandhaus-orchester
moodie
rimsky-korsakov easter festival ov.
pfitzner violin concerto
beethoven symphony 4

halle 30 november 1924
gewandhaus-orchester
beethoven symphony 4
tchaikovsky symphony 6

leipzig 4 december 1924
gewandhaus-orchester
stravinsky
berlioz le corsair overture
stravinsky concerto for piano & wind
schubert symphony 9

hamburg 5 december 1924
bpo
berlioz le corsair overture
strauss tod und verklärung
schubert symphony 9

berlin 7 and 8 december 1924
bpo
stravinsky
berlioz le corsair overture
stravinsky concerto for piano & wind
schubert symphony 9

vienna 15 and 16 december 1924
vso
singverein
engell, gallos, mayr
haydn die schöpfung

new york 3 and 4 january 1925
nypso
casals
strauss don juan
haydn cello concerto
brahms symphony 1
furtwängler's american debut

new york 11 january 1925
nypso
weber der freischütz overture
beethoven symphony 7
wagner tristan prelude and liebestod
wagner meistersinger overture

new york 15 and 16 january 1925
nypso
samaroff
handel concerto grosso 10
schumann piano concerto
tchaikovsky symphony 5

new york 18 january 1925
nypso
handel concerto grosso 10
strauss till eulenspiegel
brahms symphony 1

new york 22 and 23 january 1925
nypso
berlioz benvenuto cellini overture
schumann symphony 4
stravinsky le sacre du printemps

new york 25 january 1925
nypso
mendelssohn hebrides overture
strauss don juan
tchaikovsky symphony 5

new york 30 january 1925
nypso
haydn symphony 94
strauss tod und verklärung
beethoven symphony 5

leipzig 12 february 1925
gewandhaus-orchester
mozart symphony 38
dvorak symphony 9

leipzig 19 february 1925
gewandhaus-orchester
talen
mozart le nozze di figaro overture
mozart dies bildnis/die zauberflöte
g.schumann handel variations <u>premiere</u>
schumann symphony 4

berlin 22 and 23 february 1925
bpo
m.nikisch
g.schumann handel variations
schumann symphony 4
tchaikovsky piano concerto 1
wagner tannhäuser overture

leipzig 26 february 1925
gewandhaus-orchester
kolessa
gluck alceste overture
bortkiewicz piano concerto 1
mahler symphony 1

berlin 1 and 2 march 1925
bpo
tauber, holst
sibelius violin concerto
mozart arias from don giovanni
mahler symphony 1

berlin 8 and 9 march 1925
bpo
kolessa
bach chorales arranged by schoenberg
chopin piano concerto 1
brahms symphony 2

leipzig 12 march 1925
gewandhaus-orchester
engell
haydn symphony 88
beethoven symphony 6
vocal works by handel, schubert
and mendelssohn

leipzig 19 march 1925
gewandhaus-orchester and chorus
hansen-schulthess, weeke,
graarud, raatz-brockmann
beethoven symphony 9

hamburg 20 march 1925
bpo
<u>beethoven programme</u>
symphonies 6 and 5

berlin 22 and 23 march 1925
bpo
<u>beethoven programme</u>
symphonies 6 and 5

magdeburg 25 march 1925
bpo
<u>beethoven programme</u>
symphonies 6 and 5

leipzig 26 march 1925
gewandhaus-orchester
raatz-brockmann
handel water music suite
brahms 4 ernste gesänge
brahms symphony 2

berlin 29 and 30 march 1925
bpo
kittel choir
leonard, weeke, wilde, raatz-brockmann
beethoven symphony 9

vienna 7 and 8 april 1925
vso
singverein
foerstl, anday, wilde,
rehkemper, manowarda
bach saint matthew passion

vienna 12 april 1925
vpo
berlioz benvenuto cellini overture
bruckner symphony 9

stockholm 15 april 1925
stockholm po
beethoven coriolan overture
handel concerto grosso 5
brahms symphony 1

stockholm 19 april 1925
stockholm po
haydn symphony 88
strauss tod und verklärung
beethoven symphony 3

stockholm 21 april 1925
stockholm po
weber der freischütz overture
haydn symphony 88
tchaikovsky symphony 6

hannover 28 april 1925
bpo
handel concerto grosso 5
schumann symphony 4
tchaikovsky symphony 6

hamburg 29 april 1925
bpo
berlioz benvenuto cellini overture
schumann symphony 4
tchaikovsky symphony 6

kiel 30 april 1925
bpo
haydn symphony 88
strauss tod und verklärung
beethoven symphony 5

lübeck 1 may 1925
bpo
handel concerto grosso 5
beethoven symphony 5
strauss don juan
wagner tannhäuser overture

stettin 2 may 1925
bpo
weber der freischütz overture
brahms symphony 4
beethoven symphony 7
wagner meistersinger overture

breslau 4 may 1925
bpo
haydn symphony 88
strauss till eulenspiegel
brahms symphony 4

prague 5 may 1925
bpo
berlioz benvenuto cellini overture
schumann symphony 4
beethoven symphony 7
wagner meistersinger overture

vienna 6 may 1925
bpo
haydn symphony 88
brahms symphony 4
wagner meistersinger overture

budapest 7 may 1925
bpo
strauss don juan
schumann symphony 4
beethoven symphony 5
wagner tannhäuser overture

budapest 8 may 1925
bpo
weber der freischütz overture
brahms symphony 4
strauss till eulenspiegel
wagner meistersinger overture

munich 11 may 1925
bpo
berlioz benvenuto cellini overture
brahms symphony 4
beethoven symphony 7

nürnberg 13 may 1925
bpo
weber der freischütz overture
brahms symphony 2
beethoven symphony 5

stuttgart 14 may 1925
bpo
berlioz benvenuto cellini overture
strauss tod und verklärung
beethoven symphony 3

basel 15 may 1925
bpo
weber der freischütz overture
brahms symphony 2
beethoven symphony 5

freiburg 16 may 1925
bpo
wagner meistersinger overture
reger mozart variations
beethoven symophony 3

baden-baden 17 may 1925
bpo
handel concerto grosso 5
strauss till eulenspiegel
tchaikovsky symphony 6

pforzheim 18 may 1925
bpo
handel concerto grosso 10
schumann symphony 4
beethoven symphony 7

mannheim 19 may 1925
bpo
wagner meistersinger overture
reger mozart variations
brahms symphony 4

heidelberg 20 may 1925
bpo
handel concerto grosso 3
strauss don juan
beethoven symphony 3

frankfurt 22 may 1925
bpo
haydn symphony 88
strauss till eulenspiegel
beethoven symphony 3

wiesbaden 23 may 1925
bpo
handel concerto grosso no 10
strauss don juan
brahms symphony 4

koblenz 24 may 1925
bpo
haydn symphony 88
reger mozart variations
beethoven symphony 5

cologne 25 may 1925
bpo
brahms symphony 4
beethoven symphony 7

düsseldorf 26 may 1925
bpo
haydn symphony 88
reger mozart variations
beethoven symphony 5

wuppertal-elberfeld 27 may 1925
bpo
haydn symphony 88
strauss till eulenspiegel
beethoven symphony 3

krefeld 28 may 1925
bpo
berlioz benvenuto cellini overture
brahms symphony 2
strauss don juan
wagner tannhäuser overture

kassel 29 may 1925
bpo
haydn symphony 88
reger mozart variations
beethoven symphony 5

görlitz 7 june 1925
bpo
gieseking, leonard, liebenberg, nissen
strauss ein heldenleben
pfitzner piano concerto
bruckner te deum

görlitz 9 june 1925
bpo
hegner, nissen
wagner meistersinger overture
wagner wahn monolog/meistersinger
beethoven violin concerto
beethoven symphony 3

mannheim 29 september 1925
mannheim orchestra
bach suite 2
bartok dance suite
dvorak symphony 9

berlin 4-5 october 1925
bpo
giannini
haydn symphony 100
bartok dance suite
strauss don juan
arias by mozart and weber

222

leipzig 8 october 1925
gewandhaus-orchester
giannini
haydn symphony 100
respighi pini di roma
strauss don juan
arias by mozart and weber

leipzig 15 october 1925
gewandhaus-orchester
busch
ambrosius symphony 2
mendelssohn violin concerto
j.strauss kaiser and donau waltzes

hamburg 16 october 1925
bpo
haydn symphony 100
strauss don juan
dvorak symphony 9

berlin 18-19 october 1925
bpo
busch
respighi pini di roma
beethoven violin concerto
dvorak symphony 9

leipzig 22 october 1925
gewandhaus-orchester
borowsky
kletzki overture to a tragedy
bach piano concerto bwv 1052
brahms symphony 4

halle 26 october 1925
gewandhaus-orchester
strauss don juan
j.strauss kaiser and donau waltzes
brahms symphony 4

leipzig 29 october 1925
bpo
wittgenstein
beethoven symphony 2
strauss domestica parergon
strauss also sprach zarathustra

berlin 1-2 november 1925
bpo
wittgenstein
beethoven symphony 2
strauss domestica parergon
strauss also sprach zarathustra

vienna 9-10 november 1925
vso
singverein
foerstl-links, groenen
brahms ein deutsches requiem

leipzig 12 november 1925
gewandhaus-orchester
schnabel
mozart piano concerto 26
bruckner symphony 8

berlin 15-16 november 1925
bpo
iturbi
schumann piano concerto
bruckner symphony 8

leipzig 26 november 1926
gewandhaus-orchester
münch-holland
mozart eine kleine nachtmusik
schumann cello concerto
berlioz symphonie fantastique

hamburg 27 november 1925
bpo
mozart eine kleine nachtmusik
beethoven coriolan overture
berlioz symphonie fantastique

berlin 29-30 november 1925
bpo
borowsky
j.c.bach sinfonia in b flat
bach piano concerto bwv 1052
berlioz symphonie fantastique

leipzig 3 december 1925
gewandhaus-orchester
reger hiller variations
brahms academic festival overture
other works conducted by von baussern

berlin 6-7 december 1925
bpo
huberman
reger hiller variations
brahms violin concerto
brahms academic festival overture

vienna 12-13 december 1925
vpo
brahms academic festival overture
dvorak symphony 9
strauss sinfonia domestica

leipzig 17 december 1925
gewandhaus-orchester
reinhardt
locatelli concerto grosso 8
hindemith concerto for orchestra
wagner wesendonk-lieder
wagner fliegende holländer overture
also an aria by handel

berlin 20-21 december 1925
bpo
ivogün
gluck alceste overture
mozart eine kleine nachtmusik
braunfels prelude & prologue/die vögel
hindemith concerto for orchestra
arias by bach and handel

leipzig 1 january 1926
gewandhaus-orchester
engell
beethoven leonore 2 overture
reznicek tragische geschichte
beethoven symphony 3
vocal works by gluck, wolf & pfitzner

leipzig 7 january 1926
gewandhaus-orchester
furtwängler
gal overture to a puppet play
bach piano concerto bwv 1058
brahms symphony 3

hamburg 8 january 1926
bpo
furtwängler
beethoven leonore 2 overture
bach piano concerto bwv 1058
brahms symphony 3

berlin 10-11 january 1926
bpo
furtwängler
beethoven leonore 2 overture
bach piano concerto bwv 1058
brahms symphony 3

vienna 19-20 january 1926
vso
singverein
merz-thunner, dierolf, erb, manowarda
suter laudi di san francisco d'assisi

berlin 24-25 january 1926
bpo
kittel choir
leonard, schey
brahms ein deutsches requiem

hamburg 27 january 1926
bpo
beethoven programme
symphonies 1 and 3

new york 11-12 february 1926
nypso
beethoven egmont overture
mozart eine kleine nachtmusik
brahms symphony 4
wagner meistersinger overture

new york 13 february 1926
nypso
kindler
beethoven egmont overture
valentini cello suite
brahms symphony 4

new york 14 february 1926
nypso
kindler
dvorak symphony 9
valentini cello suite
wagner meistersinger overture

new york 18-19 february 1926
nypso
novaes
haydn symphony 88
schumann piano concerto
strauss sinfonia domestica

new york 20 february 1926
nypso
beethoven egmont overture
dvorak symphony 9

new york 21 february 1926
nypso
weber oberon overture
mozart eine kleine nachtmusik
brahms symphony 4

new york 23 february 1926
nypso
evening of light music at waldorf-
astoria hotel
mozart eine kleine nachtmusik
schubert rosamunde entr'acte
dvorak slavonic dance
brahms 2 hungarian dances
strauss kaiser-walzer

new york 25-26 february 1926
nypso
berlioz le corsair overture
respighi antiche arie e danze, suite 2
tchaikovsky symphony 6

new york 28 february 1926
nypso
szigeti
haydn symphony 88
beethoven egmont overture
brahms violin concerto
wagner meistersinger overture

new york 4-5 march 1926
nypso
mozart le nozze di figaro overture
schumann symphony 1
strauss intermezzo interlude and
    waltz scene
brahms 3 hungarian dances

new york 7 march 1926
nypso
guidi
haydn symphony 88
mendelssohn violin concerto
strauss till eulenspiegel

philadelphia 8-9 march 1926
nypso
brahms symphony 4
strauss till eulenspiegel
wagner meistersinger overture

baltimore 10 march 1926
nypso
brahms symphony 4
strauss till eulenspiegel
wagner meistersinger overture

reading pa 11 march 1926
nypso
beethoven egmont overture
strauss till eulenspiegel
tchaikovsky symphony 6

pittsburgh 12 march 1926
nypso
weber oberon overture
schumann symphony 1
respighi antiche arie e danze, suite 2
brahms 3 hungarian dances

pittsburgh 13 march 1926
nypso
haydn symphony 88
dvorak symphony 9
wagner meistersinger overture

new york 14 march 1926
nypso
backhaus
concert at metropolitan opera house
beethoven piano concerto 4
tchaikovsky symphony 6
according to rené trémine backhaus
replaced szigeti, who was to have
performed brahms violin concerto

new york 18-19 march 1926
nypso
beethoven leonore 3 overture
schoenberg verklärte nacht
dvorak husitska overture
ravel rapsodie espagnole
wagner fliegende holländer overture

new york 20 march 1926
nypso
weber oberon overture
schoenberg verklärte nacht
strauss till eulenspiegel
brahms 3 hungarian dances

new york 21 march 1926
nypso
schulz
schumann symphony 1
saint-saens cello concerto 1
beethoven leonore 3 overture

new york 25-26 march 1926
nypso
landowska
bruckner symphony 4
mozart piano concerto 26
haydn piano concerto in d
weber euryanthe overture

new york 27 march 1926
nypso
beethoven symphony 7
ravel rapsodie espagnole
wagner fliegende holländer overture

new york 28 march 1926
nypso
respighi antiche arie e danze, suite 2
ravel rapsodie espagnole
tchaikovsky symphony 6
respighi and ravel works replaced
gluck alceste overture and schoenberg
verklärte nacht originally scheduled

new york 1-2 april 1926
nypso
handel concerto grosso 5
weber aufforderung zum tanz
beethoven symphony 3

berlin 18-19 april 1926
bpo
piatigorsky
handel concerto grosso 5
dvorak cello concerto
tchaikovsky symphony 4

leipzig 22 april 1926
gewandhaus-orchester and chorus
hansen-schulthess, adam,
topitz, bockelmann
beethoven symphony 9

berlin 25-26 april 1926
bpo
beethoven symphony 4
brahms symphony 1

stettin 28 april 1926
bpo
mozart eine kleine nachtmusik
beethoven symphony 4
brahms symphony 1

hamburg 29 april 1926
bpo
beethoven symphony 4
brahms symphony 1

kiel 30 april 1926 morning
bpo
beethoven symphony 1
strauss till eulenspiegel
brahms symphony 1

braunschweig 30 april 1926 evening
bpo
beethoven symphony 1
strauss till eulenspiegel
brahms symphony 1

essen 1 may 1926
bpo
bruckner symphony 4
strauss till eulenspiegel
wagner tannhäuser overture

mülheim 2 may 1926
bpo
beethoven symphony 3
brahms symphony 4
wagner meistersinger overture

cologne 3 may 1926
bpo
beethoven symphony 1
strauss till eulenspiegel
brahms symphony 1

düsseldorf 4 may 1926
bpo
beethoven symphony 3
tchaikovsky symphony 4

kassel 5 may 1926
bpo
bruckner symphony 4
strauss till eulenspiegel
brahms 3 hungarian dances
wagner meistersinger overture

breslau 7 may 1926
bpo
beethoven symphony 1
bruckner symphony 4
wagner meistersinger overture

görlitz 8 may 1926
bpo
beethoven symphony 4
tchaikovsky symphony 4

prague 9 may 1926
bpo
beethoven symphony 1
bruckner symphony 4
wagner tannhäuser overture

vienna 10 may 1926
bpo
beethoven symphony 1
strauss till eulenspiegel
tchaikovsky symphony 4

budapest 11 may 1926
bpo
beethoven symphony 3
brahms symphony 1
brahms 3 hungarian dances

budapest 12 may 1926
bpo
weber euryanthe overture
strauss tod und verklärung
tchaikovsky symphony 4
wagner meistersinger overture

zürich 15 may 1926
bpo
beethoven symphony 1
brahms symphony 4
wagner meistersinger overture

lausanne 16 may 1926
bpo
mozart eine kleine nachtmusik
strauss tod und verklärung
beethoven symphony 3
wagner meistersinger overture

freiburg 17 may 1926
bpo
beethoven leonore 3 overture
mozart eine kleine nachtmusik
bruckner symphony 4

stuttgart 18 may 1926
bpo
weber euryanthe overture
beethoven symphony 4
tchaikovsky symphony 4

frankfurt 19 may 1926
bpo
bruckner symphony 4
strauss till eulenspiegel
wagner meistersinger overture

mannheim 20 may 1926
bpo
beethoven symphony 1
bruckner symphony 4

heidelberg 29-30 may 1926
bpo and chorus
leonard, raatz-brockmann
brahms festival
academic festival overture and
ein deutsches requiem

heidelberg 31 may 1926
bpo
busch, grümmer
brahms festival
symphony 3, double concerto and
academic festival overture

heidelberg 2 june 1926
bpo
ney
brahms festival
haydn variations, piano concerto 2
and symphony 1

mannheim 21 september 1926
mannheim orchestra
weber euryanthe overture
franck symphony in d minor
strauss till eulenspiegel
wagner siegfried idyll

berlin 26-27 september 1926
bpo
ney
franck symphony in d minor
beethoven piano concerto 5
strauss till eulenspiegel

leipzig 7 october 1926
gewandhaus-orchester
szigeti
beethoven prometheus overture
mozart violin concerto 4
honegger chant de joie
strorg artists' life
brahms symphony 2

berlin 10-11 october 1926
bpo
thibaud
weber der freischütz overture
honegger chant de joie
lalo symphonie espagnole
brahms symphony 2

leipzig 14 october 1926
gewandhaus-orchester
liebenberg
raphael symphony 1 <u>premiere</u>
schubert rosamunde entr'acte
weber euryanthe overture
vocal works by gluck and schubert

leipzig 21 october 1926
gewandhaus-orchester
horowitz
bruckner symphony 9
liszt piano concerto 2
tchaikovsky romeo and juliet

hamburg 22 october 1926
bpo
bruckner symphony 9
honegger chant de joie
weber der freischütz overture

berlin 24-25 october 1926
bpo
horowitz
bruckner symphony 9
liszt piano concerto 2
tchaikovsky romeo and juliet

leipzig 28 october 1926
gewandhaus-orchester
munch
prokofiev violin concerto 1
debussy nuages et fêtes/nocturnes
chausson poeme
beethoven symphony 4

magdeburg 29 october 1926
bpo

halle 31 october 1926
gewandhaus-orchester
weber euryanthe overture
tchaikovsky romeo and juliet
bruckner symphony 9

leipzig 4 november 1926
gewandhaus-orchester
nette-teichmüller
mozart symphony 39
jarnach morgenklangspiele <u>premiere</u>
stravinsky fireworks
schumann piano concerto
strauss ein heldenleben

berlin 7-8 november 1926
bpo
schnabel
mozart symphony 39
jarnach morgenklangspiele
brahms piano concerto 2
weber euryanthe overture

vienna 16-17 november 1926
vpo
singverein
bach matthäus-passion

berlin 21-22 november 1926
bpo
huberman
bach suite 2
beethoven violin concerto
strauss ein heldenleben

leipzig 25 november 1926
gewandhaus-orchester
rehkemper
schumann genoveva overture
schubert symphony 8
graener gothic suite
schoeck gaselen
wagner tannhäuser overture

berlin 28-29 november 1926
bpo
<u>beethoven programme</u>
egmont overture & symphonies 4 and 5

leipzig 2 december 1926
gewandhaus-orchester and chorus
balve
bach suite 2
liszt faust symphony

hamburg 3 december 1926
bpo
holst, piatigorsky
bach suite 2
brahms double concerto
strauss ein heldenleben

berlin 5-6 december 1926
bpo
oehmann
beethoven leonore 3 overture
beethoven florestan's aria/fidelio
liszt faust symphony

leipzig 9 december 1926
gewandhaus-orchester
ney
toch piano concerto
wagner siegfried idyll
schubert wanderer fantasy
beethoven symphony 8

leipzig 16 december 1926
gewandhaus-orchester
casella
berlioz carnaval romain overture
casella partita for piano & orchestra
beethoven symphony 7

berlin 19-20 december 1926
bpo
ivogün, casella
berlioz carnaval romain overture
casella partita for piano & orchestra
mozart arias
beethoven symphony 8

leipzig 31 december 1926
gewandhaus-orchester
beethoven symphony 7
schubert symphony 8
wagner tannhäuser overture

leipzig 1 january 1927
gewandhaus-orchester
mörner
marcello aria from didon
beethoven grosse fuge
brahms symphony 1
brahms lieder accompanied by furtwängler at the piano

leipzig 6 january 1927
gewandhaus-orchester
cassado
mendelssohn symphony 3
ravel daphnis et chloe, 2nd suite
saint-saens cello concerto 1
wagner meistersinger overture

berlin 9-10 january 1927
bpo
sauer
beethoven grosse fuge
schubert symphony 8
chopin piano concerto 1
wagner fliegende holländer overture

vienna 15-16 january 1927
vpo
mendelssohn symphony 3
brahms symphony 2

munich 19 january 1927
konzertvereins-orchester
brahms symphony 2
beethoven symphony 5

hamburg 21 january 1927
bpo
beethoven grosse fuge
schubert symphony 8 ٭
beethoven symphony 7

berlin 23-24 january 1927
bpo
fischer
beethoven programme
coriolan overture, piano concerto 4
and symphony 7

new york 10-11 february 1927
nypso
casals
weber der freischütz overture
schumann cello concerto
strauss ein heldenleben

new york 12 february 1927
nypso
ocko
beethoven coriolan overture
brahms violin concerto
beethoven symphony 7

new york 13 february 1927
nypso
beethoven coriolan overture
beethoven symphony 7
tchaikovsky romeo and juliet
berlioz hungarian march

new york 17-18 february 1927
nypso
berlioz carnaval romain overture
miaskovsky symphony 7 us premiere
brahms symphony 2

new york 20 february 1927
nypso
kochanski
beethoven egmont overture
brahms violin concerto
strauss ein heldenleben

new york 24-25 february 1927
nypso
mendelssohn symphony 3
sibelius tempest overture
hindemith concerto for orchestra
wagner tannhäuser overture

new york 27 february 1927
nypso
kochanski
beethoven coriolan overture
brahms violin concerto
tchaikovsky romeo and juliet
wagner tannhäuser overture

new york 1 march 1927
nypso
schumann-heink
wagner programme
lohengrin prelude, entry of the gods,
erda's warning, magic fire music,
tristan prelude and liebestod, ride
of valkyries, waltraute's narrative
and meistersinger overture

new york 3-4 march 1927
nypso
szigeti
bach brandenburg concerto 3
prokofiev violin concerto 1
beethoven leonore 2 overture
franck symphony in d minor

new york 6 march 1927
nypso
weber der freischütz overture
sibelius tempest overture
strauss don juan
brahms symphony 2

philadelphia 7 march 1927
nypso
weber der freischütz overture
sibelius tempest overture
strauss don juan
brahms symphony 2

washington 8 march 1927
nypso
weber der freischütz overture
sibelius tempest overture
strauss don juan
brahms symphony 1

baltimore 9 march 1927
nypso
weber der freischütz overture
sibelius tempest overture
strauss don juan
brahms symphony 1

harrisburg 10 march 1927
nypso
weber der freischütz overture
sibelius tempest overture
strauss don juan
brahms symphony 1

pittsburgh 11 march 1927
nypso
beethoven coriolan overture
beethoven symphony 7
tchaikovsky romeo and juliet
wagner tannhäuser overture

pittsburgh 12 march 1927
nypso
weber der freischütz overture
sibelius tempest overture
strauss don juan
brahms symphony 1

new york 13 march 1927
nypso
concert at metropolitan opera house
franck symphony in d minor
tchaikovsky romeo and juliet
berlioz carnaval romain overture

new york 15 march 1927
nypso
conductors busch and damrosch and
members of new york city so also
participated in this concert

new york 17-18 march 1927
nypso
gabrilowitsch
braunfels don juan
strauss tod und verklärung
brahms piano concerto 2

new york 19 march 1927
nypso
bach brandenburg concerto 3
hindemith concerto for orchestra
tchaikovsky symphony 4

new york 20 march 1927
nypso
schelling
bach brandenburg concerto 3
schelling fantastic suite
tchaikovsky symphony 4

new york 24-25 march 1927
nypso
gieseking
beethoven programme
grosse fuge, piano concerto 4
and symphony 5

new york 26 march 1927
nypso
schulz
strauss don juan
bruch kol nidrei
schulz berceuse for cello & orchestra
dvorak rondo for cello & orchestra
franck symphony in d minor

new york 27 march 1927
nypso
schelling
strauss don juan
schelling fantastic suite
franck symphony in d minor

new york 31 march and 1 april 1927
nypso
choral symphony society
rethberg, gange
brahms ein deutsches requiem

new york 2 april 1927
nypso
braunfels don juan
strauss tod und verklärung
beethoven symphony 5

new york 3 april 1927
nypso
choral symphony society
lerch, gange
concert at metropolitan opera house
brahms ein deutsches requiem
furtwängler's final american concert

hamburg 22 april 1927
bpo
bach brandenburg concerto 3
debussy nuages et fêtes/nocturnes
beethoven symphony 3

berlin 24-25 april 1927
bpo
bach brandenburg concerto 3
debussy nuages et fêtes/nocturnes
beethoven symphony 3

leipzig 28-29 april 1927
gewandhaus-orchester and chorus
hüni-mihacsek, dierolf, knote, schey
beethoven symphony 9

stettin 2 may 1927
bpo
beethoven egmont overture
beethoven symphony 6
wagner tristan prelude and liebestod
berlioz benvenuto cellini overture

copenhagen 4 may 1927
bpo
beethoven programme
egmont overture, symphonies 6 and 5

copenhagen 5 may 1927
bpo
weber der freischütz overture
beethoven symphony 3
wagner tristan prelude and liebestod
wagner meistersinger overture

kiel 6 may 1927
bpo
beethoven leonore 3 overture
schumann symphony 4
brahms symphony 1

braunschweig 7 may 1927
bpo
beethoven symphony 4
strauss don juan
beethoven symphony 5

mülheim 8 may 1927
bpo
beethoven leonore 3 overture
schumann symphony 4
beethoven symphony 7

dortmund 9 may 1927
bpo
berlioz benvenuto cellini overture
schumann symphony 4
beethoven symphony 3

düsseldorf 10 may 1927
bpo
weber euryanthe overture
debussy nuages et fêtes/nocturnes
strauss don juan
brahms symphony 1

cologne 11 may 1927
bpo
berlioz benvenuto cellini overture
schumann symphony 4
beethoven symphony 3

essen 12 may 1927
bpo
bach brandenburg concerto 3
schubert symphony 8
tchaikovsky symphony 4

frankfurt 13 may 1927
bpo
beethoven programme
egmont overture, symphonies 4 and 5

jena 14 may 1927
bpo
bach brandenburg concerto 3
brahms symphony 1
strauss don juan
wagner tannhäuser overture

chemnitz 15 may 1927
bpo
bach brandenburg concerto 3
schubert symphony 8
brahms symphony 1

dresden 16 may 1927
bpo
strauss don juan
schubert symphony 8
brahms symphony 1

prague 17 may 1927
bpo
weber euryanthe overture
debussy nuages et fêtes/nocturnes
strauss don juan
beethoven symphony 5

prague 18 may 1927
bpo
bach brandenburg concerto 3
schubert symphony 8
tchaikovsky symphony 4

brno 19 may 1927
bpo
bach brandenburg concerto 3
schubert symphony 8
tchaikovsky symphony 4

vienna 20 may 1927
bpo
weber euryanthe overture
beethoven symphony 4
brahms symphony 1

salzburg 22 may 1927
bpo
wagner meistersinger overture
beethoven symphony 3
strauss till eulenspiegel
brahms 3 hungarian dances

munich 23 may 1927
bpo
beethoven coriolan overture
beethoven symphony 3
strauss till eulenspiegel
brahms 3 hungarian dances

stuttgart 24 may 1927
bpo
strauss don juan
schubert symphony 8
beethoven symphony 5

zürich 25 may 1927
bpo
beethoven egmont overture
beethoven symphony 3
strauss till eulenspiegel
brahms 3 hungarian dances

bern 27 may 1927
bpo
beethoven egmont overture
schubert symphony 8
brahms symphony 1

basel 28 may 1927
bpo
bach brandenburg concerto 3
schumann symphony 4
beethoven symphony 3

pforzheim 29 may 1927
bpo
bach brandenburg concerto 3
debussy nuages et fêtes/nocturnes
strauss don juan
beethoven symphony 3

freiburg 30 may 1927
bpo
beethoven programme
egmont overture, symphonies 4 and 7

heidelberg 1 june 1927
bpo
beethoven festival
leonore 2 overture, symphonies 1 and 6

heidelberg 2 june 1927
bpo
fischer
beethoven festival
coriolan overture, piano concerto 5
and symphony 7

heidelberg 3 june 1927
bpo
beethoven festival
egmont overture, symphonies 4 and 5

frankfurt 1 july 1927
frankfurt opera orchestra
bartok
contemporary music festival
bartok piano concerto 1
nielsen symphony 5
other works conducted by scherchen
and straram

berlin 11 august 1927
bpo
wagner meistersinger overture
concert for the prussian state
government with other works conducted
by wiedemann

mannheim 30 september 1927
mannheim orchestra
haydn symphony 103
beethoven symphony 7
prokofiev chout suite

leipzig 6 october 1927
gewandhaus-orchester
morini
haydn symphony 103
beethoven leonore 2 overture
tchaikovsky violin concerto
prokofiev chout suite
tchaikovsky concerto replaced bach
violin concerto 2 played at rehearsal
by munch

berlin 9-10 october 1927
bpo
rethberg
haydn symphony 103
beethoven ah perfido!
strauss tod und verklärung
strauss 3 lieder
prokofiev chout suite

leipzig 13 october 1927
gewandhaus-orchester
rethberg
straesser symphony 6
beethoven ah perfido!
strauss 3 lieder
strauss till eulenspiegel

leipzig 20 october 1927
gewandhaus-orchester
ney
vaughan williams tallis fantasy
brahms piano concerto 1
beethoven symphony 6

hamburg 21 october 1927
bpo
beethoven symphony 6
ravel daphnis et chloe, 2nd suite
strauss till eulenspiegel

berlin 23-24 october 1927
bpo
busch
beethoven symphony 6
mozart violin concerto 5
ravel daphnis et chloe, 2nd suite

leipzig 27 october 1927
gewandhaus-orchester
hoehn
schumann manfred overture
nielsen symphony 5
beethoven piano concerto 4
beethoven egmont overture

leipzig 3-4 november 1927
gewandhaus-orchester
osterkamp
schumann symphony 2
mendelssohn arias from elijah
mendelssohn midsummer night's dream
    excerpts
stravinsky petrushka

magdeburg 5 november 1927
bpo
beethoven coriolan overture
strauss till eulenspiegel
wagner tannhäuser overture
beethoven symphony 6

leipzig 10 november 1927
gewandhaus-orchester
busch
toch comedy overture
busoni violin concerto
tchaikovsky symphony 5

berlin 13-14 november 1927
bpo
gieseking
mozart le nozze di figaro overture
mozart piano concerto 20
toch comedy overture
tchaikovsky symphony 5

vienna 19-20 november 1927
vpo
weber der freischütz overture
ravel daphnis et chloe, 2nd suite
beethoven symphony 7

vienna 22-23 november 1927
vso
singverein
peltenburg, anday, marion, manowarda
verdi requiem

berlin 27-28 november 1927
bpo
huberman
schumann symphony 2
mendelssohn violin concerto
stravinsky petrushka

hannover 30 november 1927
bpo
weber der freischütz overture
brahms symphony 2
strauss till eulenspiegel
vaughan williams tallis fantasy

london 2 december 1927
bpo
weber der freischütz overture
brahms symphony 2
strauss till eulenspiegel
wagner tannhäuser overture
<u>first visit of bpo to london</u>

manchester 3 december 1927
bpo
weber der freischütz overture
brahms symphony 2
wagner meistersinger overture
strauss till eilenspiegel
wagner tannhäuser overture

london 4 december 1927
bpo
beethoven symphony 1
vaughan williams tallis fantasy
wagner meistersinger overture
tchaikovsky symphony 5

bonn 5 december 1927
bpo
weber der freischütz overture
beethoven symphony 6
tchaikovsky symphony 5

frankfurt 6 december 1927
bpo
beethoven coriolan overture
beethoven symphony 6
tchaikovsky symphony 5

vienna 10-11 december 1927
vpo
haydn symphony 103
vaughan williams tallis fantasy
strauss also sprach zarathustra

hamburg 16 december 1927
bpo
gluck alceste overture
schumann symphony 2
strauss also sprach zarathustra

berlin 18-19 december 1927
bpo
onegin
stölzel concerto grosso a 2 cori
gluck che faro/orfeo ed euridice
brahms alto rhapsody
strauss also sprach zarathustra

leipzig 31 december 1927
gewandhaus-orchester
beethoven symphony 1
beethoven leonore 3 overture
strauss till eulenspiegel
wagner meistersinger overture

leipzig 1 january 1928
gewandhaus-orchester
schöne
mozart idomeneo ballet music
bruckner symphony 7
arias by gluck and mozart

hamburg 6 january 1928
bpo
beethoven egmont overture
bruckner symphony 7

berlin 8-9 january 1928
bpo
landowska
beethoven prometheus overture
haydn harpsichord concerto
bruckner symphony 7

vienna 14-15 january 1928
vpo
mendelssohn hebrides overture
schumann symphony 2
strauss also sprach zarathustra

vienna 17-18 january 1928
vpo
singverein
peltenburg, willer, gallos, wildhagen
handel messiah

munich 21 january 1928
konzertvereins-orchester
<u>schubert programme</u>
rosamunde overture, symphonies 8 & 9

leipzig 9 february 1928
gewandhaus-orchester
geyer
reger böcklin suite
spohr violin concerto 8
schubert symphony 9

hamburg 10 february 1928
bpo
mendelssohn hebrides overture
reger böcklin suite
tchaikovsky symphony 5

berlin 12-13 february 1928
bpo
levitzki
reger böcklin suite
schumann piano concerto
beethoven symphony 7

berlin 20 february 1928
bpo
kittel choir
leonard, dierolf, erb, bockelmann
bach matthäus-passion

leipzig 23 february 1928
gewandhaus-orchester
peltenburg, ramin
braunfels organ concerto premiere
handel arias from messiah
brahms symphony 3

vienna 25-26 february 1928
vpo
berlioz carnaval romain overture
stravinsky petrushka
brahms symphony 3

leipzig 1 march 1928
gewandhaus-orchester
kempff
hasse symphonic prelude
berlioz roméo et juliette excerpts
beethoven piano concerto 1
brahms academic festival overture

berlin 4-5 march 1928
bpo
kwast-hodapp
rathaus overture for large orchestra
berlioz roméo et juliette excerpts
brahms piano concerto 1
brahms academic festival overture

leipzig 6 march 1928
gewandhaus-orchester
brahms symphony 3
berlioz roméo et juliette excerpts
wagner meistersinger overture

leipzig 8-9 march 1928
gewandhaus-orchester
kwast-hodapp
handel concerto grosso 6
weber piano concerto 1
raphael theme, variations and rondo
liszt piano concerto 1
wagner huldigungsmarsch

leipzig 15 march 1928
gewandhaus-orchester
piatigorsky, ramin
waltershausen krippenmusik
haydn cello concerto in d
brahms symphony 4

hamburg 16 march 1928
bpo
kolessa
respighi antiche arie e danze
brahms symphony 4
chopin piano concerto 1

berlin 18-19 march 1928
bpo
vecsey
respighi antiche arie e danze
sibelius violin concerto
brahms symphony 4

leipzig 22 march 1928
gewandhaus-orchester
wollgandt, o.fischer, furtwängler
mozart symphony 40
bach brandenburg concerto 5
beethoven symphony 5

lübeck 25 march 1928
lübeck orchestra
fischer
brahms piano concerto 1
other works conducted by fischer

leipzig 29 march 1928
gewandhaus-orchester and chorus
peltenburg, dierolf, beinert,
rosenthal
beethoven symphony 9

berlin 2-3 april 1928
bpo
holst, harzer, furtwängler
mozart symphony 40
bach brandenburg concerto 5
beethoven symphony 5

vienna 11-12 april 1928
vso
singverein
leonard, dierolf, erb, rehkemper,
manowarda
bach johannes-passion

vienna 14-15 april 1928
vpo
sonnenberg, mairecker, furtwängler
bach brandenburg concerto 5
bruckner symphony 7

budapest 17 april 1928
vpo
beethoven symphony 1
beethoven leonore 3 overture
tchaikovsky symphony 5

budapest 18 april 1928
vpo
beethoven coriolan overture
beethoven symphony 7
berlioz damnation de faust excerpts
wagner siegfried idyll
wagner meistersinger overture

stettin 22 april 1928
bpo
holst, harzer, furtwängler
mozart symphony 40
bach brandenburg concerto 5
strauss don juan
wagner tannhäuser overture

copenhagen 24 april 1928
bpo
beethoven leonore 3 overture
schubert symphony 8
brahms symphony 1

copenhagen 25 april 1928
bpo
beethoven coriolan overture
beethoven symphony 7
strauss don juan
wagner tannhäuser overture

rostock 26 april 1928
bpo
holst, harzer, furtwängler
strauss don juan
bach brandenburg concerto 5
beethoven symphony 5

hamburg 27 april 1928
bpo
holst, harzer, furtwängler
mozart symphony 40
bach brandenburg concerto 5
beethoven symphony 5

braunschweig 28 april 1928
bpo
beethoven coriolan overture
mozart symphony 40
bruckner symphony 7

mülheim 29 april 1928
bpo
schubert programme
rosamunde overture, symphonies 8 & 9

wuppertal-elberfeld 30 april 1928
bpo
beethoven symphony 1
schubert symphony 8
strauss till eulenspiegel
wagner meistersinger overture

essen 1 may 1928
bpo
holst, harzer, furtwängler
beethoven coriolan overture
bach brandenburg concerto 5
bruckner symphony 7

gelsenkirchen 2 may 1928
bpo
mozart symphony 40
strauss don juan
brahms symphony 1

düsseldorf 3 may 1928
bpo
schubert programme
rosamunde overture, symphonies 8 & 9

cologne 4 may 1928
bpo
holst, harzer, furtwängler
bach brandenburg concerto 5
schubert symphony 8
beethoven symphony 5

frankfurt 5 may 1928
bpo
schubert programme
rosamunde overture, symphonies 8 & 9

mannheim 7 may 1927
bpo
beethoven symphony 5
handel concerto grosso 10
mozart symphony 40

saarbrücken 8 may 1928
bpo
mozart symphony 40
strauss till eulenspiegel
brahms symphony 1

neunkirchen 9 may 1928
bpo
handel concerto grosso 10
beethoven symphony 5
strauss till eulenspiegel
wagner meistersinger overture

paris 11 may 1928
bpo
handel concerto grosso 10
beethoven symphony 5
strauss till eulenspiegel
wagner meistersinger overture

freiburg 12 may 1928
bpo
schubert rosamunde overture
schubert symphony 8
brahms symphony 1

lucerne 13 may 1929
bpo
strauss don juan
schubert symphony 8
beethoven symphony 7

zürich 14 may 1928
bpo
schubert programme
rosamunde overture, symphonies 8 & 9

geneva 15 may 1928
bpo
beethoven coriolan overture
beethoven symphony 7
strauss till eulenspiegel
wagner meistersinger overture

basel 16 may 1928
bpo
beethoven leonore 3 overture
mozart symphony 40
schubert symphony 9

stuttgart 18 may 1928
bpo
schubert rosamunde overture
mozart symphony 40
bruckner symphony 7

munich 19 may 1928
bpo
beethoven symphony 1
bruckner symphony 7

baden-baden 20 may 1928
bpo
mozart symphony 40
beethoven leonore 3 overture
beethoven symphony 3

heidelberg 23 may 1928
bpo
schubert programme
rosamunde overture, symphonies 8 & 9

heidelberg 24 may 1928
bpo
piatigorsky
haydn cello concerto in d
strauss till eulenspiegel
bruckner symphony 7

heidelberg 25 may 1928
bpo
holst, harzer, furtwängler
mozart symphony 40
bach brandenburg concerto 5
beethoven symphony 3

238

görlitz 1 june 1928
bpo
schnabel
beethoven leonore 2 overture
mozart piano concerto 17
bruckner symphony 7

görlitz 3 june 1928
bpo
flesch, piatigorsky
strauss don juan
brahms double concerto
schubert symphony 9

hannover 16, 17 and 18 june 1928
bpo

berlin 11 august 1928
bpo
leonard
handel concerto grosso 10
bruckner psalm 150
concert for the prussian state
government with other works conducted
by baussnern

mannheim opera 30 september 1928
wagner die walküre

mannheim 1 october 1928
mannheim orchestra
schubert rosamunde overture
schubert symphony 8
bruckner symphony 4

hamburg 5 october 1928
bpo
handel concerto grosso 10
strauss don juan
bruckner symphony 4

berlin 7-8 october 1928
bpo
morini
handel concerto grosso 10
mozart violin concerto 5
brückner symphony 4

vienna staatsoper 17-19 october 1928
wagner das rheingold
wildbrunn/helletsgruber/schubert/
schipper·
first appearance at vienna staatsoper

vienna 20-21 october 1928
vpo
schubert programme
symphonies 8 and 9

vienna staatsoper 23 october 1928
wagner das rheingold
born/helletsgruber/schubert/manowarda

berlin 28-29 october 1928
bpo
flesch, piatigorsky
beethoven symphony 1
hindemith das nusch-nuschi dances
brahms double concerto
wagner fliegende holländer overture

düsseldorf 31 october 1928
bpo
handel concerto grosso 10
strauss don juan
schumann symphony 4
wagner fliegende holländer overture

cologne 1 november 1928
bpo
weber euryanthe overture
debussy nuages et fêtes/nocturnes
strauss tod und verklärung
beethoven symphony 7

hannover 2 november 1928
bpo
schubert rosamunde overture
schubert symphony 8
brahms symphony 1

london 4 november 1928
bpo
schubert rosamunde overture
schubert symphony 8
weber euryanthe overture
strauss tod und verklärung
wagner fliegende holländer overture

london 5 november 1928
bpo
debussy nuages et fêtes/nocturnes
schumann symphony 4
beethoven symphony 7

liverpool 6 november 1928
bpo
handel concerto grosso no 10
strauss don juan
brahms symphony 1

london 7 november 1928
bpo
handel concerto grosso 10
strauss don juan
brahms symphony 1

hamburg 9 november 1928
bpo
schubert rosamunde overture
schubert symphony 8
brahms symphony 1

berlin 11-12 november 1928
bpo
rachmaninov
rachmaninov piano concerto 3
brahms symphony 1

vienna staatsoper 15 november 1928
wagner das rheingold
born/helletsgruber/gallos/schipper

vienna staatsoper 20 november 1928
mozart le nozze di figaro
kern/lehmann/anday/nissen

vienna 25 november 1928
vpo
schubert anniversary concert
rosamunde overture and entr'acte,
german dances and symphony 9

vienna staatsoper 26 november 1928
mozart le nozze di figaro
schumann/lehmann/helletsgruber/
nissen/jerger

halle 29 november 1928
bpo

berlin 2-3 december 1928
bpo
schorr
schoenberg orchestral variations
premiere
schubert symphony 9
vocal works by pfitzner and weber

vienna 8-9 december 1928
vpo
beethoven symphony 1
debussy nuages et fêtes/nocturnes
bruckner symphony 4

berlin 16-17 december 1928
bpo
schnabel
debussy la mer
mozart piano concerto 19
beethoven symphony 8

vienna 22-23 december 1928
vpo
weber euryanthe overture
debussy nuages et fêtes/nocturnes
brahms symphony 1

berlin 20-21 january 1929
bpo
kreisler
schumann symphony 3
brahms violin concerto
stravinsky firebird suite

vienna 26-27 january 1929
vpo
beethoven coriolan overture
brahms symphony 3
stravinsky firebird suite
wagner meistersinger overture

vienna 29-30 january 1929
vso
singverein
bach matthäus-passion

berlin 3-4 february 1929
bpo
kempff
mendelssohn midsummer night's dream
    overture
beethoven piano concerto 1
mahler symphony 1

hamburg 5 february 1929
bpo
stravinsky firebird suite
bloch schelomo
mahler symphony 1

berlin 10-11 february 1929
bpo
kittel choir
leonard, anday, erb, rehkemper, watzke
bach matthäus-passion

vienna 16-17 february 1929
vpo
handel concerto in d
respighi antiche arie e danze
mahler symphony 1

hamburg 22 february 1929
bpo
fischer
mozart symphony 41
chopin piano concerto 2
strauss till eulenspiegel

berlin 24-25 february 1929
bpo
erb, heitmann
mozart symphony 41
beethoven aria from christus
hindemith organ concerto 2
strauss guntram closing scene
strauss till eulenspiegel

vienna 2-3 march 1929
vpo
beethoven symphony 8
korngold much ado about nothing suite
strauss till eulenspiegel

vienna 5-6 march 1929
vso
singverein
armhold, roswaenge, rössel, mosjoukine
berlioz la damnation de faust

berlin 10-11 march 1929
bpo
gabrilowitsch
haydn symphony 86
pfitzner palestrina preludes
brahms piano concerto 2
brahms 3 hungarian dances

vienna 16-17 march 1929
vpo
buxbaum
mozart symphony 41
bloch schelomo
brahms symphony 4

leipzig 20 march 1929
gewandhaus-orchester
gabrilowitsch
beethoven prometheus overture
mozart piano concerto 20
beethoven symphony 3

halle 21 march 1929
bpo
haydn symphony 86
strauss till eulenspiegel
beethoven symphony 3

hamburg 22 march 1929
bpo
haydn symphony 86
raphael theme, variations and rondo
beethoven symphony 3

berlin 24-25 march 1929
bpo
kittel choir
lamond
beethoven choral fantasy
raphael theme, variations and rondo
beethoven symphony 3

vienna 6-7 april 1929
vpo
jerger
haydn symphony 86
pfitzner herr oluf
beethoven symphony 3

budapest 8 april 1929
vpo
beethoven symphony 8
stravinsky firebird suite
brahms symphony 1

budapest 9 april 1929
vpo
beethoven symphony 3
strauss till eulenspiegel
wagner tannhäuser overture

vienna 13-14 april 1929
vpo
singverein
gerhart, kittel, pataky, mayr
beethoven programme
weihe des hauses overture and
symphony 9

hamburg 18 april 1929
bpo
beethoven symphony 1
pfitzner palestrina preludes
beethoven symphony 7

kiel 19 april 1929
bpo
berlioz benvenuto cellini overture
pfitzner palestrina preludes
beethoven symphony 3

lübeck 20 april 1929
bpo
haydn symphony 86
strauss don juan
beethoven symphony 3

stettin 21 april 1929
bpo
mendelssohn a midsummer night's dream
    overture
schumann symphony 4
beethoven symphony 7

danzig 22 april 1929
bpo
beethoven symphony 1
strauss don juan
brahms symphony 1

königsberg 23-24 april 1929
bpo

braunschweig 26 april 1929
bpo
mendelssohn a midsummer night's dream
    overture
schumann symphony 4
stravinsky firebird suite
wagner tannhäuser overture

essen 27 april 1929
bpo
berlioz benvenuto cellini overture
stravinsky firebird suite
brahms symphony 1

paris 29 april 1929
bpo
beethoven symphony 1
strauss don juan
brahms symphony 1

paris 30 april 1929
bpo
berlioz benvenuto cellini overture
schumann symphony 4
beethoven symphony 7
wagner tannhäuser overture

luxembourg 2 may 1929
bpo
mozart symphony 39
beethoven leonore 3 overture
strauss till eulenspiegel
wagner meistersinger overture

trier 3 may 1929
bpo
haydn symphony 86
strauss don juan
brahms symphony 4

saarbrücken 4 may 1929
bpo
mendelssohn midsummer night's dream
    overture
stravinsky firebird suite
beethoven symphony 7

wiesbaden 5 may 1929
bpo
haydn symphony 86
mozart symphony 39
beethoven symphony 5

frankfurt 6 may 1929
bpo
haydn symphony 86
stravinsky firebird suite
brahms symphony 4

mannheim 7 may 1929
bpo
haydn symphony 86
strauss don juan
beethoven symphony 3

baden-baden 8 may 1929
bpo
weber euryanthe overture
brahms symphony 2
stravinsky firebird suite
wagner meistersinger overture

freiburg 10 may 1929
bpo
beethoven symphony 1
pfitzner palestrina preludes
brahms symphony 2

zürich 11 may 1929
bpo
haydn symphony 86
stravinsky firebird suite
brahms symphony 1

montreux 12 may 1929
bpo
mendelssohn a midsummer night's dream
  overture
strauss don juan
schumann symphony 4
wagner meistersinger overture

geneva 13 may 1929
bpo
haydn symphony 86
beethoven leonore 3 overture
brahms symphony 1

basel 14 may 1929
bpo
flesch, piatigorsky
wagner meistersinger overture
brahms double concerto
strauss don juan
mozart symphony 39

stuttgart 15 may 1929
bpo
flesch, piatigorsky
beethoven symphony 1
beethoven leonore 3 overture
brahms double concerto
wagner meistersinger overture

munich 16 may 1929
bpo
brahms symphony 1
haydn symphony 86
stravinsky firebird suite

bamberg 17 may 1929
bpo
weber euryanthe overture
beethoven symphony 5
brahms symphony 2

heidelberg 21 may 1929
bpo
pfitzner das käthchen von heilbronn
  overture
bruckner symphony 8
erb also sang lieder at this concert

heidelberg 22 may 1929
bpo
weber euryanthe overture
schumann symphony 4
brahms symphony 2

heidelberg 23 may 1929
bpo
beethoven programme
leonore 2 overture, symphonies 5 & 8

jena 29-30 may 1929
bpo
jena choirs
peltenburg, wichmann
brahms festival
ein deutsches requiem

jena 31 may 1929
bpo
gabrilowitsch
brahms festival
haydn variations, piano concerto 1
and symphony 2

jena 2 june 1929
bpo
huberman
brahms festival
tragic overture, violin concerto
and symphony 4

berlin 4 june 1929
bpo
beethoven festival
leonore 3 overture, symphonies 1 & 5

berlin 7 june 1929
bpo
kittel choir
ginster, ellger, fidesser, hofmann
beethoven festival
symphony 9

berlin städtische oper 13 june 1929
mozart le nozze di figaro
merz/schöne/pfahl/reinmar/kipnis
performance given in schauspielhaus

berlin städtische oper 18 june 1929
wagner tristan und isolde
leider/onegin/melchior/schorr/kipnis

mannheim opera 25 june 1929
beethoven fidelio

mannheim opera 15 september 1929
wagner lohengrin

berlin städtische oper 20 sept 1929
wagner tristan und isolde
leider/onegin/melchior/schorr/kipnis

berlin städtische oper 9 & 11 oct 1929
wagner lohengrin
müller/kemp/fidesser/ditter/kipnis

berlin städtische oper 16 oct 1929
wagner lohengrin
müller/kemp/fidesser/ditter/hofmann

hamburg 18 october 1929
bpo
haydn symphony 100
bruckner symphony 8

berlin 20-21 october 1929
bpo
horowitz
bruckner symphony 8
brahms piano concerto 2

berlin städtische oper 22 october 1929
wagner lohengrin
müller/kemp/fidesser/ditter/hofmann

vienna 26-27 october 1929
vpo
handel concerto grosso 5
bruckner symphony 8

vienna 2-3 november 1929
vpo
schnabel
mozart eine kleine nachtmusik
beethoven leonore 2 overture
brahms piano concerto 2
wagner fliegende holländer overture

vienna staatsoper 6 november 1929
wagner tristan und isolde
wildbrunn/anday/graarud/manowarda

berlin 10-11 november 1929
bpo
busch
bach prelude and fugue in e flat,
    arranged by schoenberg premiere
busoni violin concerto
beethoven symphony 7

berlin städtische oper 12 nov 1929
wagner lohengrin
müller/kemp/fidesser/ditter/hofmann

vienna staatsoper 14 november 1929
wagner tristan und isolde
wildbrunn/anday/graarud/manowarda

vienna 16-17 november 1929
vpo
weber oberon overture
vaughan williams a norfolk rhapsody
prokofiev le bas d'acier
beethoven symphony 7

berlin 24-25 november 1929
bpo
ivogün
haydn symphony 100
reznicek tanz-sinfonie
saint-saens theme varié
liszt les préludes
vocal works by rameau and debussy

hannover 26 november 1929
bpo
handel concerto grosso 5
pfitzner palestrina preludes
tchaikovsky romeo and juliet
beethoven symphony 5

wuppertal-elberfeld 27 november 1929
bpo
handel concerto grosso 5
beethoven symphony 5
mendelssohn a midsummer night's dream
    overture
pfitzner palestrina preludes
stravinsky firebird suite

düsseldorf 28 november 1929
bpo
pfitzner palestrina preludes
beethoven symphony 5
stravinsky firebird suite
tchaikovsky romeo and juliet

cologne 29 november 1929
bpo
haydn symphony 100
beethoven leonore 3 overture
handel concerto grosso 5
pfitzner palestrina preludes
stravinsky firebird suite

london 1 december 1929
bpo
haydn symphony 100
beethoven leonore 3 overture
stravinsky firebird suite
tchaikovsky romeo and juliet

bristol 2 december 1929
bpo
mendelssohn a midsummer night's dream
    overture
pfitzner palestrina preludes
handel concerto grosso 5
beethoven symphony 5

london 3 december 1929
bpo
mendelssohn a midsummer night's dream
    overture
pfitzner palestrina preludes
handel concerto grosso 5
beethoven symphony 5

bremen 5 december 1929
bpo
mendelssohn a midsummer night's dream
    overture
schumann symphony 1
beethoven symphony 5

hamburg 6 december 1929
bpo
handel concerto grosso 5
respighi feste romane
schumann symphony 1

berlin 8-9 december 1929
bpo
fischer
schumann symphony 1
mozart piano concerto 20
respighi feste romane

berlin städtische oper 10 dec 1929
wagner tristan und isolde
kemp/onegin/melchior/hofmann

berlin städtische oper 12 dec 1929
wagner lohengrin
müller/helm/fidesser/ditter/hofmann

vienna 14-15 december 1929
vpo
haydn symphony 100
respighi feste romane
schumann symphony 1

berlin städtische oper 5 january 1930
wagner lohengrin
müller/helm/fidesser/prohaska/
hofmann/janssen

berlin städtische oper 11 jan 1930
wagner lohengrin
müller/kemp/fidesser/prohaska/
hofmann/heyer

berlin 19-20 january 1930
bpo
cortot
kletzki variations for orchestra
schumann piano concerto
brahms symphony 2

berlin 2-3 february 1930
bpo
wüllner
g.schumann humoreske premiere
sigwart hektors bestattung
tchaikovsky symphony 6

vienna 8-9 february 1930
vpo
mendelssohn a midsummer night's dream
    overture
prohaska passacaglia
tchaikovsky symphony 6

vienna 12 february 1930
vso
singverein
peltenburg, anday, erb, mayr
beethoven missa solemnis

vienna 15-16 february 1930
vpo
reger mozart variations
weigl fantastic intermezzo
brahms symphony 2

hamburg 21 february 1930
bpo
queling
bach suite 3
brahms symphony 2
pfitzner violin concerto

berlin 23-24 february 1930
bpo
szigeti
bach suite 3
beethoven violin concerto
stravinsky le sacre du printemps

berlin städtische oper 27 feb 1929
mozart le nozze di figaro
ivogün/reinhardt/perras/reinmar/
baumann

berlin 2-3 march 1930
bpo
kittel choir
peltenburg, anday, erb, drissen
beethoven missa solemnis

leipzig 6 march 1930
gewandhaus-orchester
mendelssohn symphony 4
strauss don juan
brahms symphony 2

hamburg 7 march 1930
bpo
reger mozart variations
mendelssohn a midsummer night's dream
    overture
mendelssohn symphony 4

berlin 9-10 march 1930
bpo
salvatini, graudan
reger mozart variations
beethoven ah perfido!
bloch schelomo
brahms symphony 3

vienna 15-16 march 1930
vpo
mozart symphony 39
strauss don juan
beethoven symphony 5

budapest 18 march 1930
vpo
mendelssohn a midsummer night's dream
    overture
reger mozart variations
tchaikovsky symphony 6

budapest 19 march 1930
vpo
mozart symphony 39
strauss don juan
beethoven symphony 5

vienna 22-23 march 1930
vpo
singverein
gerhart, szantho, pataky, mayr
beethoven symphony 9

hamburg 28 march 1930
bpo
hindemith
mozart symphony 39
hindemith konzertmusik premiere
brahms symphony 3

246

berlin 30-31 march 1930
bpo
hindemith
mozart symphony 39
hindemith konzertmusik
brahms symphony 3

berlin 13 april 1929 morning
bpo
beethoven programme
symphonies 6 and 5

berlin städtische oper 13 april 1929
mozart don giovanni
pauly/heidersbach/ivogün/fidesser/
reinmar/kipnis/hofmann

berlin 14 april 1930
bpo
beethoven programme
symphonies 6 and 5

berlin städtische oper 15 and 17
march 1930
mozart don giovanni
pauly/heidersbach/ivogün/fidesser/
reinmar/kipnis/hofmann

munich 23 april 1930
vpo
mozart eine kleine nachtmusik
smetana the moldau/ma vlast
bruckner symphony 4

stuttgart 24 april 1930
vpo
mozart eine kleine nachtmusik
strauss till eulenspiegel
bruckner symphony 4
wagner meistersinger overture

cologne 25 april 1930
vpo
mozart eine kleine nachtmusik
schubert rosamunde entr'acte
schubert symphony 8
bruckner symphony 4

london 27 april 1930
vpo
mozart eine kleine nachtmusik
schubert symphony 8
smetana the moldau/ma vlast
strauss don juan
j.strauss an der schönen blauen donau

london 29 april 1930
vpo
bruckner symphony 4
schubert rosamunde entr'acte and
    ballet music
strauss till eulenspiegel
wagner meistersinger overture

berlin 4 may 1930
bpo
debussy nuages et fêtes/nocturnes
strauss tod und verklärung
brahms symphony 3
wagner meistersinger overture

halle 5 may 1930
bpo
mozart eine kleine nachtmusik
debussy nuages et fêtes/nocturnes
strauss tod und verklärung
brahms symphony 3
wagner meistersinger overture

essen 6 may 1930
bpo
strauss tod und verklärung
mozart eine kleine nachtmusik
hindemith concerto for orchestra
brahms symphony 2

frankfurt 7 may 1930
bpo
debussy nuages et fêtes/nocturnes
brahms symphony 2
beethoven leonore 3 overture
hindemith concerto for orchestra

mannheim 8 may 1930
bpo
mendelssohn symphony 4
hindemith concerto for orchestra
beethoven symphony 5

ludwigshafen 9 may 1930
bpo
mozart eine kleine nachtmusik
debussy nuages et fêtes/nocturnes
stravinsky firebird suite
brahms symphony 2

heidelberg 10 may 1930
bpo
haydn symphony 94
stravinsky firebird suite
brahms symphony 3
wagner meistersinger overture

baden-baden 11 may 1930
bpo
mendelssohn symphony 4
beethoven leonore 3 overture
strauss tod und verklärung
wagner fliegende holländer overture

paris 13 may 1930
bpo
haydn symphony 94
hindemith concerto for orchestra
beethoven leonore 3 overture
brahms symphony 2

paris 15 may 1930
bpo
debussy nuages et fêtes/nocturnes
mendelssohn symphony 4
wagner fliegende holländer overture
wagner meistersinger overture

lyon 16 may 1930
bpo
mozart eine kleine nachtmusik
beethoven symphony 5
wagner tristan prelude and liebestod
wagner meistersinger overture

geneva 17 may 1930
bpo
mozart eine kleine nachtmusik
beethoven symphony 5
wagner tristan prelude and liebestod
wagner meistersinger overture

montreux 18 may 1930
bpo
mozart eine kleine nachtmusik
schumann symphony 1
brahms symphony 3
wagner fliegende holländer overture

basel 19 may 1930
bpo
haydn symphony 94
brahms symphony 3
stravinsky firebird suite
wagner fliegende holländer overture

freiburg 20 may 1930
bpo
mendelssohn a midsummer night's dream
    overture
schumann symphony 1
tchaikovsky symphony 6

zürich 21 may 1930
bpo
mendelssohn a midsummer night's dream
    overture
schumann symphony 1
tchaikovsky symphony 6

innsbruck 22 may 1930
bpo
haydn symphony 94
stravinsky firebird suite
beethoven symphony 5

munich 24 may 1930
bpo
mendelssohn a midsummer night's dream
    overture
schumann symphony 1
tchaikovsky symphony 6

augsburg 25 may 1930
bpo
reger mozart variations
brahms symphony 3
strauss till eulenspiegel
wagner meistersinger overture

jena 26 may 1930
bpo
haydn symphony 94
reger mozart variations
beethoven symphony 5

berlin 2 june 1930
bpo
kittel choir
peltenburg, anday, erb, drissen
beethoven missa solemnis

248

berlin städtische oper 13 june 1930
beethoven fidelio
bindernagel/erb/ditter/hofmann/kipnis

berlin 16 june 1930
bpo
kittel choir
ginster, helger, lorenz, schey
beethoven symphony 9

berlin städtische oper 17 june 1929
beethoven fidelio
bindernagel/erb/ditter/hofmann/garmo

mannheim 20 june 1930
mannheim orchestra
beethoven symphony 6
beethoven symphony 7
j.strauss kaiser-walzer

leipzig 25 june 1930
gewandhaus-orchester
beethoven egmont overture
beethoven symphony 6
strauss tod und verklärung

berlin 5-6 october 1930
bpo
müller
beethoven symphony 2
mahler 5 lieder
strauss sinfonia domestica

berlin 7 october 1930
bpo
beethoven programme
leonore 2 overture, symphonies 2 & 5

dresden 8 october 1930
bpo
beethoven programme
leonore 2 overture, symphonies 2 & 5

hamburg 17 october 1930
bpo
berlioz benvenuto cellini overture
schumann symphony 4
hindemith neues vom tage overture
strauss tod und verklärung

berlin 19-20 october 1930
bpo
elman
hindemith neues vom tage overture
schumann symphony 4
mendelssohn violin concerto
berlioz la damnation de faust excerpts

magdeburg 6 november 1930
bpo
hagedorn-chevalley
beethoven egmont overture
schumann piano concerto
strauss tod und verklärung
beethoven symphony 4

hamburg 7 november 1930
bpo
holst, goldberg
beethoven egmont overture
beethoven symphony 4
k.marx double violin concerto
ravel boléro

berlin 9-10 november 1930
bpo
huberman
beethoven egmont overture
beethoven symphony 4
tchaikovsky violin concerto
ravel boléro

berlin 12 november 1930
bpo
beethoven egmont overture
beethoven symphony 4
strauss don juan
berlioz la damnation de faust excerpts

berlin 24 november 1930 _morning_
bpo
mozart eine kleine nachtmusik
mozart le nozze di figaro overture
brahms symphony 4
wagner meistersinger overture

berlin 24 november 1930
bpo
kittel choir
peltenburg, klose, fidesser, schey
gluck alceste overture
pfitzner das dunkle reich
mozart requiem

berlin 30 november-1 december 1930
bpo
holst, goldberg
berlioz benvenuto cellini overture
k.marx double violin concerto
brahms symphony 4

lübeck 11 december 1930
bpo
queling
beethoven symphony 8
brahms violin concerto
brahms symphony 4

hamburg 12 december 1930
bpo
mozart eine kleine nachtmusik
trapp symphony 4
beethoven symphony 8

berlin 14-15 december 1930
bpo
bertram, eisler, osborn, kreutzer
trapp symphony 4
bach concerto for 4 pianos
beethoven symphony 8

berlin 18-19 january 1931
bpo
kittel choir
peltenburg, wittrisch, schey
haydn die schöpfung

berlin 25-26 january 1931
bpo
cassado
kodaly summer night
schubert arpeggione sonata
tchaikovsky symphony 4

berlin 28 january 1931
bpo
bach brandenburg concerto 3
brahms symphony 4
hindemith neues vom tage overture
stravinsky firebird suite

dresden 29 january 1931
bpo
bach brandenburg concerto 3
brahms symphony 4
hindemith neues vom tage overture
stravinsky firebird suite

breslau 30 january 1931
bpo
beethoven symphony 8
stravinsky firebird suite
brahms symphony 4

leipzig 5 february 1931
gewandhaus-orchester
haydn symphony 104
toch kleine theatersuite
tchaikovsky symphony 4

hamburg 6 february 1931
bpo
toch kleine theatersuite
haydn symphony 104
brahms symphony 4

berlin 8-9 february 1931
bpo
gieseking
haydn symphony 104
franck variations symphoniques
toch kleine theatersuite
strauss burleske
liszt hungarian rhapsody 1

berlin 22-23 february 1931
bpo
schlusnus
mozart symphony 38
bruckner symphony 3
vocal works by gluck and handel

hannover 24 february 1931
bpo
beethoven egmont overture
beethoven symphony 4
brahms symphony 4
wagner meistersinger overture

wuppertal-elberfeld 25 february 1931
bpo
bach brandenburg concerto 3
schumann symphony 4
hindemith neues vom tage overture
strauss tod und verklärung

brussels 26 february 1931
bpo
beethoven programme
egmont overture, symphonies 4 and 5

brussels 27 february 1931
bpo
bach brandenburg concerto 3
schumann symphony 4
hindemith neues vom tage overture
strauss tod und verklärung
stravinsky firebird suite
wagner meistersinger overture

london 1 march 1931
bpo
bach brandenburg concerto 3
brahms symphony 4
hindemith neues vom tage overture
strauss tod und verklärung

birmingham 2 march 1931
bpo
bach brandenburg concerto 3
beethoven symphony 7
strauss tod und verklärung
wagner meistersinger overture

liverpool 3 march 1931
bpo
mozart eine kleine nachtmusik
beethoven symphony 7
sibelius en saga
wagner meistersinger overture

newcastle 4 march 1931
bpo
bach brandenburg concerto 3
beethoven symphony 7
strauss tod und verklärung
wagner meistersinger overture

glasgow 5 march 1931
bpo
mozart eine kleine nachtmusik
brahms symphony 4
sibelius en saga
wagner meistersinger overture

dundee 6 march 1931
bpo
beethoven egmont overture
sibelius en saga
berlioz hungarian march
schubert symphony 9
wagner tannhäuser overture

edinburgh 7 march 1931
bpo
beethoven coriolan overture
beethoven symphony 7
sibelius en saga
berlioz la damnation de faust excerpts

london 8 march 1931
bpo
beethoven coriolan overture
beethoven symphony 7
sibelius en saga
berlioz la damnation de faust excerpts

den haag 9 march 1931
bpo
bach brandenburg concerto 3
beethoven symphony 7
stravinsky firebird suite
wagner meistersinger overture

amsterdam 10 march 1931
bpo
beethoven egmont overture
brahms symphony 4
hindemith neues vom tage overture
strauss tod und verklärung
wagner meistersinger overture

bremen 11 march 1931
bpo
beethoven egmont overture
bach brandenburg concerto 3
stravinsky firebird suite
brahms symphony 4

hamburg 13 march 1931
bpo
kulenkampff
debussy prélude a l'apres-midi
taneyev suite for violin & orchestra
schubert symphony 9

berlin 15-16 march 1931
bpo
kulenkampff
debussy prélude a l'apes-midi
taneyev suite for violin and orchestra
schubert symphony 9

vienna 21-22 march 1931
vpo
singverein
gerhart, rünger, krauss, mayr
beethoven programme
leonore 2 overture and symphony 9

berlin 29-30 march 1931
bpo
beethoven programme
prometheus overture, grosse fuge,
leonore 3 overture and symphony 3

berlin 18 april 1931
bpo
flesch, havemann
bach brandenburg concerto 3
bach double violin concerto
brahms symphony 4

berlin 19 april 1931
bpo
schubert symphony 9
debussy prélude a l'apres-midi
strauss till eulenspiegel
wagner tannhäuser overture

prague 22 april 1931
bpo
bach brandenburg concerto 3
beethoven symphony 7
debussy prélude a l'apres-midi
strauss till eulenspiegel
wagner meistersinger overture

halle 23 april 1931
bpo
bach brandenburg concerto 3
schumann symphony 4
debussy prélude a l'apres-midi
brahms symphony 4

leipzig 24 april 1931
bpo
bach brandenburg concerto 3
debussy prélude a l'apres-midi
strauss till eulenspiegel
brahms symphony 4

braunschweig 25 april 1931
bpo
haydn symphony 104
strauss till eulenspiegel
beethoven symphony 5

mülheim 26 april 1931
bpo
haydn symphony 104
beethoven leonore 2 overture
bruckner symphony 3

essen 27 april 1931
bpo
schubert symphony 9
debussy prélude a l'apres-midi
berlioz la damnation de faust excerpts
strauss till eulenspiegel

düsseldorf 28 april 1931
bpo
beethoven symphony 3
debussy prélude a l'apres-midi
berlioz la damnation de faust excerpts
strauss till eulenspiegel

cologne 29 april 1931
bpo
bach brandenburg concerto 3
brahms symphony 4
debussy prélude a l'apres-midi
strauss till eulenspiegel
wagner tannhäuser overture

frankfurt 30 april 1931
bpo
schubert symphony 9
debussy prélude a l'apres-midi
strauss till eulendpiegel
wagner meistersinger overture

heidelberg 1 may 1931
bpo
haydn symphony 104
beethoven leonore 2 overture
bruckner symphony 3

ludwigshafen 2 may 1931
bpo
bach brandenburg concerto 3
schumann symphony 4
beethoven symphony 3

baden-baden 3 may 1931
bpo
schubert symphony 9
debussy prélude a l'apres-midi
berlioz la damnation de faust excerpts
wagner tannhäuser overture

paris 5 may 1931
bpo
bach brandenburg concerto 3
stravinsky firebird suite
beethoven symphony 3
berlioz la damnation de faust excerpts

paris 7 may 1931
bpo
schubert symphony 9
debussy prélude a l'apres-midi
strauss till eulenspiegel
wagner tannhäuser overture
wagner meistersinger overture

lyon 8 may 1931
bpo
bach brandenburg concerto 3
schumann symphony 4
strauss till eulenspiegel
wagner tannhäuser overture
berlioz la damnation de faust excerpts

marseille 9 may 1931
bpo
bach brandenburg concerto 3
schumann symphony 4
strauss till eulenspiegel
wagner tannhäuser overture
debussy prélude a l'apres-midi
berlioz la damnation de faust excerpts

geneva 11 may 1931
bpo
schumann symphony 4
bach brandenburg concerto 3
debussy prélude a l'apres-midi
strauss till eulenspiegel
berlioz la damnation de faust excerpts

zürich 12 may 1931
bpo
bruckner symphony 3
strauss till eulenspiegel
wagner tannhäuser overture

freiburg 13 may 1931
bpo
bach brandenburg concerto 3
mozart symphony 40
beethoven symphony 5

stuttgart 15 may 1931
bpo
haydn symphony 104
stravinsky firebird suite
beethoven symphony 5

munich 16 may 1931
bpo
bach brandenburg concerto 3
strauss till eulenspiegel
schubert symphony 9

augsburg 17 may 1931
bpo
mozart symphony 40
beethovven leonore 2 overture
bruckner symphony 3

jena 18 may 1931
bpo
mozart symphony 40
strauss till eulenspiegel
bruckner symphony 3

görlitz 21 may 1931
bpo
holst, goldberg
bach brandenburg concerto 3
k.marx double violin concerto
stravinsky firebird suite
wagner meistersinger overture
schumann symphony 4

görlitz 24 may
bpo
fischer
beethoven programme
egmont overture, choral fantasy,
piano concerto 5 and symphony 5

kiel 27 may 1931
bpo
mozart symphony 40
stravinsky firebird suite
beethoven symphony 7

bayreuth 23 july & 3 august 1931
wagner tristan und isolde
larsen-todsen/helm/melchior/
bockelmann/manowarda

bayreuth 4 august 1931
bayreuth festival orchestra
siegfried wagner memorial concert
beethoven symphony 3
other works conducted by elmendorff;
toscanini conducted only at morning
rehearsal

bayreuth 18 august 1931
wagner tristan und isolde
larsen-todsen/helm/pistor/
bockelmann/manowarda

mannheim 6 october 1931
mannheim orchestra
brahms haydn variations
sekles symphony 1
beethoven symphony 5

berlin 11-12 october 1931
bpo
morini
brahms haydn variations
schubert symphony 8
glazunov violin concerto
stravinsky petrushka

hamburg 23 october 1931
bpo
schuster
vogel 2 studies
dvorak cello concerto
beethoven symphony 6

berlin 25-26 october 1931
bpo
milstein
vogel 2 studies
dvorak violin concerto
beethoven symphony 6

berlin staatsoper 12 november 1931
pfitzner das herz
reinhardt/klose/soot/kullmann/
helgers/grossmann

berlin 15-16 november 1931
bpo
kittel choir
erdmann
debussy 3 nocturnes
beethoven piano concerto 2
schumann introduction and allegro
  appassionato
brahms symphony 1

berlin staatsoper 17 november 1931
pfitzner das herz
heidersbach/klose/soot/scheidl

berlin staatsoper 21 november 1931
pfitzner das herz
reinhardt/klose/soot/helgers/
grossmann

berlin 24 november 1931
bpo
beethoven symphony 6
brahms symphony 1

berlin staatsoper 25 november 1931
pfitzner das herz
heidersbach/booth/soot/helgers/
grossmann

berlin 30 november 1931
bpo
kittel choir
peltenburg, hammer, patzak, schey
handel messiah

halle 2 december 1931
bpo
haydn symphony 99
beethoven leonore 3 overture
tchaikovsky francesca da rimini
wagner tannhäuser overture
stravinsky scherzo fantastique

magdeburg 3 december 1931
bpo
haydn symphony 99
stravinsky scherzo fantastique
schubert symphony 8
tchaikovsky francesca da rimini

254

hamburg 4 december 1931
bpo
haydn symphony 99
schubert symphony 8
stravinsky scherzo fantastique
tchaikovsky francesca da rimini

berlin 6-7 december 1931
bpo
huberman
haydn symphony 99
brahms violin concerto
stravinsky scherzo fantastique
tchaikovsky francesca da rimini

berlin staatsoper 8 december 1931
pfitzner das herz
heidersbach/klose/soot/grossmann/
abendroth

vienna 15-16 december 1931
vso
singverein
handel messiah

berlin staatsoper 18 december 1931
pfitzner das herz
reinhardt/klose/soot/grossmann/
abendroth

berlin 20-21 december 1931
bpo
kempff
graener die flöte von sanssouci
schumann piano concerto
beethoven symphony 7

berlin staatsoper 14 january 1932
pfitzner das herz
reinhardt/klose/soot/scheidl/
abendroth

berlin 19 january 1932
bpo
haydn symphony 104
beethoven grosse fuge
schubert symphony 9

hannover 21 january 1932
bpo
armhold
mozart symphony 40
mozart aria from il re pastore
mahler symphony 4

hamburg 22 january 1932
bpo
armhold
mozart symphony 40
mahler symphony 4

berlin staatsoper 23 january 1932
pfitzner das herz
reinhardt/klose/soot/scheidl/
abendroth

berlin 24-25 january 1932
bpo
armhold
mozart symphony 40
mozart aria from il re pastore
beethoven leonore 3 overture
mahler symphony 4

bielefeld 26 january 1932
bpo
beethoven symphony 6
brahms symphony 1
wagner meistersinger overture

dortmund 27 january 1932
bpo
haydn symphony 104
debussy nuages et fêtes/nocturnes
strauss don juan
schubert symphony 9

brussels 28 january 1932
bpo
haydn symphony 104
debussy nuages et fêtes/nocturnes
brahms symphony 1

brussels 29 january 1932
bpo
beethoven symphony 6
strauss don juan
wagner meistersinger overture
wagner fliegende holländer overture

london 1 february 1932
bpo
schubert programme
rosamunde overture, symphonies 8 & 9

london 2 february 1932
bpo
huberman
brahms programme
haydn variations, violin concerto
and symphony 1

liverpool 3 february 1932
bpo
brahms haydn variations
schubert symphony 8
beethoven grosse fuge
beethoven symphony 5

london 4 february 1932
bpo
beethoven programme
grosse fuge, symphonies 6 and 5

glasgow 5 february 1932
bpo
haydn symphony 104
wagner siegfried idyll
strauss don juan
brahms symphony 1

edinburgh 6 february 1932
bpo
haydn symphony 104
beethoven grosse fuge
tchaikovsky symphony 6

london 7 february 1932
bpo
haydn symphony 104
wagner siegfried idyll
wagner fliegende holländer overture
tchaikovsky symphony 6

den haag 8 february 1932
bpo
beethoven programme
grosse fuge, symphonies 6 and 5

amsterdam 9 february 1932
bpo
beethoven programme
grosse fuge, symphonies 6 and 5

bremen 11 february 1932
bpo
beethoven symphony 6
beethoven grosse fuge
wagner tristan prelude and liebestod
wagner meistersinger overture

hamburg 12 february 1932
bpo
kreutzer
brahms haydn variations
beethoven piano concerto 3
bruckner symphony 9

berlin 14-15 february 1932
bpo
schnabel
beethoven piano concerto 1
bruckner symphony 9

berlin 16 february 1932
bpo
brahms haydn variations
wagner siegfried idyll
wagner fliegende holländer overture
tchaikovsky symphony 6

berlin 18 february 1932
bpo
handel concerto grosso 10
schubert symphony 8
beethoven symphony 7

berlin staatsoper 19 february 1932
pfitzner das herz
reinhardt/klose/soot/grossmann/
abendroth

berlin staatsoper 5 march 1932
pfitzner das herz
heidersbach/klose/soot/scheidl/
abendroth

berlin 6-7 march 1932
bpo
graveure, schuster
gabrieli sonata pian e forte
boccherini cello concerto
brahms symphony 3
vocal works by handel and haydn

leipzig 9 march 1932
gewandhaus-orchester
schubert symphony 8
schubert rosamunde overture
beethoven symphony 7

berlin 15 march 1932
bpo
haydn symphony 102
strauss till eulenspiegel
brahms symphony 3

breslau 16 march 1932
bpo
brahms symphony 3
strauss till eulenspiegel
beethoven symphony 7

magdeburg 17 march 1932
bpo
haydn symphony 102
debussy nuages et fêtes/nocturnes
beethoven symphony 7

hamburg 18 march 1932
bpo
gabrieli sonata pian e forte
haydn symphony 102
brahms symphony 3

berlin 20-21 march 1932
bpo
haydn symphony 102
beethoven coriolan overture
strauss don juan
concert also included ravel piano
concerto in g played by m.long
and conducted by composer

berlin staatsoper 31 march 1932
wagner tristan und isolde
leider/branzell/pistor/kipnis/janssen

hamburg 1 april 1932
bpo
ettinger old english suite
beethoven grosse fuge
beethoven symphony 7

berlin 3-4 april 1932
bpo
bertram, eisner, osborn
ettinger old english suite
bach concerto for 3 pianos
beethoven symphony 5

berlin staatsoper 5 april 1932
wagner tristan und isolde
leider/branzell/soot/kipnis/janssen

vienna 9-10 april 1932
bpo
bruckner symphony 7
strauss till eulenspiegel
wagner tannhäuser overture

berlin staatsoper 12 april 1932
wagner tristan und isolde
leider/branzell/soot/list/prohaska

berlin 14-15 april 1932
bpo
bpo 50th anniversary concerts
bach suite 2
hindemith philharmonic concerto
    premiere
bruckner symphony 7

berlin 17-18 april 1932
bpo
kittel choir
ginster, dierolf, roswaenge,
bockelmann
bpo 50th anniversary concerts
beethoven symphony 9

düsseldorf 21 april 1932
bpo
weber der freischütz overture
brahms symphony 4
hindemith neues vom tage·overture
ravel daphnis et chloé, 2nd suite
wagner tristan prelude and liebestod

wuppertal-elberfeld 22 april 1932
bpo
haydn symphony 88
berlioz roméo et juliette excerpts
berlioz carnaval romain overture
brahms symphony 4

cologne 23 april 1932
bpo
haydn symphony 88
berlioz roméo et juliette excerpts
berlioz carnaval romain overture
beethoven symphony 7

neunkirchen 24 april 1932
bpo
brahms symphony 2
ravel daphnis et chloé, 2nd suite
beethoven symphony 5

paris 26 april 1932
bpo
haydn symphony 88
beethoven symphony 5
berlioz carnaval romain overture
berlioz roméo et juliette excerpts
wagner tannhäuser overture

paris 28 april 1932
bpo
weber der freischütz overture
brahms symphony 4
ravel daphnis et chloé, 2nd suite
wagner tristan prelude and liebestod
wagner tannhäuser overture
wagner meistersinger overture

strasbourg 29 april 1932
bpo
beethoven coriolan overture
beethoven symphony 7
stravinsky firebird suite
wagner tannhäuser overture
weber der freischütz overture

freiburg 30 april 1932
bpo
beethoven coriolan overture
brahms symphony 4
strauss don juan
wagner tristan prelude and liebestod

turin 2 may 1932
bpo
cherubini anacreon overture
beethoven symphony 5
stravinsky firebird suite
wagner tannhäuser overture
weber der freischütz overture

florence 4 may 1932
bpo
weber der freischütz overture
brahms symphony 4
strauss don juan
wagner tristan prelude and liebestod
wagner meistersinger overture

rome 6 may 1932
bpo
cherubini anacreon overture
brahms symphony 2
hindemith neues vom tage overture
strauss till eulenspiegel
wagner tannhäuser overture
weber der freischütz overture

rome 8 may 1932
bpo
haydn symphony 88
stravinsky firebird overture
beethoven symphony 5
wagner meistersinger overture

florence 9 may 1932
bpo
haydn symphony 88
debussy nuages et fêtes/nocturnes
berlioz carnaval romain overture
beethoven symphony 5
wagner tannhäuser overture

turin 10 may 1932
bpo
beethoven coriolan overture
brahms symphony 2
strauss don juan
wagner tristan prelude and liebestod
wagner meistersinger overture

milan 11 may 1932
bpo
cherubini anacreon overture
brahms symphony 2
hindemith neues vom tage overture
stravinsky firebird suite
wagner tannhäuser overture

milan 12 may 1932
bpo
haydn symphony 88
debussy nuages et fêtes/nocturnes
strauss till eulenspiegel
beethoven symphony 5
wagner meistersinger overture

zürich 14 may 1932
bpo
haydn symphony 88
debussy nuages et fêtes/nocturnes
berlioz carnaval romain overture
beethoven symphony 5

vevey 15 may 1932
bpo
haydn symphony 88
beethoven coriolan overture
strauss till eulenspiegel
wagner tristan prelude and liebestod
wagner meistersinger overture

geneva 17 may 1932
bpo
haydn symphony 88
wagner tristan prelude and liebestod
beethoven symphony 7

basel 18 may 1932
bpo
haydn symphony 88
debussy nuages et fêtes/nocturnes
strauss till eulenspiegel
brahms symphony 4

baden-baden 19 may 1932
bpo
haydn symphony 88
debussy nuages et fêtes/nocturnes
strauss don juan
beethoven symphony 7

stuttgart 20 may 1932
bpo
weber der freischütz overture
brahms symphony 2
beethoven symphony 7

heidelberg 21 may 1932
bpo
berlioz carnaval romain overture
haydn symphony 88
debussy nuages et fêtes/nocturnes
beethoven symphony 7

wiesbaden 22 may 1932
bpo
beethoven symphony 1
stravinsky firebird suite
brahms symphony 2

frankfurt 23 may 1932
bpo
beethoven programme
coriolan overture, symphonies 1 & 7

halle 24 may 1932
bpo
haydn symphony 88
berlioz carnaval romain overture
wagner tristan prelude and liebestod
brahms symphony 2

paris opéra 7 and 9 june 1932
wagner tristan und isolde
leider/olszewska/melchior/kipnis/
janssen

paris 10 june 1932
private chamber concert
furtwängler participated together
with other eminent musicians

berlin staatsoper 7 october 1932
wagner die meistersinger von nürnberg
lehmann/wolff/kipnis/janssen/
bockelmann

berlin staatsoper 9 october 1932
wagner tristan und isolde
leider/melchior/kipnis/bockelmann

berlin staatsoper 14 october 1932
wagner die meistersinger von nürnberg
heidersbach/wolff/kipnis/janssen/
bockelmann

berlin 16-17 october 1932
bpo
piatigorsky
reger mozart variations
schumann cello concerto
brahms symphony 2

berlin staatsoper 21 october 1932
wagner die meistersinger von nürnberg
heidersbach/wolff/kipnis/janssen/
bockelmann

berlin staatsoper 25 october 1932
wagner die meistersinger von nürnberg
lehmann/wolff/kipnis/janssen/
bockelmann

berlin 27 october 1932
bpo
goldberg, hindemith
mozart sinfonia concertante
beethoven symphony 4
berlioz harold en italie

hamburg 28 october 1932
bpo
goldberg, hindemith
beethoven symphony 4
mozart sinfonia concertante
berlioz harold en italie

berlin 30-31 october 1932
bpo
prokofiev, hindemith
beethoven symphony 4
prokofiev piano concerto 5 premiere
berlioz harold en italie

berlin staatsoper 2 november 1932
wagner die meistersinger von nürnberg
heidersbach/wolff/kipnis/janssen/
bockelmann

berlin 6-7 november 1932
bpo
kittel choir
ginster, thorborg, patzak, schey,
bockelmann
bach johannes-passion

halle 9 november 1932
bpo
fischer
brahms haydn variations
brahms piano concerto 2
beethoven symphony 7

wuppertal-elberfeld 10 november 1932
bpo
fischer
brahms haydn variations
brahms piano concerto 2
beethoven symphony 8

frankfurt 11 november 1932
bpo
fischer
brahms haydn variations
brahms piano concerto 2
beethoven symphony 8

heidelberg 12 november 1932
bpo
fischer
mozart symphony 38
brahms piano concerto 2
beethoven symphony 8

karlsruhe 13 november 1932
bpo
mozart symphony 38
schubert symphony 8
beethoven symphony 7

munich 14 november 1932
bpo
fischer
brahms haydn variations
brahms piano concerto 2
beethoven symphony 7

vienna 19-20 november 1932
vpo
beethoven programme
egmont overture, symphonies 6 and 7

berlin staatsoper 22 november 1932
wagner die meistersinger von nürnberg
heidersbach/wolff/kipnis/janssen/
bockelmann

berlin 24 november 1932
bpo
mozart die zauberflöte overture
mozart symphony 38
bruckner symphony 4

berlin 27-28 november 1932
bpo
schlusnus
mozart symphony 38
bruckner symphony 4
vocal works by durante, gluck,
   giordani and carissimi

berlin staatsoper 29 november,
4 and 9 december 1932
wagner die meistersinger von nürnberg
heidersbach/wolff/kipnis/janssen/
bockelmann

berlin staatsoper 16 december 1932
wagner die meistersinger von nürnberg
reinhardt/wolff/list/krenn/bockelmann

berlin 18-19 december 1932
bpo
ivogün
k.marx passacaglia premiere
beethoven symphony 8
vocal works by gluck and beethoven

berlin 20 december 1932
bpo
reger mozart variations
beethoven symphony 8
beethoven leonore 3 overture

berlin staatsoper 26 december 1932
wagner die meistersinger von nürnberg
reinhardt/wolff/kipnis/krenn/
bockelmann

berlin staatsoper 15 january 1933
wagner die meistersinger von nürnberg
reinhardt/wolff/list/janssen/prohaska

berlin 16 january 1933
bpo
beethoven symphony 1
stravinsky suite 1
dukas l'apprenti sorcier
schubert symphony 9

breslau 17 january 1933
bpo
beethoven symphony 1
stravinsky suite 1
dukas l'apprenti sorcier
schubert symphony 9

dresden 18 january 1933
bpo
beethoven symphony 1
beethoven coriolan overture
schubert symphony 9

leipzig 19 january 1933
bpo
beethoven symphony 1
stravinsky suite 1
dukas l'apprenti sorcier
brahms symphony 4

hamburg 20 january 1933
bpo
beethoven symphony 1
stravinsky suite 1
dukas l'apprenti sorcier
schubert symphony 9

berlin 22-23 january 1933
bpo
fischer
stravinsky suite 1
dukas l'apprenti sorcier
beethoven piano concerto 3
schubert symphony 9

magdeburg 1 february 1933
bpo
müller variations and fugue
wagner tristan prelude and liebestod
wagner meistersinger overture
tchaikovsky symphony 5

leipzig 2 february 1933
bpo
müller variations and fugue
schubert symphony 8
tchaikovsky symphony 5

berlin 5-6 february 1933
bpo
goldberg
müller variations and fugue
beethoven violin concerto
tchaikovsky symphony 5

münster 7 february 1933
bpo
cherubini anacreon overture
beethoven symphony 3
debussy prélude a l'apres-midi
strauss till eulenspiegel
wagner tannhäuser overture

dortmund 8 february 1933
bpo
cherubini anacreon overture
beethoven symphony 3
dukas l'apprenti sorcier
debussy prélude a l'apres-midi
liszt les préludes

brussels 9 february 1933
bpo
schubert symphony 9
debussy prélude a l'apres-midi
dukas l'apprenti sorcier
liszt les préludes

brussels 10 february 1933
bpo
cherubini anacreon overture
beethoven symphony 3
strauss till eulenspiegel
wagner tannhäuser overture

antwerp 11 february 1933
bpo
beethoven symphony 1
hindemith philharmonic concerto
wagner tristan prelude and liebestod
strauss till eulenspiegel
liszt les préludes

london 13 february 1933
bpo
beethoven coriolan overture
beethoven symphony 1
beethoven symphony 3
wagner meistersinger overture

london 14 february 1933
bpo
weber der freischütz overture
hindemith philharmonic concerto
wagner tristan prelude and liebestod
tchaikovsky symphony 5

newcastle 15 february 1933
bpo
mozart symphony 40
ettinger old english suite
strauss till eulenspiegel
wagner tristan prelude and liebestod
wagner tannhäuser overture

edinburgh 16 february 1933
bpo
mozart symphony 40
strauss don juan
beethoven symphony 3

manchester 17 february 1933
bpo
cherubini anacreon overture
beethoven symphony 3
strauss don juan
wagner tristan prelude and liebestod

bristol 18 january 1933
bpo
mozart symphony 40
ettinger old english suite
wagner lohengrin prelude
strauss till eulenspiegel
liszt les préludes
wagner meistersinger overture

london 19 february 1933
bpo
mozart symphony 40
ettinger old english suite
strauss don juan
wagner lohengrin prelude
liszt les préludes

den haag 21 february 1933
bpo
mozart symphony 40
strauss don juan
schubert symphony 9

bielefeld 22 february 1933
bpo
mozart symphony 40
brahms tragic overture
beethoven symphony 3

hannover 23 february 1933
bpo
hoehn
brahms programme
tragic overture, piano concerto 1
and symphony 4

hamburg 24 february 1933
bpo
hoehn
brahms programme
tragic overture, piano concerto 1
and symphony 4

berlin 26-27 february 1933
bpo
flesch
brahms centenary concert
tragic overture, violin concerto
and symphony 4

vienna 4-5 march 1933
vpo
haydn symphony 101
heger variations on a theme by verdi
tchaikovsky symphony 5

berlin 12 march 1933
bpo
kolessa
beethoven symphony 1
beethoven leonore 2 overture
liszt piano concerto 1
wagner siegfried idyll
wagner götterdämmerung trauermarsch

berlin 13 march 1933
bpo
kolessa
beethoven symphony 1
beethoven leonore 2 overture
liszt piano concerto 1
wagner siegfried idyll
wagner tannhäuser overture

berlin staatsoper 21 march 1933
wagner die meistersinger von nürnberg
heidersbach/wolff/list/krenn/
bockelmann

berlin staatsoper 22 march 1933
strauss elektra
pauly/ursuleac/klose/wittrisch/
grossmann

leipzig 23 march 1933
bpo
kulenkampff
schubert symphony 9
brahms violin concerto
wagner meistersinger overture

hamburg 24 march 1933
bpo
kulenkampff
schumann symphony 4
brahms violin concerto
strauss till eulenspiegel

berlin 26-27 march 1933
bpo
ney
honegger mouvement symphonique 3
schumann symphony 4
beethoven piano concerto 4
strauss till eulenspiegel

berlin staatsoper 29 march 1933
strauss elektra
pauly/ursuleac/klose/wittrisch/
grossmann

berlin staatsoper 2 april 1933
wagner die meistersinger von nürnberg
lemnitz/wolff/kipnis/krenn/bockelmann

berlin staatsoper 4 april 1933
strauss elektra
pauly/ursuleac/klose/soot/grossmann

berlin 9-10 april 1933
bpo
borries, harzer, furtwängler
haydn symphony 101
bach brandenburg concerto 5
beethoven symphony 3

berlin staatsoper 12 april 1933
strauss elektra
münchow/ursuleac/klose/wittrisch/
grossmann

berlin 21 april 1933
bpo
weber der freischütz overture
brahms symphony 3
beethoven symphony 5

263

essen 22 april 1933
bpo
haydn symphony 101
beethoven leonore 2 overture
brahms symphony 1

düsseldorf 23 april 1933
bpo
brahms academic festival overture
brahms symphony 3
beethoven symphony 7

cologne 24 april 1933
bpo
haydn symphony 101
beethoven leonore 2 overture
brahms symphony 1

frankfurt 25 april 1933
bpo
haydn symphony 101
strauss don juan
wagner meistersinger overture
brahms symphony 3

mannheim 26 april 1933
bpo
brahms symphony 3
wagner lohengrin prelude
wagner tannhäuser bacchanale
wagner fliegende holländer overture
bpo augmented by members of the
mannheim orchestra

saarbrücken 27 april 1933
bpo
brahms academic festival overture
brahms symphony 3
strauss don juan
wagner lohengrin prelude
wagner fliegende holländer overture

karlsruhe 28 april 1933
bpo
beethoven egmont overture
beethoven symphony 6
wagner lohengrin prelude
wagner tannhäuser bacchanale
wagner meistersinger overture

baden-baden 29 april 1933
bpo
beethoven egmont overture
beethoven symphony 6
dukas l'apprenti sorcier
wagner tannhäuser bacchanale
wagner fliegende holländer overture

paris 2 may 1933
bpo
beethoven egmont overture
beethoven symphony 6
dukas l'apprenti sorcier
strauss don juan
wagner fliegende holländer overture

paris 4 may 1933
bpo
brahms academic festival overture
brahms symphony 3
wagner lohengrin prelude
wagner tannhäuser overture
wagner meistersinger overture

marseille 6 may 1933
bpo
beethoven egmont overture
beethoven symphony 6
wagner huldigungsmarsch
wagner lohengrin prelude
wagner tannhäuser bacchanale
wagner meistersinger overture

lyon 7 may 1933
bpo
beethoven egmont overture
beethoven symphony 6
brahms academic festival overture
wagner huldigungsmarsch
wagner lohengrin prelude
wagner tannhäuser bacchanale
wagner meistersinger overture

geneva 8 may 1933
bpo
beethoven egmont overture
beethoven symphony 6
wagner lohengrin prelude
strauss don juan

basel 9 may 1933
bpo
haydn symphony 101
dukas l'apprenti sorcier
brahms symphony 3
wagner meistersinger overture

freiburg 10 may 1933
bpo
beethoven egmont overture
beethoven symphony 7
brahms symphony 1

zürich 11 may 1933
bpo
beethoven programme
egmont overture, symphonies 6 and 7

munich 12 may 1933
bpo
haydn symphony 101
beethoven leonore 2 overture
brahms symphony 1

vienna 16-17 may 1933
vso
singverein
armhold, manowarda
brahms centenary concerts
ein deutsches requiem

vienna 19 may 1933
vpo
huberman, casals
brahms centenary concerts
tragic overture, symphony 3, double
concerto and academic festival ov.

vienna 21 may 1933
vpo
schnabel
brahms centenary concerts
haydn variations, piano concerto 2
and symphony 1

berlin 24 may 1933
bpo
fischer
brahms centenary concert
piano concerto 2 and symphony 1

berlin staatsoper 28 may 1933
wagner tristan und isolde
leider/branzell/grahl/list/bockelmann

berlin staatsoper 30 may 1933
wagner die meistersinger von nürnberg
müller/wo]ff/kipnis/janssen/
bockelmann

paris opéra 8 and 10 june 1933
wagner tristan und isolde
leider/kalter/melchior/kipnis/
janssen

paris opéra 13 and 15 june 1933
wagner die walküre
leider/lehmann/kalter/melchior/
kipnis/schorr
lehmann probably only sang on 15 june

berlin staatsoper 9 september 1933
wagner die meistersinger von nürnberg
heidersbach/wolff/kipnis/janssen/
bockelmann

berlin staatsoper 17 september 1933
wagner die meistersinger von nürnberg
heidersbach/lorenz/kipnis/krenn/
bockelmann

berlin staatsoper 24 september 1933
wagner tristan und isolde
leider/branzell/grahl/kipnis/
bockelmann

berlin staatsoper 12 october 1933
strauss arabella
ursuleac/heidersbach/wittrisch/
krenn/prohaska
berlin premiere of the opera

berlin 15-16 october 1933
bpo
gieseking
schillings oedipus rex prelude
beethoven piano concerto 5
bruckner symphony 5

berlin staatsoper 17 october 1933
strauss arabella
ursuleac/heidersbach/kullmann/
krenn/prohaska

berlin staatsoper 18 october 1933
wagner die meistersinger von nürnberg
heidersbach/lorenz/list/krenn/
bockelmann

berlin staatsoper 20 october 1933
strauss arabella
ursuleac/heidersbach/wittrisch/
krenn/prohaska

berlin staatsoper 25 october 1933
strauss arabella
dobay/fischer/kullmann/neumann/
prohaska

hamburg 27 october 1933
bpo
mozart symphony 39
schubert symphony 8
strauss also sprach zarathustra

berlin 29-30 october 1933
bpo
lehmann
mozart symphony 39
strauss also sprach zarathustra
vocal works by goetz and strauss

berlin staatsoper 31 october 1933
strauss arabella
ursuleac/heidersbach/roswaenge/
krenn/prohaska

berlin staatsoper 8 november 1933
wagner die meistersinger von nürnberg
heidersbach/lorenz/kipnis/janssen/
grossmann

berlin staatsoper 11 november 1933
strauss arabella
dobay/fischer/wittrisch/krenn/prohaska

berlin 15 november 1933 morning
bpo
opening concert of reichskulturkammer
beethoven egmont overture
other works conducted by strauss and
kittel

berlin staatsoper 15 november 1933
strauss arabella
dobay/heidersbach/wittrisch/krenn/
prohaska

berlin 19-20 november 1933
bpo
backhaus
graener sinfonia breve
schubert symphony 8
brahms piano concerto 2
brahms academic festival overture

berlin staatsoper 29 november 1933
wagner das rheingold
klose/krenn/kipnis/bockelmann

berlin staatsoper 30 november 1933
wagner die walküre
leider/ursuleac/klose/lorenz/
kipnis/bockelmann

hamburg 1 december 1933
bpo
m.nikisch
trapp symphonic suite
chopin piano concerto 1
beethoven symphony 6

berlin 3-4 december 1933
bpo
pellicia
trapp symphonic suite
respighi concerto gregoriano
beethoven symphony 6

berlin staatsoper 5 december 1933
wagner das rheingold
klose/krenn/kipnis/bockelmann

berlin staatsoper 6 december 1933
wagner die walküre
leider/ursuleac/klose/lorenz/
kipnis/bockelmann

berlin staatsoper 8 december 1933
strauss arabella
ursuleac/heidersbach/wittrisch/
neumann/prohaska

berlin 11 december 1933
bpo
beethoven symphony 1
beethoven leonore 2 overture
brahms symphony 1

berlin staatsoper 14 december 1933
wagner das rheingold
klose/krenn/kipnis/bockelmann

berlin staatsoper 15 december 1933
wagner die walküre
leider/reinhardt/klose/wolff/
kipnis/bockelmann

berlin 17-18 december 1933
bpo
moodie, queling
debussy la mer
bach double violin concerto
brahms symphony 4

berlin staatsoper 19 december 1933
wagner tristan und isolde
leider/klose/melchior/kipnis/
bockelmann

berlin staatsoper 11 january 1934
wagner die walküre
leider/ursuleac/klose/völker/kipnis/
bockelmann

hamburg 12 january 1934
bpo
moodie
müller heitere musik
bach violin concerto 1
tchaikovsky symphony 6

berlin 14-15 january 1934
bpo
völker
müller heitere musik
tchaikovsky symphony 6
vocal works by méhul, weber & haydn

berlin 16 january 1934
bpo
bach suite 3
schumann symphony 4
tchaikovsky symphony 6

dresden 17 january 1934
bpo
bach suite 3
schumann symphony 4
brahms symphony 3
wagner meistersinger overture

leipzig 18 january 1934
bpo
bach suite 3
schumann symphony 4
brahms symphony 3
wagner meistersinger overture

magdeburg 19 january 1934
bpo
beethoven symphony 2
reger mozart variations
brahms symphony 3
wagner meistersinger overture

hannover 20 january 1934
bpo
mozart eine kleine nachtmusik
reger mozart variations
beethoven symphony 7
wagner meistersinger overture

london 22 january 1934
bpo
bach suite 3
schumann symphony 4
beethoven symphony 7

london 23 january 1934
bpo
beethoven symphony 2
reger mozart variations
brahms symphony 3
wagner meistersinger overture

newcastle 24 january 1934
bpo
weber euryanthe overture
strauss don juan
strauss couperin suite
strauss tod und verklärung
beethoven symphony 7

glasgow 25 january 1934
bpo
mozart eine kleine nachtmusik
schumann symphony 4
brahms symphony 3
weber euryanthe overture

manchester 26 january 1934
bpo
weber euryanthe overture
strauss couperin suite
strauss tod und verklärung
beethoven symphony 7

bristol 27 january 1934
bpo
mozart eine kleine nachtmusik
schubert symphony 8
weber euryanthe overture
strauss couperin suite
wagner meistersinger overture

london 28 january 1934
bpo
mozart eine kleine nachtmusik
schubert symphony 8
weber euryanthe overture
strauss couperin suite
strauss tod und verklärung

den haag 30 january 1934
bpo
mozart eine kleine nachtmusik
schumann symphony 4
brahms symphony 3
wagner meistersinger overture

brussels 31 january 1934
bpo
reger mozart variations
beethoven leonore 2 overture
brahms symphony 3
berlioz benvenuto cellini overture

antwerp 1 february 1934
bpo
bach suite 3
schumann symphony 4
brahms symphony 3
wagner meistersinger overture

dortmund 2 february 1934
bpo
mozart eine kleine nachtmusik
beethoven symphony 7
strauss couperin suite
strauss tod und verklärung
wagner meistersinger overture

wuppertal-elberfeld 3 february 1934
bpo
beethoven leonore 2 overture
reger mozart variations
brahms symphony 3
brahms academic festival overture

essen 4 february 1934
bpo
weber euryanthe overture
reger mozart variations
brahms symphony 3
brahms academic festival overture

bielefeld 5 february 1934
bpo
bach suite 3
schubert symphony 8
beethoven symphony 7

berlin 11-12 february 1934
bpo
weber euryanthe overture
mendelssohn a midsummer night's dream
    excerpts
beethoven symphony 7

berlin staatsoper 14 february 1934
strauss elektra
pauly/ursuleac/klose/soot/grossmann

berlin staatsoper 16 february 1934
strauss arabella
ursuleac/heidersbach/wittrisch/
krenn/prohaska

berlin 18 february 1934
bpo
day of the german composer
schillings ingwelde prelude
strauss till eulenspiegel
other works conducted by pfitzner,
hindemith and others

berlin staatsoper 20 february 1934
wagner die meistersinger von nürnberg
heidersbach/lorenz/kipnis/krenn/
grossmann

berlin staatsoper 21 february 1934
strauss elektra
pauly/ursuleac/klose/soot/grossmann

VEREIN WIENER TONKÜNSTLER-ORCHESTER

**Donnerstag 29. und Freitag, 30. September 1921
pünktlich 7 Uhr**

I. Abonnement-Konzert

im Großen Musikvereins-Saale

Dirigent:

WILHELM FURTWÄNGLER

— — —

PROGRAMM:

Beethoven . . . . . Ouvertüre „Leonore Nr. 2".

Brahms . . . . . · . Variationen über ein Thema
von Jos. Haydn.

Mahler . . . . . . Sinfonie Nr. 1, D-dur.

II. ABONNEMENT-KONZERT
Donnerstag 10. und Freitag, 11. November 1921
Dirigent: **WILHELM FURTWÄNGLER**
Händel . . . . Concerto grosso in B-dur.
Bruckner . . . . IV. Sinfonie Es-dur (Romantische).

---

hamburg 23 february 1934
bpo
weber euryanthe overture
pfitzner symphony op 36
beethoven symphony 7

berlin 25-26 february 1934
bpo
fischer
bach suite 3
pfitzner symphony op 36
schumann piano concerto
wagner götterdämmerung trauermarsch

berlin staatsoper 28 february 1934
strauss arabella
ursuleac/heidersbach/rosvaenge/
krenn/prohaska

berlin staatsoper 1 march 1934
strauss elektra
pauly/ursuleac/klose/soot/grossmann

berlin staatsoper 4 march 1934
wagner tristan und isolde
a.konetzni/klose/grahl/kipnis/janssen

berlin staatsoper 8 march 1934
strauss arabella
ursuleac/heidersbach/kullmann/
krenn/prohaska

berlin 11-12 march 1934
grümmer
hindemith mathis der maler symphony
   premiere
c.p.e.bach cello concerto
brahms symphony 3

berlin staatsoper 18 march 1934
strauss arabella
dobay/fischer/wittrisch/krenn/
prohaska

berlin staatsoper 20 march 1934
weber der freischütz
müller/berger/wittrisch/bohnen/
janssen/prohaska

halle 21 march 1934
bpo
beethoven programme
coriolan overture, symphonies 2 & 5

leipzig 22 march 1934
bpo
rehberg
reger mozart variations
brahms piano concerto 1
beethoven symphony 7

hamburg 23 march 1934
bpo
beethoven programme
coriolan overture, symphonies 2 & 5

berlin staatsoper 24 march 1934
weber der freischütz
müller/berger/wittrisch/bohnen/
janssen/grossmann

berlin 25-26 march 1934
bpo
beethoven programme
coriolan overture, symphonies 2 & 5

berlin staatsoper 27 march 1934
wagner die meistersinger von nürnberg
heidersbach/lorenz/fuchs/kipnis/
grossmann

berlin staatsoper 28 march and
3 april 1934
weber der freischütz
müller/berger/wittrisch/bohnen/
janssen/grossmann

berlin staatsoper 4 april 1934
wagner tristan und isolde
a.konetzni/klose/grahl/kipnis/janssen

vienna 7-8 april 1934
vpo
singverein
schumann, szantho, maikl, duhan
beethoven symphony 9

berlin 11 april 1934
bpo
beethoven symphony 1
beethoven grosse fuge
beethoven leonore 3 overture
strauss couperin suite
wagner siegfried idyll
wagner fliegende holländer overture

weimar 12 april 1934
bpo
mozart eine kleine nachtmusik
schumann symphony 4
beethoven symphony 5

düsseldorf 13 april 1934
bpo
beethoven symphony 1
beethoven grosse fuge
beethoven leonore 3 overture
ravel pavane pour une infante défunte
strauss also sprach zarathustra

cologne 14 april 1934
bpo
debussy nuages et fêtes/nocturnes
strauss also sprach zarathustra
beethoven grosse fuge
beethoven symphony 5

mülheim 15 april 1934
bpo
mozart eine kleine nachtmusik
strauss also sprach zarathustra
beethoven symphony 7

paris 17 april 1934
bpo
mozart eine kleine nachtmusik
schumann symphony 4
ravel pavane pour une infante défunte
debussy nuages et fêtes/nocturnes
strauss also sprach zarathustra

paris 19 april 1934
bpo
beethoven symphony 1
beethoven grosse fuge
beethoven leonore 3 overture
wagner götterdämmerung trauermarsch
wagner siegfried idyll
wagner fliegende holländer overture
debussy fêtes/nocturnes

lyon 20 april 1934
bpo
mozart eine kleine nachtmusik
schubert symphony 8
beethoven leonore 3 overture
wagner siegfried idyll
wagner meistersinger overture
debussy nuages et fêtes/nocturnes
wagner fliegende holländer overture

marseille 21 april 1934
bpo
handel concerto grosso 5
strauss tod und verklärung
wagner meistersinger overture
strauss couperin suite
wagner fliegende holländer overture

nice 22 april 1934
bpo
handel concerto grosso 5
brahms symphony 1
strauss couperin suite
strauss tod und verklärung
wagner fliegende holländer overture
wagner meistersinger overture

rome 24 april 1934
bpo
handel concerto grosso 10
strauss tod und verklärung
brahms symphony 1
wagner meistersinger overture

rome 26 april 1934
bpo
mozart eine kleine nachtmusik
pfitzner palestrina preludes
beethoven leonore 3 overture
beethoven symphony 7
wagner meistersinger overture

florence 27 april 1934
bpo
mozart eine kleine nachtmusik
schumann symphony 4
beethoven leonore 3 overture
beethoven symphony 7
wagner tannhäuser overture

baden-baden 29 april 1934
bpo
beethoven grosse fuge
brahms symphony 1
schubert symphony 8

neunkirchen 30 april 1934
bpo
beethoven symphony 7
schubert symphony 8
brahms symphony 1

luxembourg 1 may 1934
bpo
weber oberon overture
beethoven symphony 8
wagner lohengrin prelude
wagner siegfried idyll
wagner fliegende holländer overture
wagner tannhäuser overture

frankfurt 2 may 1934
bpo
weber oberon overture
pfitzner palestrina preludes
schumann symphony 4
beethoven symphony 5

heidelberg 3 may 1934
bpo
mozart eine kleine nachtmusik
pfitzner palestrina preludes
beethoven leonore 3 overture
brahms symphony 1

stuttgart 4 may 1934
bpo
beethoven grosse fuge
schubert symphony 8
brahms symphony 3
wagner meistersinger overture

zürich 5 may 1934
bpo
beethoven symphony 8
schubert symphony 8
brahms symphony 3

munich 7 may 1934
bpo
mozart eine kleine nachtmusik
brahms symphony 3
beethoven symphony 5

bamberg 8 may 1934
bpo
weber oberon overture
beethoven symphony 8
schumann symphony 4
strauss tod und verklärung
wagner meistersinger overture

jena 9 may 1934
bpo
beethoven symphony 1
schubert symphony 8
brahms symphony 3
wagner meistersinger overture

berlin staatsoper 10 may 1934
wagner das rheingold
klose/krenn/fuchs/bockelmann

berlin staatsoper 11 may 1934
wagner die walküre
leider/müller/klose/wolff/helgers/
bockelmann

berlin staatsoper 15 may 1934
weber der freischütz
müller/berger/wittrisch/bohnen/
grossmann

berlin staatsoper 16 may 1934
wagner die meistersinger von nürnberg
heidersbach/lorenz/fuchs/krenn/
bockelmann

berlin 18 may 1934
bpo
mozart eine kleine nachtmusik
pfitzner palestrina preludes
beethoven leonore 3 overture
brahms symphony 1

berlin staatsoper 23 may 1934
wagner tristan und isolde
leider/branzell/melchior/andresen/
prohaska

paris opéra 29 and 31 may 1934
wagner tristan und isolde
leider/rünger/melchior/kipnis/janssen

paris opéra 5 and 7 june 1934
wagner die meistersinger von nürnberg
lehmann/lorenz/kipnis/janssen/
bockelmann

vienna 10 june 1934
vpo
schumann
strauss 70th birthday
don juan, 4 lieder & ein heldenleben

berlin staatsoper 15 june 1934
strauss elektra
rössler-keuschnigg/ursuleac/klose/
soot/grossmann

berlin staatsoper 17 june 1934
strauss arabella
ursuleac/tegetthoff/krenn/prohaska

berlin staatsoper 20 september 1934
wagner tristan und isolde
leider/klose/strack/janssen/hofmann

berlin staatsoper 26 september 1934
weber der freischütz
lemnitz/berger/wittrisch/bohnen/
janssen

stettin 28 september 1934
bpo
beethoven egmont overture
beethoven symphony 1
bruckner symphony 9

berlin 30 september & 1 october 1934
bpo
rethberg
bruckner symphony 9
weber oberon overture
vocal works by bach, mozart & weber

berlin staatsoper 6 october 1934
wagner siegfried
leider/klose/loιenz/zimmermann/
bockelmann

berlin staatsoper 16 october 1934
wagner götterdämmerung
leider/lorenz/janssen/hofmann

berlin staatsoper 20 october 1934
wagner das rheingold
klose/zimmermann/krenn/fuchs/
bockelmann

berlin staatsoper 21 october 1934
wagner die walküre
leider/müller/klose/völker/kipnis/
bockelmann

berlin staatsoper 24 october 1934
wagner siegfried
leider/klose/lorenz/zimmermann/
bockelmann

berlin staatsoper 26 october 1934
wagner götterdämmerung
leider/lorenz/fuchs/janssen/hofmann

berlin 28-29 october 1934
bpo
gieseking
handel concerto grosso 7
pfitzner piano concerto
beethoven symphony 3

berlin staatsoper 1 november 1934
weber der freischütz
lemnitz/berger/wittrisch/bohnen/
hiller

berlin 11-12 november 1934
bpo
cortot
schumann manfred overture
schumann symphony 1
chopin piano concerto 2
ravel la valse

berlin staatsoper 14 november 1934
wagner das rheingold
klose/lemnitz/zimmermann/fuchs/
krenn/bockelmann

berlin staatsoper 15 november 1934
wagner die walküre
leider/ursuleac/klose/völker/kipnis/
bockelmann

berlin staatsoper 18 november 1934
wagner siegfried
leider/arndt-ober/lorenz/zimmermann/
fuchs/bockelmann

berlin staatsoper 21 november 1934
wagner götterdämmerung
leider/heidersbach/klose/lorenz/
fuchs/janssen/hofmann

hamburg 23 november 1934
bpo
erdmann
schumann manfred overture
brahms symphony 1
pfitzner piano concerto

berlin 25-26 november 1934
bpo
francescatti
kaminski dorische musik
bach violin concerto 1
paganini violin concerto 1
brahms symphony 1

berlin staatsoper 2 december 1934
wagner tristan und isolde
leider/klose/pistor/janssen/kipnis

budapest 12 april 1935
vpo
beethoven programme
egmont overture, symphonies 6 and 5

vienna 13-14 april 1935
vpo
beethoven programme
egmont overture, symphonies 6 and 5

vienna 16-17 april 1935
vso
singverein
peltenburg, szantho, patzak,
watzke, manowarda
bach matthäus-passion

berlin 25 april 1935
bpo
beethoven programme
egmont overture, symphonies 6 and 5

hamburg 26 april 1935
bpo
beethoven programme
egmont overture, symphonies 6 and 5

berlin 3 may 1935
bpo
beethoven programme
egmont overture, symphonies 6 and 5

london covent garden 20 and 24
june 1935
wagner tristan und isolde
leider/kalter/melchior/janssen/kipnis

paris opéra 30 may 1935
wagner tristan und isolde
leider/kalter/melchior/hann/list

paris 1 june 1935 morning
private chamber concert
honegger & roussel also participated

paris opéra 1 june 1935
wagner tristan und isolde
leider/kalter/melchior/list/hann

paris opéra 4 june 1935
wagner die walküre
leider/lehmann/kalter/melchior/
kipnis/schorr

munich 7 june 1935
bpo
beethoven programme
egmont overture, symphonies 6 and 5

stuttgart 9 june 1935
bpo
beethoven programme
egmont overture, symphonies 6 and 5

munich staatsoper 10 june 1935
wagner tristan und isolde
trundt/olszewska/pölzer/weber/nissen

vienna staatsoper 16 june 1935
wagner tristan und isolde
a.konetzni/szantho/pistor/kipnis/
hofmann

hamburg staatsoper 23 june 1935
wagner die meistersinger von nürnberg
müller/lorenz/bockelmann/manowarda

lübeck 26 june 1935
bpo
brahms haydn variations
sibelius symphony 7
beethoven symphony 5

nürnberg opera 8 september 1935
wagner die meistersinger von nürnberg
müller/kronenberg/w.frantz/manowarda

hamburg 27 september 1935
bpo
cassado
weber oberon overture
pfitzner cello concerto
schubert symphony 9

berlin 29-30 september 1935
bpo
erdmann
trapp concerto for orchestra premiere
beethoven piano concerto 3
schubert symphony 9

vienna staatsoper 13 & 15 october 1935
wagner tannhäuser
bathy/thorborg/pistor/maikl/sved

vienna staatsoper 18 october 1935
wagner tannhäuser
h.konetzni/thorborg/pistor/maikl/sved

vienna 19-20 october 1935
vpo
haydn symphony 94
beethoven coriolan overture
bruckner symphony 7

vienna 22-23 october 1935
vso
singverein
vincent, sved
brahms ein deutsches requiem

berlin 27, 28 and 30 october 1935
bpo
kittel choir
**heidersbach, pitzinger, ludwig,
watzke**
beethoven symphony 9

berlin schauspielhaus 7 november 1935
goethe egmont
furtwängler conducted beethoven's
incidental music

berlin staatsoper 8 november 1935
wagner die walküre
leider/müller/klose/lorenz/prohaska/
manowarda

berlin schauspielhaus 9 november 1935
goethe egmont
furtwängler conducted beethoven's
incidental music

berlin 24-25 november 1935
bpo
kolberg
sibelius symphony 7
tchaikovsky violin concerto
brahms symphony 1

hannover 26 november 1935
bpo
handel concerto grosso 10
sibelius symphony 7
weber euryanthe overture
brahms symphony 1

wuppertal-elberfeld 27 november 1935
bpo
beethoven egmont overture
schubert symphony 9
stravinsky firebird suite
wagner tannhäuser overture

london 29 november 1935
bpo
beethoven egmont overture
schubert symphony 9
stravinsky firebird suite
wagner tannhäuser overture

london 30 november 1935
bpo
handel concerto grosso 5
sibelius symphony 7
weber euryanthe overture
brahms symphony 1

brighton 2 december 1935
bpo
weber euryanthe overture
stravinsky firebird suite
schubert symphony 9

bristol 2 december 1935
bpo
haydn symphony 94
stravinsky firebird suite
brahms symphony 1

birmingham 3 december 1935
bpo
handel concerto grosso 5
reger der geigende eremit
weber euryanthe overture
schubert symphony 9

manchester 4 december 1935
bpo
haydn symphony 94
stravinsky firebird suite
brahms symphony 1

sheffield 5 manchester 1935
bpo
handel concerto grosso 5
reger der geigende eremit
smetana the moldau/ma vlast
tchaikovsky symphony 4

newcastle 6 december 1935
bpo
haydn symphony 94
reger der geigende eremit
smetana the moldau/ma vlast
tchaikovsky symphony 4

edinburgh 7 december 1935
bpo
handel concerto grosso 5
stravinsky firebird suite
brahms symphony 1

london 8 december 1935
bpo
haydn symphony 94
reger der geigende eremit
smetana the moldau/ma vlast
tchaikovsky symphony 4

dortmund 10 december 1935
bpo
handel concerto grosso 5
haydn symphony 94
tchaikovsky symphony 4

bielefeld 11 december 1935
bpo
haydn symphony 94
smetana the moldau/ma vlast
tchaikovsky symphony 4

bremen 12 december 1935
bpo
haydn symphony 94
stravinsky firebird suite
schubert symphony 9

hamburg 13 december 1935
bpo
handel concerto grosso 5
sibelius symphony 7
tchaikovsky symphony 4

berlin 15-16 december 1935
bpo
kulenkampff
pfitzner käthchen von heilbronn ov.
brahms violin concerto
tchaikovsky symphony 4

vienna staatsoper 18 december 1935
wagner tannhäuser
h.konetzni/thorborg/lorenz/maikl/
sved/jerger

munich staatsoper 25 december 1935
wagner die meistersinger von nürnberg
reich/branzell/krauss/nissen/weber/
hann

munich staatsoper 1 january 1936
wagner tristan und isolde
bäumer/branzell/hartmann/weber/nissen

vienna 4-5 january 1936
vpo
schumann manfred overture
schumann symphony 1
beethoven symphony 7

budapest 7 january 1936
vpo
schumann manfred overture
schumann symphony 1
beethoven symphony 7

vienna staatsoper 9 january 1936
wagner tannhäuser
müller/thorborg/lorenz/maikl/
sved/jerger

vienna 11-12 january 1936
vpo
singverein
bathy, rutschka, pataky, watzke
beethoven symphony 9

halle 15 january 1936
bpo
schumann manfred overture
schumann symphony 1
wagner tristan prelude and liebestod
brahms symphony 3

leipzig 16 january 1936
bpo
fischer
schumann manfred overture
beethoven piano concerto 4
schubert symphony 9

magdeburg 17 january 1936
bpo
haydn symphony 101
pfitzner palestrina preludes
beethoven symphony 7

frankfurt 18 january 1936
bpo
schumann manfred overture
schumann symphony 1
beethoven symphony 7

weimar 19 january 1936
bpo
fischer
weber euryanthe overture
brahms piano concerto 1
beethoven symphony 7

dresden 20 january 1936
bpo
weber euryanthe overture
brahms symphony 3
beethoven symphony 7

breslau 21 january 1936
bpo
handel concerto grosso 5
schumann symphony 1
brahms symphony 3

warsaw 22 january 1936
bpo
handel concerto grosso 5
brahms symphony 3
beethoven symphony 7

posen 23 january 1936
bpo
handel concerto grosso 5
brahms symphony 3
beethoven symphony 7

vienna 8-9 february 1936
vpo
handel concerto in d
schmidt variations on a husar's song
tchaikovsky symphony 4

vienna staatsoper 13 february 1936
wagner die walküre
müller/a.konetzni/anday/völker/
jerger/kipnis

vienna staatsoper 17 february 1936
wagner die walküre
müller/a.konetzni/thorborg/völker/
kipnis/jerger

berlin 19, 20, 21 & 23 february 1936
bpo
kittel choir
vincent, szantho, erb, löffel, drissen
bach matthäus-passion

stettin 16 april 1936
bpo
furtwängler
gluck alceste overture
mozart piano concerto 23
brahms symphony 2

hamburg 17 april 1936
bpo
furtwängler
gluck alceste overture
mozart piano concerto 23
brahms symphony 2

berlin 19-20 april 1936
bpo
furtwängler
gluck alceste overture
mozart piano concerto 23
beethoven symphony 3

düsseldorf 22 april 1936
bpo
furtwängler
weber oberon overture
mozart piano concerto 23
beethoven symphony 3

essen 23 april 1936
bpo
handel concerto grosso 5
wagner siegfried idyll
wagner fliegende holländer overture
beethoven symphony 7

cologne 24 april 1936
bpo
handel concerto grosso 5
beethoven symphony 8
brahms symphony 2

frankfurt 25 april 1936
bpo
furtwängler
pfitzner käthchen von heilbronn ov.
mozart piano concerto 23
brahms symphony 2

heidelberg 26 april 1936
bpo
gluck alceste overture
haydn symphony 101
beethoven symphony 3

ludwigshafen 27 april 1936
bpo
furtwängler
handel concerto grosso 5
mozart piano concerto 23
beethoven symphony 7

wiesbaden 28 april 1936
bpo
weber oberon overture
smetana the moldau/ma vlast
wagner tannhäuser bacchanale
beethoven symphony 3

karlsruhe 29 april 1936
bpo
haydn symphony 101
beethoven leonore 2 overture
brahms symphony 2

baden-baden 30 april 1936
bpo
haydn symphony 101
pfitzner palestrina preludes
brahms symphony 3
wagner meistersinger overture

saarbrücken 2 may 1936
bpo
beethoven symphony 8
pfitzner palestrina preludes
brahms symphony 2

freiburg 3 may 1936
bpo
haydn symphony 101
beethoven leonore 2 overture
beethoven symphony 3

stuttgart 4 may 1936
bpo
furtwängler
gluck alceste overture
mozart piano concerto 23
beethoven symphony 3

lucerne 5 may 1936
bpo
furtwängler
handel concerto grosso 5
mozart piano concerto 23
beethoven symphony 7
weber oberon overture

basel 6 may 1936
bpo
beethoven leonore 2 overture
beethoven symphony 8
brahms symphony 2

zürich 7 may 1936
bpo
beethoven coriolan overture
haydn symphony 101
brahms symphony 2

munich 8 may 1936
bpo
beethoven symphony 8
beethoven coriolan overture
brahms symphony 2

berlin 9 may 1936
bpo
beethoven programme
coriolan overture, symphonies 8 & 7

paris opéra 19 may 1936
wagner die meistersinger von nürnberg
müller/lorenz/prohaska/fuchs/hofmann

zürich stadttheater 24 & 26 may 1936
wagner tristan und isolde
leider/onegin/seibert/mrakitsch

paris opéra 28 may 1936
wagner die meistersinger von nürnberg
müller/lorenz/prohaska/fuchs/hofmann

berlin staatsoper 1 june 1936
wagner die meistersinger von nürnberg
m.fuchs/lorenz/manowarda/bockelmann

vienna staatsoper 15 june 1936
wagner tannhäuser
lehmann/lorenz/maikl/sved/hofmann

bayreuth 19 july 1936
wagner lohengrin
müller/klose/völker/manowarda/
janssen/prohaska

bayreuth 20 july 1936
wagner parsifal
m.fuchs/rosvaenge/andresen/janssen/
manowarda

bayreuth 21 july 1936
wagner lohengrin
müller/klose/völker/manowarda/
janssen/prohaska

bayreuth 23 july 1936
wagner das rheingold
heidersbach/klose/burg/manowarda/
bockelmann

bayreuth 24 july 1936
wagner die walküre
leider/müller/klose/völker/
manowarda/bockelmann

bayreuth 25 july 1936
wagner siegfried
leider/lorenz/zimmermann/burg/
bockelmann

bayreuth 27 july 1936
wagner götterdämmerung
leider/klose/lorenz/manowarda/
burg/prohaska

bayreuth 29 july 1936
wagner parsifal
m.fuchs/rosvaenge/andresen/janssen/
manowarda

bayreuth 30 july 1936
wagner lohengrin
müller/klose/lorenz/manowarda/
janssen/prohaska

bayreuth 18, 27 and 30 august 1936
wagner parsifal
m.fuchs/rosvaenge/andresen/janssen/
manowarda

berlin 10 february 1937
bpo
weber der freischütz overture
beethoven symphony 5
brahms symphony 4

berlin 21-22 february 1937
bpo
weber der freischütz overture
brahms symphony 4
beethoven symphony 7

leipzig 4-5 march 1937
violin sonata recital with kolberg
sonatas by mozart and beethoven and
premiere of furtwängler's sonata
in d minor

berlin 8 march 1937
violin sonata recital with kolberg
sonatas by mozart, beethoven and
furtwängler

munich 16 march 1937
violin sonata recital with kolberg
sonatas by mozart, beethoven and
furtwängler

vienna 20-21 march 1937
vpo
rosé, niedermayer, furtwängler
weber der freischütz overture
bach brandenburg concerto 5
brahms symphony 2

london 25 march 1937
lpo
philharmonic choir
berger, pitzinger, ludwig, watzke
beethoven symphony 9

berlin staatsoper 10 april 1937
wagner das rheingold
klose/zimmermann/fuchs/janssen/
bockelmann

berlin staatsoper 11 april 1937
wagner die walküre
leider/müller/klose/völker/
manowarda/bockelmann

berlin staatsoper 13 april 1937
wagner siegfried
leider/arndt-ober/lorenz/zimmermann/
bockelmann

berlin staatsoper 15 april 1937
wagner götterdämmerung
leider/müller/klose/lorenz/janssen/
manowarda

berlin 18-19 april 1937
bpo
kittel choir
berger, pitzinger, ludwig, watzke
beethoven symphony 9

halle 21 april 1937
bpo

bielefeld 22 april 1937
bpo

dortmund 23 april 1937
bpo

düsseldorf 24 april 1937
bpo

cologne 25 april 1937
bpo

paris 27 april 1937
bpo
haydn symphony 104
bach brandenburg concerto 5
ravel la valse
wagner tannhäuser overture & bacchanale
wagner meistersinger overture

paris 29 april 1937
bpo
reger mozart variations
beethoven symphony 7
strauss till eulenspiegel
wagner fliegende holländer overture

london 1 may 1937
bpo
philharmonic choir
berger, pitzinger, ludwig, watzke
beethoven symphony 9

london 2 may 1937
bpo
beethoven coriolan overture
haydn symphony 104
bruckner symphony 7

london covent garden 13 may 1937
wagner das rheingold
klose/bockelmann/fuchs/weber

london covent garden 17 may 1937
wagner die walküre
leider/müller/klose/völker/weber/
bockelmann

london covent garden 19 may 1937
wagner siegfried
leider/lorenz/zimmermann/fuchs/
bockelmann

london covent garden 21 may 1937
wagner götterdämmerung
leider/klose/lorenz/fuchs/weber/
janssen

london covent garden 24 may 1937
wagner das rheingold
thorborg/fuchs/weber/bockelmann

london covent garden 26 may 1937
wagner die walküre
flagstad/müller/thorborg/völker/
weber/bockelmann

london covent garden 28 may 1937
wagner siegfried
flagstad/melchior/zimmermann/fuchs/
bockelmann

london covent garden 1 june 1937
wagner götterdämmerung
flagstad/thorborg/melchior/weber/
fuchs/janssen

bayreuth 23 july 1937
wagner parsifal
m.fuchs/lorenz/janssen/burg/
manowarda

bayreuth 26 july 1937
wagner das rheingold
klose/zimmermann/hofmann/burg/
bockelmann

bayreuth 27 july 1937
wagner die walküre
leider/müller/klose/lorenz/hofmann/
bockelmann

bayreuth 28 july 1937
wagner siegfried
leider/szantho/lorenz/zimmermann/
burg/bockrlmann

bayreuth 29 july 1937
wagner götterdämmerung
leider/lorenz/prohaska/hofmann/burg

bayreuth 1, 5 and 11 august 1937
wagner parsifal
m.fuchs/lorenz/janssen/burg/
manowarda

bayreuth 13 august 1937
wagner das rheingold
klose/zimmermann/manowarda/burg/
bockelmann

bayreuth 14 august 1937
wagner die walküre
leider/müller/klose/lorenz/
hofmann/bockelmann

bayreuth 15 august 1937
wagner siegfried
leider/szantho/lorenz/zimmermann/
burg/bockelmann

bayreuth 16 august 1937
wagner götterdämmerung
leider/lorenz/prohaska/burg/hofmann

bayreuth 20 august 1937
wagner parsifal
m.fuchs/wolff/manowarda/burg/janssen

salzburg 27 august 1937
vpo
vienna opera chorus
ginster, anday, rosvaenge, alsen
beethoven symphony 9

paris 7 september 1937
bpo
kittel choir
berger, hochreiter, ludwig, watzke
beethoven symphony 9

paris opéra 8 and 11 september 1937
wagner die walküre
leider/müller/klose/völker/
manowarda/bockelmann

hamburg 15 october 1937
bpo
kulenkampff, mainardi
brahms programme
symphony 3, double concerto, academic
festival overture & 3 hungarian dances

berlin 16, 17, 18 and 19 october 1937
bpo
kulenkampff, mainardi
brahms programme
symphony 3, double concerto, academic
festival overture & 3 hungarian dances

munich 26 october 1937
bpo
fischer
handel concerto grosso 5
furtwängler symphonic concerto
    premiere
beethoven symphony 8

stuttgart 27 october 1937
bpo

leipzig 28 october 1937
bpo
fischer
beethoven symphony 1
furtwängler symphonic concerto

halle 29 october 1937
bpo

magdeburg 30 october 1937
bpo

berlin 31 october & 1-2 nov 1937
bpo
fischer
beethoven symphony 8
furtwängler symphonic concerto

berlin staatsoper 10 & 13 nov 1937
wagner tannhäuser
lemnitz/lorenz/manowarda/schlusnus

berlin 14-15 november 1937
bpo
röhn
schmidt variations on a hussar's song
mozart adelaide concerto
schubert symphony 9

berlin staatsoper 16 november 1937
wagner tannhäuser
lemnitz/lorenz/manowarda/schlusnus

vienna 20-21 november 1937
vpo
singverein
rethy, basilides, rosler, alsen
beethoven symphony 9

vienna staatsoper 25 november 1937
wagner die meistersinger von nürnberg
reining/lorenz/kamann/alsen

berlin 28 and 29 november 1937
bpo
handel concerto grosso 5
tchaikovsky symphony 6
programme also included kaminski
concerto conducted by the composer

berlin staatsoper 30 november 1937
wagner tannhäuser
lemnitz/lorenz/manowarda/fuchs

berlin staatsoper 3 december 1937
wagner tannhäuser
lemnitz/lorenz/manowarda/schlusnus

vienna 7-8 december 1937
vso
singverein
berger, pataky, alsen
haydn die schöpfung

vienna staatsoper 9 december 1937
wagner die meistersinger von nürnberg
reining/lorenz/maikl/jerger/alsen

vienna 12 december 1937
vpo
beethoven programme for 125th
anniversary of gesellschaft der
musikfreunde
egmont overture, symphonies 5 and 6

budapest 15 december 1937
budapest po
wagner meistersinger overture
brahms haydn variations
strauss tod und verklärung
beethoven symphony 5

vienna 18-19 december 1937
vpo
schubert rosamunde overture
berlioz roméo et juliette excerpts
strauss till eulenspiegel
tchaikovsky symphony 6

budapest 20 december 1937
vpo
schubert rosamunde overture
berlioz roméo et juliette excerpts
strauss till eulenspiegel
tchaikovsky symphony 6

vienna staatsoper 3 january 1938
wagner die meistersinger von nürnberg
reining/seider/kamann/alsen

hamburg 7 january 1938
bpo
beethoven symphony 1
bruckner symphony 8

berlin 8, 9 & 10 january 1938
bpo
backhaus
bruckner symphony 8
beethoven piano concerto 5

breslau 12 january 1938
bpo

dresden 13 january 1938
bpo

leipzig 14 january 1938
bpo
kolberg, harzer, furtwängler
gluck alceste overture
bach brandenburg concerto 5
bruckner symphony 8

weimar 15 january 1938
bpo

frankfurt 16 january 1938
bpo
kolberg, harzer, furtwängler
gluck alceste overture
bach brandenburg concerto 5
brahms symphony 2

wuppertal 17 january 1938
bpo

dortmund 18 january 1938
bpo

cologne 19 january 1938
bpo

london 21 january 1938
bpo
kolberg, harzer, furtwängler
bach brandenburg concerto 5
beethoven leonore 2 overture
brahms symphony 3

bristol 22 january 1938
bpo
schubert rosamunde overture and
    entr'actes
beethoven symphony 5
pfitzner käthchen von heilbronn ov.
wagner tristan prelude & liebestod
strauss till eulenspiegel

london 23 january 1938
bpo
schubert rosamunde overture and
    entr'actes
beethoven symphony 5
pfitzner käthchen von heilbronn ov.
wagner tristan prelude & liebestod
strauss till eulenspiegel

den haag 25 january 1938
bpo

brussels 26 january 1938
bpo
kolberg, harzer, furtwängler
gluck alceste overture
bach brandenburg concerto 5
schumann symphony 4
wagner tristan prelude & liebestod
wagner meistersinger overture

düsseldorf 27 january 1938
bpo

bielefeld 28 january 1938
bpo

berlin 30-31 january 1938
bpo
erdmann
bartok strings, percussion & celesta
schumann symphony 4
goetz piano concerto
strauss till eulenspiegel

potsdam 1 february 1938
bpo
brahms symphony 2
beethoven symphony 5

berlin 2 february 1938
bpo
baum
concert to initiate pfitzner society
käthchen von heilbronn overture,
herr oluf & 3 lieder
pfitzner also conducted symphony in c

berlin 3 february 1938
bpo
young peoples' concert
gluck alceste overture
schubert rosamunde entr'actes
strauss till eulenspiegel

vienna staatsoper 4 march 1938
wagner die meistersinger von nürnberg
reining/thorborg/kalenberg/
kamann/alsen

berlin staatsoper 20 march 1938
wagner tannhäuser
müller/lorenz/manowarda/arnold

bremen 31 march 1938
bpo

hamburg 1 april 1938
bpo
beethoven programme
leonore 2 overture, symphonies 4 & 3

berlin 3, 4 and 5 april 1938
bpo
beethoven programme
leonore 2 overture, symphonies 4 & 5

vienna staatsoper 20 april 1939
wagner die meistersinger von nürnberg
reining/kalenberg/hofmann/alsen

berlin 22-23 april 1938
vpo
schubert symphony 8
bruckner symphony 7
j.strauss kaiser-walzer

wiesbaden 26 april 1938
bpo

heidelberg 27 april 1938
bpo
beethoven egmont overture
brahms haydn variations
bruckner symphony 8

freiburg 28 april 1938
bpo

rome 30 april 1938
bpo
brahms haydn variations
schumann symphony 4
wagner tristan prelude & liebestod
beethoven symphony 5

florence 1 may 1938
bpo
beethoven egmont overture
bruckner symphony 8
strauss till eulenspiegel
wagner meistersinger overture

florence 2 may 1938
bpo
cherubini anacreon overture
schumann symphony 4
wagner tristan prelude & liebestod
beethoven symphony 5

zürich 5 may 1938
bpo
brahms haydn variations
bruckner symphony 8

basel 6 may 1938
bpo
beethoven symphony 5
schumann symphony 4
ravel daphnis et chloé, 2nd suite
cherubini anacreon overture

paris 8 may 1938
bpo
cherubini anacreon overture
schumann symphony 4
schubert rosamunde overture
ravel daphnis et chloé, 2nd suite
strauss don juan

paris 10 may 1938
bpo
brahms haydn variations
wagner parsifal prelude
beethoven symphony 5
wagner tannhäuser overture

london covent garden 18 may 1938
wagner das rheingold
thorborg/zimmermann/vogel/bockelmann

london covent garden 20 may 1938
wagner die walküre
a.konetzni/h.konetzni/melchior/
weber/bockelmann

london covent garden 24 may 1938
wagner siegfried
a.konetzni/melchior/zimmermann/
bockelmann

london covent garden 27 may 1938
wagner götterdämmerung
a.konetzni/thorborg/melchior/
janssen/weber

london covent garden 30 may 1938
wagner das rheingold
branzell/laufkötter/vogel/
janssen/kamann

london covent garden 1 june 1938
wagner die walküre
leider/lemnitz/melchior/kamann/schirp

london covent garden 3 june 1938
wagner siegfried
leider/melchior/laufkötter/vogel/
kamann

london covent garden 7 june 1938
wagner götterdämmerung
leider/thorborg/melchior/vogel/
schirp/janssen

zürich stadttheater 12-14 june 1938
beethoven fidelio
h.konetzni/stig/hirzel/rothmüller

paris opéra 21-23 june 1938
wagner tristan und isolde
lubin/klose/sattler/janssen/alsen

berlin staatsoper 25 june 1938
wagner tannhäuser
lemnitz/leider/lorenz/hüsch/
manowarda

potsdam 27 june 1938
bpo
fischer, furtwängler, erdmann
bach suite 2
bach concerto for 3 pianos
mozart symphony 40

salzburg 23 july 1938
wagner die meistersinger von nürnberg
reining/svanholm/zimmermann/
alsen/grossmann

salzburg 10 august 1938
wagner die meistersinger von nürnberg
reining/svanholm/zimmermann/
alsen/kamann

salzburg 19 august 1938
wagner die meistersinger von nürnberg
reining/seider/zimmermann/
alsen/kamann

284

salzburg 28 august 1938
vpo
pfitzner käthchen von heilbronn ov.
schubert symphony 8
bruckner symphony 7

salzburg 29 august 1938
wagner die meistersinger von nürnberg
reining/svanholm/zimmermann/
alsen/kamann

nürnberg opernhaus 5 september 1938
wagner die meistersinger von nürnberg
vpo/lemnitz/laholm/zimmermann/
manowarda/bockelmann

flensburg 19 october 1938
bpo

hamburg 21-22 october 1938
bpo
purcell king arthur suite
mozart symphony 40
brahms symphony 1

berlin 23, 24 & 25 october 1938
bpo
purcell king arthur suite
mozart symphony 40
brahms symphony 1

hannover 3 november 1938
bpo

magdeburg 4 november 1938
bpo

berlin 5, 6 & 7 november 1938
bpo
dohnanyi
beethoven piano concerto 4
bruckner symphony 5

leipzig 8-9 november 1938
bpo
beethoven leonore 2 overture
bruckner symphory 5

vienna 12-13 november 1938
vpo
bach suite 2
bruckner symphony 5

budapest 16 november 1938
budapest po
beethoven egmont overture
beethoven symphony 6
wagner tristan prelude & liebestod
strauss don juan

vienna 19-20 november 1938
vpo
mozart symphony 40
schmidt notre dame intermezzo
ravel daphnis et chloé, 2nd suite
beethoven symphony 6

vienna 22-23 november 1938
vso
singverein
vincent, klose, tulder, hüsch
bach matthäus-passion

berlin 26, 27 & 28 november 1938
bpo
cassado
brehme tryptychon
haydn cello concerto in d
beethoven symphony 6

dresden 29 november 1938
bpo

paris 3 december 1938
orchestre de la société philharmonique
beethoven coriolan overture
brahms symphony 2
strauss tod und verklärung
pfitzner käthchen von heilbronn ov.

paris 5 december 1938
orchestre de la société philharmonique
mozart symphony 40
beethoven symphony 6
strauss tod und verklärung
debussy nuages et fêtes/nocturnes
wagner fliegende holländer overture

kiel 8 december 1938
bpo

hamburg 9 december 1938
bpo
haydn symphony 101
stravinsky baiser de la fée
beethoven symphony 6

stettin 10 december 1938
bpo

berlin 11, 12 & 13 december 1938
bpo
cortot
haydn symphony 101
beethoven leonore 3 overture
franck variations symphoniques
stravinsky baiser de la fée
ravel left hand concerto
wagner fliegende holländer overture

pressburg 16 december 1938
vpo
mozart symphony 40
beethoven leonore 2 overture
brahms symphony 4

vienna 17-18 december 1938
vpo
prohaska
pfitzner käthchen von heilbronn ov.
pfitzner herr oluf
strauss also sprach zarathustra
brahms symphony 4

munich 19 december 1938
vpo
mozart symphony 40
beethoven leonore 2 overture
brahms symphony 4

paris opéra 27 and 29 december 1938
wagner siegfried
lubin/sattler/zimmermann/
fuchs/bockelmann

leipzig 5-6 january 1939
bpo
brahms haydn variations
schubert symphony 8
strauss also sprach zarathustra

berlin 7, 8 & 9 january 1939
bpo
kolberg, troester
brahms haydn variations
pfitzner double concerto
wagner parsifal prelude and good
    friday music
strauss also sprach zarathustra

vienna 14-15 january 1939
vpo
fischer
beethoven symphony 1
furtwängler symphonic concerto

breslau 17 january 1939
bpo

dresden 18 january 1939
bpo

berlin 19 january 1939
bpo
fischer
beethoven symphony 1
furtwängler symphonic concerto

hamburg 20 january 1939
bpo
fischer
beethoven symphony 1
furtwängler symphonic concerto

bielefeld 21 january 1939
bpo

essen 22 january 1939
bpo

düsseldorf 23 january 1939
bpo

cologne 25 january 1939
bpo

duisburg 26 january 1939
bpo

krefeld 27 january 1939
bpo

mönchen-gladbach 28 january 1939
bpo

wuppertal 29 january 1939
bpo
concerts between 25-29 january
replaced a cancelled british tour

den haag 31 january 1939
bpo

brussels 1 february 1939
bpo
haydn symphony 101
debussy nuages et fêtes/nocturnes
strauss tod und verklärung
beethoven symphony 3

berlin 5, 6 & 7 february 1939
bpo
borries
h.schubert prelude and toccata
schumann violin concerto
tchaikovsky symphony 5

berlin 8 february 1939
bpo
borries
beethoven leonore 3 overture
schumann violin concerto
tchaikovsky symphony 5

vienna 11-12 february 1939
vpo
schneiderhan
beethoven programme
coriolan overture, violin romance 2,
symphonies 2 and 3

halle 20 april 1939
bpo

hamburg 21 april 1939
bpo
beethoven programme
coriolan overture, symphonies 2 & 3

berlin 22, 23 and 24 april 1939
bpo
beethoven programme
coriolan overture, symphonies 2 & 3

potsdam 26 april 1939
bpo
fischer
beethoven symphony 1
furtwängler symphonic concerto

weimar 27 april 1939
bpo

frankfurt 28 april 1939
bpo
fischer
beethoven symphony· 1
furtwängler symphonic concerto

heidelberg 29 april 1939
bpo

munich 30 april 1939
bpo

stuttgart 2 may 1939
bpo

freiburg 3 may 1939
bpo

basel 4 may 1939
bpo
haydn symphony 101
stravinsky firebird suite
beethoven symphony 3

karlsruhe 5 may 1939
bpo

berlin 13-14 april 1939
bpo
kittel choir
fahrni, rohs, erb, watzke
bach matthäus-passion

munich 15 may 1939
bpo
kittel choir
fahrni, rohs, erb, watzke
bach matthäus-passion

florence 17-18 may 1939
bpo
kittel choir
fahrni, rohs, erb, watzke
bach matthäus-passion

düsseldorf 21 may 1939
bpo

potsdam 31 may 1939
bpo
kempff, fischer, furtwängler
mozart piano concerto 27
bach concerto for 3 pianos
beethoven symphony 7

zürich stadttheater. 4-7 june 1939
wagner die meistersinger von nürnberg
hellwig/svanholm/emmerich/berglund

zürich stadttheater 9 june 1939
wagner die walküre
flagstad/lubin/branzell/lorenz/
emmerich/berglund

triebschen 10 june 1939
tonhalle-orchester
flagstad
wagner concert in villa wesendonk
wesendonk-lieder and siegfried idyll

zürich stadttheater 13 june 1939
wagner die walküre
flagstad/lubin/branzell/lorenz/
emmericn/berglund

vienna 5 july 1939
vpo
bruckner symphony 8

berlin 13 september 1939
bpo
radio concert
handel concerto grosso 5
beethoven symphony 5

berlin 1 october 1939
radio concert/beethoven programme
egmont overture and symphony 3

vienna 14-15 october 1939
vpo
mozart symphony 39
strauss till eulenspiegel
schubert symphony 9

munich 17 october 1939
vpo
haydn symphony 88
strauss till eulenspiegel
schubert symphony 9

hamburg 20 october 1939
bpo
beethoven egmont overture
hessenberg concerto grosso
strauss till eulenspiegel
schubert symphony 9

berlin 22-23 october 1939
bpo
beethoven egmont overture
hessenberg concerto grosso
strauss till eulenspiegel
schubert symphony 9

dresden 24 october 1939
bpo

berlin 29, 30 and 31 october 1939
bpo
gieseking
weber oberon overture
franck symphony in d minor
brahms piano concerto 2
wagner meistersinger overture

halle 1 november 1939
bpo

winterthur 8 november 1939
stadtorchester winterthur
beethoven programme
coriolan overture, symphonies 4 & 3

zürich 14 november 1939
tonhalle-orchester
strauss don juan
schumann symphony 4
brahms symphony 1

hamburg 17 november 1939
bpo
schumann genoveva overture
pfitzner symphony op 44 premiere
tchaikovsky symphony 4

berlin 19, 20 and 21 november 1939
bpo
hotter
schumann genoveva overture
pfitzner herr oluf
pfitzner symphony op 44
pfitzner aria from der arme heinrich
tchaikovsky symphony 4

budapest 24, 25 & 26 november 1939
budapest po
trapp concerto for orchestra
strauss till eulenspiegel
brahms symphony 2

vienna staatsoper 29 november 1939
wagner die walküre
a.konetzni/h.konetzni/lorenz/
kamann/manowarda

berlin 3, 4 and 5 december 1939
bpo
arrau
trapp concerto for orchestra
schumann piano concerto
brahms symphony 4

vienna 9-10 december 1939
vpo
trapp concerto for orchestra
wagner siegfried idyll
wagner götterdämmerung trauermarsch
tchaikovsky symphony 4

munich 11-12 december 1939
vpo
weber oberon overture
beethoven symphony 4
tchaikovsky symphony 4

hamburg 15 december 1939
bpo
müller concerto for large orchestra
smetana the moldau/ma vlast
beethoven symphony 7

berlin 17, 18 and 19 december 1939
bpo
kulenkampff
müller concerto for large orchestra
beethoven violin concerto
beethoven symphony 7

berlin 21 december 1939
bpo
workers' concert
beethoven egmont overture
strauss till eulenspiegel
smetana the moldau/ma vlast
wagner meistersinger overture

vienna staatsoper 1 january 1940
wagner die walküre
h.konetzni/a.konetzni/sattler/
alsen/kamann

berlin 5, 6, 7 and 8 january 1940
bpo
de machula
sibelius symphony 2
dvorak cello concerto
beethoven symphony 1

copenhagen 12 january 1940
royal danish orchestra
weber der freischütz overture
tchaikovsky symphony 5
strauss tod und verklärung

copenhagen 16 january 1940
royal danish orchestra
beethoven programme
leonore 3 overture, symphonies 1 & 5

braunschweig 18 january 1940
bpo

bielefeld 19 january 1940
bpo

wuppertal 20 january 1940
bpo

mülheim 21 january 1940 morning
bpo

hagen 21 january 1940 evening
bpo

düsseldorf 22 january 1940
bpo

den haag 23 january 1940
bpo

cologne 25 january 1940
bpo

hamburg 26 january 1940
bpo
haydn symphony 88
rimsky-korsakov scheherazade
brahms symphony 2

berlin 28, 29 and 30 january 1940
bpo
haydn symphony 88
rimsky-korsakov scheherazade
brahms symphony 2

leipzig 31 january 1940
bpo
haydn symphony 88
smetana the moldau/ma vlast
brahms symphony 1

weimar 1 february 1940
bpo

chemnitz 2 february 1940
bpo

vienna staatsoper 7 february 1940
wagner tristan und isolde
a.konetzni/klose/lorenz/schöffler

munich 19 february 1940
violin sonata recital with
kulenkampff
sonatas by handel, beethoven and
furtwängler (premiere of d major
sonata)

hamburg 23 february 1940
bpo
handel concerto grosso 10
wagner götterdämmerung trauermarsch
bruckner symphony 9

berlin 25, 26 and 27 february 1940
bpo
schlüter
bruckner symphony 9
gluck divinités du styx/alceste
wagner götterdämmerung trauermarsch
and immolation

dresden 28 february 1940
bpo

leipzig 29 february 1940
bpo
handel concerto grosso 10
wagner götterdämmerung trauermarsch
bruckner symphony 9

vienna 2 march 1940
vpo
singverein
rethy, bugarinovic, lorenz, manowarda
beethoven symphony 9

vienna 3 march 1940 morning
vpo
singverein
rethy, bugarinovic, lorenz, manowarda
beethoven symphony 9

vienna 3 march 1940 evening
vpo
mozart die zauberflöte overture
played at government cultural
function

vienna 4 march 1940
vpo
singverein
rethy, bugarinovic, lorenz, manowarda
beethoven symphony 9

vienna staatsoper 5 march 1940
wagner tristan und isolde
a.konetzni/klose/lorenz/schöffler/
manowarda

bremen 14 march 1940
bpo

hamburg 15 march 1940
bpo
beethoven programme
grosse fuge, symphonies 5 and 8

berlin 17, 18 and 19 march 1940
bpo
beethoven programme
grosse fuge, cavatina and symphonies
5 and 8

hannover 20 march 1940
bpo

oslo 1 april 1940
oslo po
haydn symphony 88
strauss tod und verklärung
beethoven symphony 7

copenhagen 5 april 1940
royal danish orchestra
beethoven programme
leonore 3 overture, symphonies 6 & 5
rehearsal also held for a further
concert on 10 april which was
subsequently cancelled

berlin 20 april 1940
bpo
lorenz
radio concert/wagner programme
tannhäuser bacchanale and siegfried
schmiedelieder

berlin 28 april 1940
bpo
bruckner symphony 9

breslau 2 may 1940
bpo

chemnitz 3 may 1940
bpo

prague 4 may 1940
bpo
bruckner symphony 9
beethoven symphony 5

vienna 5 may 1940
bpo
bruckner symphony 9
beethoven symphony 5

potsdam 3-4 june 1940
bpo
fischer, kempff, furtwängler
gluck iphigenie in aulis overture
bach concerto for 3 pianos
beethoven symphony 6

salzburg 29-30 july 1940
vpo
beethoven symphony 8
wagner götterdämmerung trauermarsch
brahms symphony 1

berlin 2 october 1940
bpo
hansen, kempff, furtwängler
concert for the red cross
bach concerto for 3 pianos
strauss tod und verklärung
beethoven symphony 5

berlin 13, 14 and 15 october 1940
bpo
erdmann
weber oberon overture
chopin piano concerto 2
pfitzner symphony op 46
tchaikovsky symphony 6

vienna 26-27 october 1940
vpo
sauer
reznicek chamisso variations
schumann piano concerto
tchaikovsky symphony 6

vienna staatsoper 30 october 1940
wagner götterdämmerung
a.konetzni/reich/lorenz/schöffler/
manowarda

hamburg 1 november 1940
bpo
troester
reznicek chamisso variations
schumann cello concerto
tchaikovsky symphony 6

berlin 3, 4 and 5 november 1940
bpo
mainardi
beethoven symphony 6
reznicek chamisso variations
schumann cello concerto
wagner tannhäuser overture

leipzig 6 november 1940
bpo
troester
reznicek chamisso variations
schumann cello concerto
tchaikovsky symphony 6

prague 7 november 1940
bpo

zürich 12 and 17 november 1940
tonhalle-orchester
beethoven symphony 1
bruckner symphony 7

winterthur 20 november 1940
stadtorchester winterthur
haydn symphony 88
strauss tod und verklärung
brahms symphony 2

vienna 23-24 november 1940
vpo
beethoven symphony 6
pfitzner symphony op 46
strauss tod und verklärung

vienna staatsoper 26 november 1940
wagner götterdämmerung
a.konetzni/sattler/schöffler/manowarda

vienna 5 december 1940
violin sonata recital with
kulenkampff
sonatas by tartini, beethoven and
furtwängler

munich 6 december 1940
violin sonata recital with
kulenkampff
sonatas by tartini, beethoven and
furtwängler

leipzig 11 december 1940
violin sonata recital with
kulenkampff
sonatas by tartini, beethoven and
furtwängler

berlin 15, 16 and 17 december 1940
bpo
harzer, borries, furtwängler
berger rondino giocoso
bach brandenburg concerto 5
brahms symphony 1

vienna 21-22 november 1940
vpo
schneiderhan, niedermayer, furtwängler
berger rondino giocoso
bach brandenburg concerto 5
brahms symphony 2

vienna staatsoper 5 january 1941
wagner tristan und isolde
a.konetzni/klose/lorenz/
alsen/schöffler

hamburg 10 january 1941
bpo
schumann symphony 1
brahms symphony 1

berlin 12, 13 and 14 january 1941
bpo
fischer
schumann symphony 1
strauss tod und verklärung
brahms piano concerto 1

munich 16 january 1941
bpo
harzer, borries, furtwängler
strauss don juan
bach brandenburg concerto 5
brahms symphony 1

milan 18 january 1941
bpo
harzer, borries, furtwängler
strauss don juan
bach brandenburg concerto 5
brahms symphony 1
wagner meistersinger overture

turin 19 january 1941
bpo
harzer, borries, furtwängler
wagner meistersinger overture
bach brandenburg concerto 5
beethoven symphony 7
wagner tannhäuser overture

genua 20 january 1941
bpo
beethoven egmont overture
brahms symphony 1
berger rondino giocoso
strauss don juan
wagner tannhäuser overture

rome 22 january 1941
bpo
harzer, borries, furtwängler
wagner meistersinger overture
bach brandenburg concerto 5
brahms symphony 1
wagner fliegende holländer overture

naples 23 january 1941
bpo
beethoven egmont overture
beethoven symphony 7
berger rondino giocoso
strauss don juan
wagner tannhäuser overture
wagner meistersinger overture

rome 24 january 1941
bpo
beethoven egmont overture
beethoven symphony 7
berger rondino giocoso
wagner tannhäuser overture
rossini barbiere di siviglia overture

florence 26 january 1941
bpo
harzer, borries, furtwängler
strauss don juan
bach brandenburg concerto 5
brahms symphony 1

bologna 27 january 1941
bpo
harzer, borries, furtwängler
strauss don juan
bach brandenburg concerto 5
brahms symphony 1
wagner meistersinger overture
wagner fliegende holländer overture

trieste 28 january 1941
bpo
harzer, borries, furtwängler
strauss don juan
bach brandenburg concerto 5
brahms symphony 1

venice 29 january 1941
bpo
harzer, borries, furtwängler
strauss don juan
bach brandenburg concerto 5
brahms symphony 1

berlin 2, 3 and 4 february 1941
bpo
roehn
smetana bartered bride overture
zilcher violin concerto premiere
schubert rondo for violin & orchestra
bruckner symphony 7

dresden 5 february 1941
bpo

vienna 8-9 february 1941
vpo
mozart serenade for 13 wind
bruckner symphony 7

munich 10 february 1941
vpo
mozart serenade for 13 wind
bruckner symphony 7

concerts in vienna on 22-23 february
(vpo/kempff) cancelled due to sickness

berlin 5 march 1941
bpo
strauss don juan
wagner tristan prelude & liebestod
beethoven symphony 7

concerts for remainder of 1940-1941
season cancelled following furtwängler's skiing accident: these
included performances of tristan
scheduled for may 1941 at the
maggio musicale in florence

berlin 19, 20 and 21 october 1941
bpo
hoelscher
weber euryanthe overture
höller cello concerto premiere
beethoven symphony 3

hamburg 22 october 1941
bpo
kempff
weber euryanthe overture
beethoven piano concerto 4
beethoven symphony 3

berlin 2, 3 and 4 november 1941
bpo
kempff
haydn symphony 100
berger ballade for orchestra premiere
beethoven piano concerto 4
beethoven leonore 3 overture

leipzig 5 november 1941
bpo
haydn symphony 100
berger ballade for orchestra
beethoven symphony 3

zürich 11 and 16 november 1941
tonhalle-orchester
beethoven programme
symphonies 6 and 5

bern 17-18 november 1941
stadtorchester bern
handel concerto grosso 5
schubert symphony 8
brahms symphony 3
wagner meistersinger overture

vienna 22-23 november 1941
vpo
handel concerto grosso 5
reger mozart variations
brahms symphony 3
brahms 3 hungarian dances

budapest 24 november 1941
vpo
handel concerto grosso 5
reger mozart variations
brahms symphony 3
wagner meistersinger overture

berlin 29-30 november and
1 december 1941
bpo
reger mozart variations
dvorak symphony 9
programme also included a bach solo
chaconne played by taschner

vienna 5 december 1941
vpo
singverein
reining, klose, sabel, alsen
150th anniversary of mozart's death
mozart requiem

vienna 6 december 1941
vpo
singverein
reining, klose, sabel, hann
mozart requiem

berlin 10-11 december 1941
bpo
kittel choir
eipperle, fischer, ludwig, greindl
mozart requiem

berlin 14, 15 and 16 december 1941
bpo
mozart serenade for 13 wind
bruckner symphony 4

hamburg 17 december 1941
bpo
mozart serenade for 13 wind
bruckner symphony 4

vienna staatsoper 25 december 1941
and 1 january 1942
wagner tristan und isolde
a.konetzni/klose/lorenz/alsen/
schöffler

vienna 3-4 january 1942
vpo
mozart serenade for 13 wind
bruckner symphony 4

vienna staatsoper 7 january 1942
beethoven fidelio
braun/lorenz/alsen/hotter

berlin 11, 12 and 13 january 1942
bpo
bustabo
handel concerto grosso 5
bruch violin concerto 1
brahms symphony 3
brahms 3 hungarian dances

hamburg 14 january 1942
bpo
reger mozart variations
brahms symphony 3

vienna 16 january 1942
beethoven fidelio
braun/lorenz/alsen/hotter

vienna 17-18 january 1942
vpo
schubert rosamunde overture
schubert symphony 8
casella also conducted his own
symphony op 63

copenhagen 23 january 1942
royal danish orchestra
sibelius en saga
beethoven leonore 2 overture
schumann symphony 4
wagner tannhäuser overture

stockholm 27-28 january 1942
stockholm po
reger mozart variations
beethoven leonore 3 overture
brahms symphony 1

stockholm 5 february 1942
bpo

uppsala 6 february 1942
bpo

stockholm 8 february 1942
bpo
handel concerto grosso 5
strauss till eulenspiegel
beethoven symphony 3

malmo 9 february 1942
bpo

copenhagen 10 february 1942
bpo
taschner, de machula
weber oberon overture
brahms double concerto
beethoven symphony 7

copenhagen 11 february 1942
bpo
handel concerto grosso 5
strauss till eulenspiegel
beethoven symphony 3

berlin 13 february 1942
bpo
handel concerto grosso 5
strauss till eulenspiegel
beethoven symphony 3

berlin 15, 16 and 17 february 1942
bpo
anders
jarnach symphonic variations
schumann symphony 4
strauss 4 songs with orchestra
strauss don juan

vienna staatsoper 20 february 1942
beethoven fidelio
braun/lorenz/alsen/hotter

vienna staatsoper 24 february 1942
beethoven fidelio
braun/lorenz/alsen/jerger

berlin 26 february 1942 morning
bpo
workers' concert
schubert symphony 8
strauss till eulenspiegel
wagner meistersinger overture

berlin 1, 2 and 3 march 1942
bpo
gieseking
hoffer bach variations
schumann piano concerto
beethoven symphony 7

vienna staatsoper 13 march 1942
beethoven fidelio
braun/lorenz/rus/jerger

berlin 21, 22, 23 and 24 march 1942
bpo
kittel choir
briem, höngen, anders, watzke
kittel choir 40th birthday concert
beethoven symphony 9

vienna 28 march 1942 morning
vpo
beethoven weihe des hauses overture
vpo centenary commemoration

vienna 28 march 1942
vpo
a.konetzni, boskovsky
vpo centenary concert
schubert symphony 3
beethoven violin romance 1
mozart non temer amato bene
nicolai lustigen weiber overture

vienna 29-30 march 1942
vpo
bruckner symphony 8

berlin 19 april 1942
bpo
kittel choir
berger, pitzinger, roswaenge, watzke
bach air/suite 3
beethoven symphony 9

vienna 21, 22, 23 and 24 april 1942
vpo
singverein
rokyta, schürhoff, maikl, alsen
beethoven symphony 9

berlin 31 may and 1 june 1942
bpo
cortot
schumann manfred overture
schumann piano concerto
schubert symphony 9

basel 4 june 1942
bpo
beethoven leonore 3 overture
beethoven symphony 1
schubert symphony 9

bern 5 june 1942
bpo
brahms symphony 4
beethoven symphony 7

geneva 6 june 1942
bpo
beethoven programme
leonore 3 overture, symphonies 1 & 7

lausanne 7 june 1942
bpo
beethoven symphony 1
brahms symphony 4
wagner meistersinger overture

zürich 8 june 1942
bpo
brahms symphony 4
beethoven symphony 7

zürich stadttheater 11 & 14 june 1942
wagner götterdämmerung
flagstad/lorenz/weber/rothmüller

berlin 21-22 june 1942
bpo
taschner
brahms programme
tragic overture, violin concerto
and symphony 4

potsdam 29-30 june 1942
bpo

berlin 25, 26, 27 & 28 october 1942
bpo
de machula
gluck alceste overture
schumann cello concerto
bruckner symphony 5

vienna 31 october & 1 november 1942
vpo
schneiderhan
brahms violin concerto
bruckner symphony 5

vienna staatsoper 4 november 1942
beethoven fidelio
braun/lorenz/alsen/hotter

berlin 8-9 november 1942
bpo
fischer
frommel symphony in e flat premiere
brahms piano concerto 2
wagner tristan prelude & liebestod

berlin 10-11 november 1942
bpo
bork
frommel symphony in e flat
brahms piano concerto 2
wagner tristan prelude & liebestod

vienna staatsoper 12 november 1942
beethoven fidelio
braun/lorenz/alsen/jerger

vienna 14-15 november 1942
vpo
kempff
sibelius en saga
beethoven piano concerto 4
dvorak symphony 9

stockholm opera 20-22 november 1942
wagner die walküre
hertzberg/björck/svanholm/björker/
berglund

stockholm 25-27 november 1942
stockholm po
beethoven symphony 6
strauss don juan
wagner tristan prelude & liebestod

stockholm 29 november 1942
stockholm po
brahms haydn variations
bruckner symphony 5

gothenburg 2 december 1942
gothenburg so
wagner meistersinger overture
sibelius en saga
beethoven symphony 3

berlin 6, 7 and 8 december 1942
bpo
berger, ludwig, heitmann
h.schubert hymnisches konzert premiere
mozart non che sei capace, aria
schubert symphony 9

berlin staatsoper 12 december 1942
wagner die meistersinger von nürnberg
müller/lorenz/fuchs/manowarda/
bockelmann
new production for re-opening of
staatsoper after bomb damage

berlin staatsoper 16 december 1942
wagner die meistersinger von nürnberg
müller/lorenz/fuchs/manowarda/
prohaska

vienna 19-20 december 1942
vpo
reger hiller variations
schubert symphony 9

vienna staatsoper 26 december 1942
beethoven fidelio
braun/lorenz/alsen/schöffler

vienna staatsoper 2 & 5 january 1943
wagner tristan und isolde
a.konetzni/klose/lorenz/alsen/
schöffler
new production which furtwängler
conducted and directed

berlin staatsoper 8 january 1943
wagner die meistersinger von nürnberg
müller/lorenz/fuchs/greindl/prohaska

berlin 10, 11 and 12 january 1943
bpo
anda
reger hiller variations
franck variations symphoniques
beethoven symphony 1

winterthur 16 january 1943
stadtorchester winterthur
haydn symphony 101
bruckner symphony 4

zürich 20 and 24 january 1943
tonhalle-orchester
haydn symphony 101
strauss tod und verklärung
schubert symphony 9

bern 26 january 1943
stadtorchester bern
beethoven symphony 1
beethoven coriolan overture
bruckner symphony 4

berlin 7, 8, 9 & 10 february 1943
bpo
kulenkampff
sibelius en saga
sibelius violin concerto
brahms symphony 2

berlin staatsoper 11 february 1943
wagner die meistersinger von nürnberg
müller/lorenz/fuchs/greindl/prohaska

vienna 13-14 february 1943
vpo
weber euryanthe overture
schumann symphony 4
strauss sinfonia domestica

vienna staatsoper 16 february 1943
wagner tristan und isolde
a.konetzni/klose/lorenz/roth/schöffler

vienna 20-21 february 1943
vpo
kodaly peacock variations
schubert symphony 9

budapest 22 february 1943
vpo
kodaly peacock variations
schubert symphony 9
weber euryanthe overture

copenhagen 6 may 1943
vpo
schubert programme
rosamunde overture, symphonies 8 & 9

copenhagen 8 may 1943
vpo
beethoven symphony 3
berger rondino giocoso
pfitzner käthchen von heilbronn ov.
strauss till eulenspiegel
j.strauss kaiser-walzer
wagner meistersinger overture

malmo 10 may 1943
vpo
schubert programme
rosamunde overture, symphonies 8 & 9

gothenburg 11 may 1943
vpo
schubert programme
rosamunde overture, symphonies 8 & 9

stockholm 12 may 1943
vpo
schubert rosamunde overture
schubert symphony 8
schubert symphony 9
j.strauss kaiser-walzer

uppsala 13 may 1943
vpo
schubert programme
rosamunde overture, symphonies 8 & 9

stockholm 14 may 1943
vpo
beethoven symphony 3
berger rondino giocoso
pfitzner käthchen von heilbronn ov.
strauss till eulenspiegel
j.strauss kaiser-walzer & blue danube
wagner meistersinger overture

berlin 17 may 1943 morning
bpo
workers' concert
schubert symphony 8
strauss till eulenspiegel
j.strauss kaiser-walzer

berlin 17 may 1943 evening
bpo
pfitzner käthchen von heilbronn ov.
schubert symphony 8
beethoven symphony 3
j.strauss kaiser-walzer

vienna 22-23 may 1943
vpo
beethoven programme
coriolan overture, symphonies 4 & 3

potsdam 24-25 june 1943
bpo
ney
beethoven programme
coriolan overture, piano concerto 5
and symphony 5

berlin 27, 28, 29 & 30 june 1943
bpo
beethoven programme
coriolan overture, symphonies 4 & 5
one of these was a radio concert

bayreuth 15, 18, 21 & 24 july 1943
wagner die meistersinger von nürnberg
müller/kallab/lorenz/fuchs/krenn/
nissen (schöffler)

zürich 18 august 1943
tonhalle-orchester
beethoven programme
symphonies 4 and 3

zürich 21 august 1943
tonhalle-orchester
mozart serenade for 13 wind
sibelius en saga
dvorak symphony 9

munich 30 september 1943
munich po
beethoven programme
symphonies 6 and 5

vienna 15, 16 and 17 october 1943
vpo
schneiderhan, krotschak
brahms programme
haydn variations, double concerto
and symphony 4

vienna 23, 24 and 25 october 1943
vpo
a.konetzni
bruckner symphony 6
wagner götterdämmerung trauermarsch
   and immolation

berlin staatsoper 27 october 1943
wagner die meistersinger von nürnberg
müller/lorenz/krenn/greindl/prohaska

berlin 31 october and 1, 2 & 3
november 1943
bpo
hansen
pepping symphony 2
beethoven piano concerto 4
beethoven symphony 7

vienna 5, 6 and 7 november 1943
vpo
mozart symphony 40
strauss till eulenspiegel
strauss also sprach zarathustra
this concert may have been
repeated in budapest

berlin 13, 14, 15 & 16 november 1943
bpo
fournier
bruckner symphony 6
schumann cello concerto
strauss till eulenspiegel

vienna staatsoper 21 november 1943
wagner tristan und isolde
braun/lorenz/alsen/schöffler

gothenburg 26 november 1943
gothenburg so
beethoven symphony 1
beethoven leonore 3 overture
brahms symphony 1

stockholm 1 december 1943
stockholm po
handel concerto grosso 5
schumann symphony 4
wagner götterdämmerung trauermarsch
wagner tannhäuser overture

stockholm 5, 7 and 8 december 1943
stockholm po and chorus
schymberg, tunell, bäckelin, björling
beethoven symphony 9
fred prieberg also mentions guest
performances of vienna staatsoper in
stockholm in december 1943, at which
furtwängler was to have conducted
wagner meistersinger von nürnberg

berlin 12, 13, 14 & 15 december 1943
bpo
aeschbacher
brahms programme
haydn variations, piano concerto 2
and symphony 4

vienna 18, 19 and 20 december 1943
vpo
beethoven programme
symphonies 6 and 5

vienna staatsoper 2 january 1944
wagner tristan und isolde
a.konetzni/lorenz/alsen/schöffler

vienna 6 january 1943
wagner tristan und isolde
a.konetzni/pölzer/alsen/schöffler

berlin 9, 10, 11 & 12 january 1944
bpo
roehn
beethoven violin concerto
strauss sinfonia domestica
final concerts in alte philarmonie

lausanne 17 january 1944
suisse romande orchestra
mozart serenade for 13 wind
strauss don juan
beethoven symphony 5
wagner tristan prelude & liebestod

geneva 19 january 1944
suisse romande orchestra
mozart serenade for 13 wind
strauss don juan
beethoven symphony 5
wagner tristan prelude & liebestod

bern 24-25 january 1944
stadtorchester bern
beethoven programme
symphonies 6 and 5

berlin 7-8 february 1944
bpo
handel concerto grosso 10
mozart symphony 40
beethoven symphony 5
concert given in staatsoper; two
performances of the programme on
each of the dates

berlin 12 february 1944
bpo
handel concerto grosso 10
beethoven symphony 5
concert given in berliner dom

vienna staatsoper 20 february 1944
wagner tristan und isolde
a.konetzni/pölzer/alsen/schöffler

vienna 10, 11 and 12 march 1944
vpo
schubert symphony 8
pfitzner symphony op 46
ravel daphnis et chloé, 2nd suite
wagner tannhäuser overture

budapest 13 march 1944
vpo
schubert symphony 8
pfitzner symphony op 46
ravel daphnis et chloé, 2nd suite
wagner tannhäuser overture

budapest 14 march 1944
vpo
beethoven programme
symphonies 6 and 5

prague 16 march 1944
bpo
dvorak symphony 9
beethoven symphony 5

berlin 20-21 march 1944
bpo
weber der freischütz overture
ravel daphnis et chlooé, 2nd suite
beethoven symphony 6
concerts given in staatsoper; concert
on 21 march played twice

postsdam 22 march 1944
bpo
weber der freischütz overture
ravel daphnis et chloè, 2nd suite
beethoven symphony 6

vienna 2-3 june 1944
vpo
beethoven leonore 3 overture
mozart symphony 40
schubert rosamunde overture and
    entr'actes
3 june was a radio concert

zürich stadttheater 14 & 18 june 1944
wagner siegfried
m.fuchs/lorenz/zimmermann/schöffler

potsdam 19 and 22 june 1944
bpo

bayreuth 18 and 22 july 1944
wagner die meistersinger von nürnberg
kupper/kallab/lorenz/krenn/
dalberg/prohaska

salzburg 14 august 1944
vpo
bruckner symphony 8

lucerne 22 august 1944
lucerne festival orchestra
brahms haydn variations
schumann symphony 4
strauss till eulenspiegel
wagner parsifal good friday music
wagner tannhäuser overture

lucerne 6 september 1944
lucerne festival orchestra
beethoven programme
leonore 2 overture, symphonies 1 & 3

berlin 7 october 1944
bpo
radio concert
bruckner symphony 9

st florian 11 october 1944
bruckner-orchester linz
bruckner symphony 9

vienna 14, 15 and 16 october 1944
vpo
beethoven leonore 2 overture
bruckner symphony 8

vienna 17 october 1944
vpo
radio concert
bruckner symphony 8

potsdam 21 october 1944
bpo
westermann divertimento premiere
beethoven leonore 2 overture
brahms symphony 3

berlin 22-23 october 1944
bpo
lemnitz
westermann divertimento
arias by mozart
brahms symphony 3
concerts given in staatsoper

berlin staatsoper 29 october 1944
wagner götterdämmerung
schlüter/klose/lorenz/hofmann/prohaska
c.p. Prologue & act III

berlin 10-11 december 1944
bpo
schneiderhan
hessenberg symphony 2
brahms violin concerto
beethoven leonore 3 overture
concerts given in admiralspalast

berlin 12 december 1944
bpo
schneiderhan
schubert symphony 8
brahms violin concerto
beethoven leonore 3 overture
concert given in admiralspalast

vienna 16, 17 and 18 december 1944
vpo
beethoven programme
symphonies 1 and 3

vienna 19-20 december 1944
vpo
beethoven programme for radio concerts
symphonies 1 and 3

berlin 22-23 january 1945
bpo
mozart die zauberflöte overture
mozart symphony 40
brahms symphony 1
concerts given in staatsoper; mozart
symphony interrupted by air-raid on
23 january

vienna 27, 28 and 29 january 1945
vpo
franck symphony in d minor
brahms symphony 2

geneva 12 february 1945
suisse romande orchestra
beethoven symphony 1
beethoven leonore 2 overture
brahms symphony 2

lausanne 14 february 1945
suisse romande orchestra
beethoven symphony 1
beethoven leonore 2 overture
brahms symphony 2

winterthur 23 february 1945
stadtorchester winterthur
bruckner symphony 8

concerts announced in zürich with the
tonhalle-orchester on 20 and 25
february cancelled by the municipal
authorities

rome 6 april 1947
santa cecilia orchestra
beethoven leonore 2 overture
schubert symphony 8
brahms symphony 2
furtwängler's first post-war concert

rome 9 april 1947
santa cecilia orchestra
haydn symphony 101
strauss tod und verklärung
beethoven symphony 5

florence 13 april 1947
maggio musicale orchestra
brahms haydn variations
beethoven leonore 3 overture
beethoven symphony 3

florence 20 april 1947
maggio musicale orchestra
haydn symphony 101
wagner tristan prelude & liebestod
beethoven symphony 5
wagner tannhäuser overture

berlin 25, 26, 27 and 29 may 1947
bpo
beethoven programme
egmont overture, symphonies 6 and 5
first post-war concerts in berlin

berlin 31 may and 1-2 june 1947
staatskapelle
beethoven symphony 1
strauss till eulenspiegel
tchaikovsky symphony 6

potsdam 3 june 1947
bpo
beethoven programme
egmont overture, symphonies 6 and 5

berlin 4 june 1947
staatskapelle
beethoven symphony 1
strauss till eulenspiegel
tchaikovsky symphony 6

hamburg 9 june 1947
philharmonisches staatsorchester
beethoven leonore 2 overture
strauss tod und verklärung
brahms symphony 2

munich 12-13 june 1947
bpo
beethoven programme
egmont overture, symphonies 6 and 5

salzburg 10 august 1947
vpo
weber der freischütz overture
strauss tod und verklärung
schubert symphony 9

salzburg 13 august 1947
vpo
menuhin
hindemith symphonic metamorphoses
brahms violin concerto
brahms symphony 1

lucerne 20 august 1947
lucerne festival orchestra & chorus
schwarzkopf, hotter
brahms ein deutsches requiem

lucerne 27 august 1947
lucerne festival orchestra
aeschbacher
beethoven leonore 3 overture
beethoven piano concerto 1
brahms symphony 1

lucerne 30 august 1947
lucerne festival orchestra
menuhin
wagner lohengrin prelude
beethoven violin concerto
brahms symphony 1

berlin 14, 15 and 16 september 1947
bpo
hindemith symphonic metamorphoses
strauss don juan
brahms symphony 2

potsdam 17 september 1947
bpo
hindemith symphonic metamorphoses
strauss don juan
brahms symphony 2

hamburg 22 september 1947
nwdr orchestra
roehn, troester
mendelssohn a midsummer night's
    dream excerpta
brahms double concerto
beethoven symphony 7

berlin 28-29 september 1947
bpo
menuhin
mendelssohn a midsummer night's
    dream overture
beethoven violin concerto
beethoven symphony 7

berlin 2 october 1947
staatskapelle
menuhin
gluck alceste overture
beethoven violin concerto
wagner tristan prelude & liebestod

berlin staatsoper 3 october 1947
wagner tristan und isolde
schlüter/klose/suthaus/frick/prohaska

stockholm 8 october 1947
stockholm philharmonic
hindemith symphonic metamorphoses
strauss don juan
brahms symphony 2

stockholm 10 and 12 october 1947
stockholm philharmonic
beethoven symphony 1
beethoven coriolan overture
tchaikovsky symphony 6

munich 15, 17 and 18 october 1947
munich philharmonic
weber der freischütz overture
hindemith symphonic metamorphoses
brahms symphony 1

berlin 21 october 1947
staatskapelle
gluck alceste overture
wagner tristan prelude & liebestod
tchaikovsky symphony 6

berlin staatsoper 24 october 1947
wagner tristan und isolde
schlüter/klose/suthaus/frick/prohaska

berlin 26-27 october 1947
bpo
haydn symphony 101
strauss metamorphosen
tchaikovsky symphony 5

berlin staatsoper 30 october 1947
wagner tristan und isolde
büchner/klose/suthaus/frick/prohaska

leipzig 4 november 1947
gewandhaus-orchester
mendelssohn hebrides overture
mendelssohn symphony 4
beethoven symphony 3

vienna 8-9 november 1947
vpo
schneiderhan
mendelssohn midsummer night's
    dream overture
mendelssohn violin concerto
beethoven symphony 3

vienna 15-16 november 1947
vpo
hindemith symphonic metamorphoses
strauss don juan
brahms symphony 1

vienna 29-30 november 1947
vpo
beethoven programme
symphonies 6 and 5

vienna 3-4 december 1947
vso
singverein
schwarzkopf, schöffler
brahms ein deutsches requiem

geneva 12-13 december 1947
suisse romande orchestra
beethoven programme
coriolan overture, symphonies 6 & 7

winterthur 17 december 1947
stadtorchester winterthur
brahms haydn variations
beethoven leonore 3 overture
beethoven symphony 7

schaffhausen 19 december 1947
stadtorchester winterthur
brahms haydn variations
beethoven leonore 3 overture
beethoven symphony 7

bern 12-13 january 1948
stadtorchester bern
bruckner symphony 8

paris 24-25 january 1948
conservatoire orchestra
beethoven symphony 5
debussy nuages et fêtes/nocturnes
strauss till eulenspiegel
wagner tristan prelude & liebestod

vienna 31 january & 1 february 1948
vpo
beethoven programme
leonore 3 overture, symphonies 8 & 7

vienna 4-5 february 1948
vso
handel concerto grosso 5
ravel daphnis et chloé, 2nd suite
tchaikovsky symphony 6

berlin 15-16 february 1948
bpo
handel concerto grosso 5
schumann symphony 4
debussy nuages et fêtes/nocturnes
stravinsky firebird suite

berlin 22-23 february 1948
bpo
handel concerto grosso 5
furtwängler symphony 2 premiere

london 29 february 1948
lpo
vaughan williams tallis fantasia
schumann symphony 4
beethoven symphony 7
covent garden sunday concert given
in the royal opera house

london 4 march 1948
lpo
zareska
mendelssohn hebrides overture
mahler lieder eines fahrenden gesellen
strauss tod und verklärung
brahms symphony 1

birmingham 5 march 1948
lpo
mendelssohn hebrides overture
beethoven symphony 7
brahms symphony 1

leicester 6 march 1948
lpo
mendelssohn hebrides overture
beethoven symphony 7
brahms symphony 1

watford 8 march 1948
lpo
zareska
mendelssohn hebrides overture
mahler lieder eines fahrenden gesellen
strauss tod und verklärung
brahms symphony 1

wimbledon 9 march 1948
lpo
zareska
mendelssohn hebrides overture
mahler lieder eines fahrenden gesellen
strauss tod und verklärung
brahms symphony 1

london 11 march 1948
lpo
haydn symphony 101
sibelius en saga
brahms symphony 2

london 14 march 1948
lpo
weber oberon overture
brahms symphony 3
ravel daphnis et chloé, 2nd suite
wagner tannhäuser overture
covent garden sunday concert given
in the royal opera house

london 18 march 1948
lpo
gluck alceste overture
brahms symphony 4
strauss till eulenspiegel
wagner tristan prelude & liebestod

london 25 march 1948
lpo
lpo choir
hammond, jarred, jones, parsons
beethoven symphony 9

buenos aires 6 april 1948
teatro colon orchestra
beethoven symphony 1
strauss tod und verklärung
brahms symphony 1

buenos aires 10 april 1948
teatro colon orchestra
handel concerto grosso 5
schumann symphony 4
ravel daphnis et chloé, 2nd suite
wagner tannhäuser overture

buenos aires 14 april 1948
teatro colon orchestra
mendelssohn hebrides overture
strauss ein heldenleben
beethoven symphony 5

buenos aires 17 april 1948
teatro colon orchestra
bruckner symphony 4
wagner siegfried idyll
wagner götterdämmerung trauermarsch
wagner meistersinger overture

buenos aires 24 april 1948
teatro colon orchestra
mozart symphony 40
beethoven leonore 3 overture
stravinsky firebird suite
wagner tristan prelude & liebestod

buenos aires 28 april 1948
teatro colon orchestra
haydn symphony 101
respighi pini di roma
buchardo escenas argentinas
tchaikovsky symphony 6

buenos aires 29 april 1948
teatro colon orchestra
beethoven symphony 1
beethoven leonore 3 overture
tchaikovsky symphony 6
wagner meistersinger overture

buenos aires 4 may 1948
teatro colon orchestra and chorus
hoffmann, negroni, pataky, mattiello
handel concerto grosso 5
beethoven symphony 9

rome 12 may 1948
santa cecilia orchestra
cherubini anacreon overture
schumann symphony 4
ravel daphnis et chloé, 2nd suite
wagner tannhäuser overture

rome 16 may 1948
santa cecilia orchestra
beethoven programme
coriolan overture, symphonies 6 & 7

florence 19 may 1948
teatro communale orchestra
weber der freischütz overture
frazzi cicilia
wagner parsifal karfreitagszauber
brahms symphony 1

florence 21 may 1948
teatro communale orchestra
respighi fontane di roma
strauss tod und verklärung
beethoven symphony 7
wagner meistersinger overture

milan 26 may 1948
la scala orchestra
weber der freischütz overture
respighi fontane di roma
strauss till eulenspiegel
brahms symphony 1

milan 29 may 1948
la scala orchestra
mainardi
beethoven coriolan overture
beethoven symphony 6
schumann cello concerto
wagner götterdämmerung trauermarsch
wagner meistersinger overture

basel 3 june 1948
vpo
mozart serenade for 13 wind
schumann symphony 4
beethoven symphony 5

geneva 4 june 1948
vpo
mozart serenade for 13 wind
schumann symphony 4
beethoven symphony 5

montreux 5 june 1948
vpo
mozart serenade for 13 wind
schubert symphony 8
beethoven symphony 3

lausanne 6 june 1948
vpo
schubert rosamunde overture
schubert symphony 8
beethoven symphony 5

bern 7 june 1948
vpo
schubert programme
rosamunde overture, symphonies 8 & 9

zürich 8 june 1948
vpo
schubert rosamunde overture
schubert symphony 8
schubert symphony 9
j.strauss kaiser-walzer

salzburg 31 july & 3 august 1948
beethoven fidelio
schlüter/della casa/patzak/edelmann

salzburg 5 august 1948
vpo
uhl introduction and variations
pfitzner palestrina preludes
stravinsky petrushka
strauss ein heldenleben

salzburg 6 august 1948
beethoven fidelio
schlüter/della casa/patzak/edelmann

lucerne 18 august 1948
lucerne festival orchestra
wagner meistersinger overture
wagner siegfried idyll
wagner götterdämmerung trauermarsch
bruckner symphony 4

lucerne 28-29 august 1948
lucerne festival orchestra & chorus
schwarzkopf, cavelti, haefliger,
schöffler
beethoven symphony 9

lucerne 30 august 1948
lucerne festival orchestra
beethoven symphony 1
wagner siegfried idyll
wagner götterdämmerung trauermarsch
wagner meistersinger overture

edinburgh 8 september 1948
santa cecilia orchestra
michelangeli, de vito, mainardi
cherubini anacreon overture
brahms symphony 2
beethoven triple concerto
beethoven leonore 2 overture

edinburgh 9 september 1948
santa cecilia orchestra
ghedini partita
strauss tod und verklärung
beethoven symphony 5

vienna 24, 25 & 26 september 1948
vpo
beethoven programme
egmont overture, symphonies 4 and 6

london 28 september 1948
vpo
beethoven cycle
egmont overture, symphonies 6 and 5

london 30 september 1948
vpo
beethoven cycle
leonore 3 overture, symphonies 8 & 7

london 2 october 1948
vpo
beethoven cycle
coriolan overture, symphonies 4 & 3

london 3 october 1948
vpo
menuhin
beethoven cycle
violin concerto, symphonies 1 & 2

london 6 october 1948
vpo
bbc choral society
welitsch, höngen, patzak, walker
beethoven cycle
symphony 9

hamburg 17-18 october 1948
philharmonisches staatsorchester
furtwängler symphony 2
other work conducted by jochum

berlin 22 october 1948
bpo
radio concert
bach suite 3
brahms symphony 4

berlin 24, 25 & 26 october 1948
bpo
bach suite 3
schubert symphony 8
brahms symphony 4

london 3 november 1948
bpo
hess
bach suite 3
beethoven piano concerto 4
brahms symphony 4

liverpool 4 november 1948
bpo
bach suite 3
strauss till eulenspiegel
schubert symphony 9

birmingham 5 november 1948
bpo
bach suite 3
strauss till eulenspiegel
brahms symphony 4

oxford 7 november 1948
bpo
schubert programme
rosamunde overture, symphonies 8 & 9

stockholm 13 november 1948
stockholm po
beethoven programme
leonore 3 overture, symphonies 8 & 7

stockholm 17, 18 & 19 november 1948
stockholm po and chorus
lindberg-torlind, sönnerstedt
brahms ein deutsches requiem

paris 27-28 november 1948
conservatoire orchestra
strauss don juan
schumann symphony 4
beethoven symphony 7

vienna 4, 5 & 6 december 1948
vpo
weber der freischütz overture
walton symphony 1
tchaikovsky symphony 5

vienna 18, 19 & 20 december 1948
vpo
kamesch
j.marx nordland-rapsodie
strauss oboe concerto
brahms symphony 4

vienna 21 and 22 december 1948
vso
schneiderhan
brahms violin concerto
bruckner symphony 4

geneva 19 january 1949
suisse romande orchestra
schubert symphony 9
strauss till eulenspiegel
wagner siegfried idyll
wagner meistersinger overture

lausanne 20 january 1949
suisse romande orchestra
schubert symphony 9
strauss till eulenspiegel
wagner siegfried idyll
wagner meistersinger overture

freiburg 21 january 1949
suisse romande orchestra
schubert symphony 9
strauss till eulenspiegel
wagner siegfried idyll
wagner meistersinger overture

munich 26, 27, 28 & 29 january 1949
munich po
beethoven symphony 4
tchaikovsky symphony 6

paris 5-6 february 1949
conservatoire orchestra
mozart serenade for 13 wind
wagner siegfried idyll
wagner götterdämmerung trauermarsch
brahms symphony 2

vienna 8 february 1949
vpo
bella, badura-skoda
mozart prograame for wiener
mozartgemeinde
serenade for 13 wind, double piano
concerto and symphony 40

vienna 12, 13 & 14 february 1949
vpo
pfitzner funeral march/die rose
   vom liebesgarten
bruckner symphony 5

vienna 19, 20 & 21 february 1949
vpo
singverein
schwarzkopf, höngen, patzak,
schöffler
beethoven symphony 9

bern 28 february & 1 march 1949
stadtorchester bern
weber der freischütz overture
barber adagio for strings
strauss till eulenspiegel
tchaikovsky symphony 6

winterthur 9 march 1949
stadtorchester winterthur
haydn symphony 88
furtwängler symphony 2

berlin 13, 14 and 15 march 1949
bpo
bruckner symphony 8
14 march was a radio concert

munich 19, 20 and 21 march 1949
munich po and chorus
ebers, fischer, fehenberger, watzke
beethoven symphony 9

florence 14 may 1949
teatro communale orchestra
mozart serenade for 13 wind
debussy nuages et fêtes/nocturnes
strauss till eulenspiegel
brahms symphony 2
wagner fliegende holländer overture

rome 18 may 1949
santa cecilia orchestra
beethoven programme
egmont overture, symphonies 4 and 5

rome 22 may 1949
santa cecilia orchestra·and chorus
fleri, ʻibacchi, berdini, bruscantini
beethoven symphony 9

milan 25 may 1949
la scala orchestra
cherubini anacreon overture
brahms symphony 2
hindemith symphonic metamorphoses
strauss tod und verklärung

milan 28 may 1949
la scala orchestra and chorus
cecil, simionato, prandelli, siepi
beethoven symphony 9

hamburg 1 june 1949
bpo
pfitzner palestrina preludes
mozart symphony 40
strauss till eulenspiegel
brahms symphony 4

hamburg 2 june 1949
bpo
beethoven programme
coriolan overture, symphonies 6 & 5

hildesheim 3 june 1949
bpo
pfitzner palestrina preludes
mozart symphony 40
strauss till eulenspiegel
brahms symphony 4

hannover 4 june 1949
bpo
beethoven programme
coriolan overture, symphonies 6 & 5

bielefeld 5 june 1949
bpo
pfitzner palestrina preludes
beethoven symphony 6
beethoven symphony 5

bad pyrmont 6 june 1949
bpo
pfitzner palestrina preludes
mozart symphony 40
strauss till eulenspiegel
brahms symphony 4

viersen 7 june 1949
bpo
pfitzner palestrina preludes
beethoven symphony 6
beethoven symphony 5

wuppertal 8 june 1949
bpo
pfitzner palestrina preludes
mozart symphony 40
strauss till eulenspiegel
brahms symphony 4

düsseldorf 9 june 1949
bpo
beethoven programme
coriolan overture, symphonies 6 & 5

wiesbaden 10 june 1949
bpo
pfitzner palestrina preludes
mozart symphony 40
strauss till eulenspiegel
brahms symphony 4

frankfurt 12 june 1949 afternoon
bpo
pfitzner palestrina preludes
beethoven symphony 6
beethoven symphony 5

wiesbaden 12 june 1949 evening
bpo
pfitzner palestrina preludes
beethoven symphony 6
beethoven symphony 5

heidelberg 13 june 1949
bpo
pfitzner palestrina preludes
mozart symphony 40
strauss till eulenspiegel
brahms symphony 4

baden-baden 14 june 1949
bpo
pfitzner palestrina preludes
beethoven symphony 6
beethoven symphony 5

berlin 18 june 1949
bpo
pfitzner palestrina preludes
beethoven symphony 6
beethoven symphony 5
concert given twice on this date

berlin 19 june 1949
bpo
mozart symphony 40
strauss till eulenspiegel
beethoven symphony 5

salzburg 27 july 1949
mozart die zauberflöte
seefried/lipp/w.ludwig/greindl

salzburg 30 july & 3 august 1949
beethoven fidelio
flagstad/seefried/patzak/greindl

salzburg 5 august 1949
mozart die zauberflöte
seefried/lipp/w.ludwig/greindl

salzburg 7 august 1949
vpo
pfitzner symphony op 46
bruckner symphony 8

salzburg 8 august 1949
beethoven fidelio
flagstad/seefried/patzak/greindl

salzburg 11 august 1949
mozart die zauberflöte
seefried/lipp/w.ludwig/greindl

salzburg 16 and 19 august 1949
beethoven fidelio
flagstad/seefried/patzak/greindl

salzburg 20 august 1949
mozart die zauberflöte
seefried/lipp/w.ludwig/greindl

lucerne 24 august 1949
lucerne festival orchestra
schneiderhan, mainardi
brahms double concerto
strauss till eulenspiegel
tchaikovsky symphony 4

lucerne 27-28 august 1949
lucerne festival orchestra & chorus
seefried, w.ludwig, christoff
haydn die schöpfung

besançon 9 september 1949
colonne orchestra
hirt
weber der freischütz overture
hindemith piano concerto
schubert symphony 9

vienna 24-25 september 1949
vpo
strauss tod und verklärung
wagner faust overture
brahms haydn variations
brahms symphony 1

london 28 september 1949
vpo
bbc chorus
jarred
goethe bi-centenary concert
wagner faust overture
schubert gesang der geister
brahms alto rhapsody
beethoven egmont overture
beethoven symphony 7

london 29 september 1949
vpo
strauss tod und verklärung
mendelssohn violin concerto
tchaikovsky symphony 5

oxford 30 september 1949
vpo
beethoven coriolan overture
schubert symphony 8
brahms haydn variations
berlioz marche hongroise
j.strauss kaiser-walzer

london 1 october 1949
vpo
radio concert
beethoven coriolan overture
schubert symphony 8
brahms haydn variations
j.strauss kaiser-walzer

london 4 october 1949
vpo
menuhin
brahms programme
haydn variations, violin concerto
and symphony 1

london 5 october 1949
vpo
lpo choir
hammond, watson, patzak, hotter
beethoven symphony 9

paris 8 october 1949
vpo
wagner faust overture
strauss tod und verklärung
brahms symphony 1
j.strauss kaiser-walzer

paris 9 october 1949
vpo
beethoven programme
leonore 3 overture, symphonies 4 & 7

geneva 11 october 1949
vpo
beethoven egmont overture
strauss tod und verklärung
brahms symphony 1

zürich 12 october 1949
vpo
beethoven programme
leonore 3 overture, symphonies 4 & 7

berlin 16, 17 and 18 october 1949
bpo
hoelscher
beethoven leonore 2 overture
hoeller cello concerto 2
bruckner symphony 7

basel 25-26 october 1949
stadtorchester basel
handel concerto grosso 10
beethoven leonore 2 overture
bruckner symphony 7

potsdam 17 december 1949
bpo
mozart serenade for 13 wind
schumann manfred overture
brahms symphony 3
wagner meistersinger overture

berlin 18, 19 and 20 december 1949
bpo
taschner
schumann manfred overture
brahms symphony 3
fortner violin concerto
wagner götterdämmerung trauermarsch
wagner meistersinger overture

leipzig 23 december 1949
gewandhaus orchester
beethoven programme
leonore 2 overture, symphonies 4 & 5

munich 8 and 10 january 1950
munich po
handel concerto grosso 5
furtwängler symphony 2

vienna 14-15 january 1950
vpo
schumann manfred overture
korngold symphonic serenade premiere
beethoven symphony 7

vienna 16 january 1950
vpo
j.strauss blue danube
played at philharmonikerball

vienna 28-29 january 1950
vpo
weber oberon overture
shostakovich symphony 9
tchaikovsky symphony 4

vienna 11-12 february 1950
vpo
reznicek, barylli, furtwängler
bach brandenburg concerto 5
beethoven symphony 3

milan la scala 2 and 4 march 1950
wagner das rheingold
höngen/treptow/pernerstorfer/frantz

milan la scala 9 march 1950
wagner die walküre
flagstad/h.konetzni/höngen/
treptow/frantz/weber

milan la scala 11 march 1950
wagner das rheingold
höngen/treptow/pernerstorfer/frantz

milan la scala 13 and 16 march 1950
wagner die walküre
flagstad/h.konetzni/höngen/
treptow/frantz/weber

milan la scala 22, 24 & 26 march 1950
wagner siegfried
flagstad/svanholm/herrmann/weber

milan la scala 2, 4 and 6 april 1950
wagner götterdämmerung
flagstad/lorenz/weber/pernerstorfer

buenos aires 14 april 1950
teatro colon orchestra
haydn symphony 104
debussy nuages et fêtes/nocturnes
strauss till eulenspiegel
beethoven symphony 7

buenos aires 20 april 1950
teatro colon orchestra
ugarte preludio
strauss also sprach zarathustra
brahms symphony 4

buenos aires 23 april 1950
teatro colon orchestra
handel concerto grosso 10
bartok concerto for orchestra
tchaikovsky symphony 4

buenos aires 29 april and 2 may 1950
teatro colon orchestra and chorus
hoffmann, klose, dermota, greindl
bach matthäus-passion

buenos aires 5 may 1950
teatro colon orchestra
dermota
castro obertura para una opera comica
schubert rosamunde overture
mahler lieder eines fahrenden gesellen
beethoven symphony 3
dermota sang in place of klose

buenos aires 6 and 7 may 1950
teatro colon orchestra and chorus
hoffmann, klose, dermota, greindl
bach matthäus-passion

buenos aires 10 may 1950
teatro colon orchestra
beethoven prometheus overture
brahms symphony 4
wagner parsifal prelude
wagner götterdämmerung rheinfahrt
wagner tristan prelude and liebestod
wagner meistersinger overture

buenos aires 14 may 1950
orquesta sinfonica de buenos aires
levy, caracciolo, furtwängler
bach brandenburg concerto 5
beethoven symphony 6
beethoven symphony 5

london 22 may 1950
philharmonia
flagstad
wagner meistersinger overture
wagner siegfried idyll
strauss 4 letzte lieder premiere
wagner tristan prelude & liebestod
wagner götterdämmerung rheinfahrt
   and immolation

wiesbaden 24 may 1950
bpo
brahms haydn variations
beethoven leonore 2 overture
bruckner symphony 7

frankfurt 25 may 1950
bpo
handel concerto grosso 10
beethoven leonore 2 overture
schubert symphony 9

munich 26 may 1950
bpo
beethoven symphony 1
beethoven leonore 2 overture
bruckner symphony 7

stuttgart 27 may 1950
bpo
beethoven programme
leonore 3 overture, symphonies 1 & 3

montreux 28 may 1950
bpo
beethoven symphony 1
strauss till eulenspiegel
schubert symphony 9

lausanne 29 may 1950
bpo
handel concerto grosso 10
brahms haydn variations
beethoven symphony 3

geneva 30 may 1950
bpo
handel concerto grosso 10
beethoven symphony 1
beethoven leonore 3 overture
hindemith concerto for orchestra
wagner tristan prelude & liebestod
wagner meistersinger overture

bern 31 may 1950
bpo
brahms haydn variations
beethoven leonore 2 overture
bruckner symphony 7

basel 1 june 1950
bpo
beethoven programme
leonore 3 overture, symphonies 1 & 3

paris 3 june 1950
bpo
handel concerto grosso 10
brahms haydn variations
strauss till eulenspiegel
schubert symphony 9
wagner tannhäuser overture

paris 4 june 1950
bpo
beethoven leonore 2 overture
beethoven symphony 1
beethoven symphony 3
wagner tristan prelude

cologne 6 june 1950
bpo
beethoven symphony 1
beethoven leonore 3 overture
bruckner symphony 7

viersen 7 june 1950
bpo
brahms haydn variations
strauss till eulenspiegel
schubert symphony 9

düsseldorf 8 june 1950
bpo
beethoven programme
leonore 3 overture, symphonies 1 & 3

bielefeld 9 june 1950
bpo
handel concerto grosso 5
beethoven leonore 3 overture
schubert symphony 9

münster 10 june 1950
bpo
handel concerto grosso 10
brahms haydn variations
bruckner symphony 7

bremen 11 june 1950
bpo
beethoven symphony 1
beethoven leonore 2 overture
bruckner symphony 7

hamburg 12 june 1950
bpo
handel concerto grosso 10
hindemith concerto for orchestra
strauss don juan
beethoven symphony 3

hamburg 13 june 1950
bpo
beethoven symphony 1
brahms haydn variations
bruckner symphony 7

lübeck 14 june 1950
bpo
bork
beethoven symphony 1
furtwängler symphonic concerto

hannover 15 june 1950
bpo
beethoven symphony 1
beethoven leonore 2 overture
schubert symphony 9

berlin 17, 18 and 19 june 1950
bpo
beethoven symphony 1
strauss till eulenspiegel
schubert symphony 9

berlin 20 june 1950
bpo
handel concerto grosso 10
brahms haydn variations
hindemith concerto for orchestra
beethoven symphony 3

amsterdam 13 july 1950
concertgebouw orchestra
beethoven symphony 1
beethoven leonore 3 overture
brahms symphony 1

scheveningen 14 july 1950
concertgebouw orchestra
beethoven symphony 1
beethoven leonore 3 overture
brahms symphony 1

salzburg 27 july 1950
mozart don giovanni
schwarzkopf/welitsch/seefried/
dermota/kunz/gobbi

salzburg 29 july 1950
mozart die zauberflöte
seefried/lipp/w.ludwig/kunz/greindl

salzburg 31 july 1950
mozart don giovanni
schwarzkopf/welitsch/seefried/
dermota/kunz/gobbi

salzburg 3 august 1950
mozart die zauberflöte
seefried/lipp/w.ludwig/kunz/greindl

salzburg 4 august 1950
mozart don giovanni
schwarzkopf/welitsch/seefried/
dermota/kunz/gobbi

salzburg 5 august 1950
beethoven fidelio
flagstad/schwarzkopf/patzak/greindl

lucerne 9 august 1950
lucerne festival orchestra
primrose
gluck alceste overture
brahms haydn variations
hindemith der schwanendreher
beethoven symphony 5

salzburg 11 and 14 august 1950
beethoven fidelio
flagstad/schwarzkopf/patzak/greindl

salzburg 15 august 1950
vpo
stravinsky symphony in 3 movements
strauss till eulenspiegel
brahms symphony 4

salzburg 16 august 1950
mozart die zauberflöte
seefried/lipp/w.ludwig/kunz/greindl

salzburg 17 august 1950
beethoven fidelio
flagstad/schwarzkopf/patzak/greindl

salzburg 18 august 1950
mozart don giovanni
schwarzkopf/welitsch/seefried/
dermota/kunz/gobbi

salzburg 21 august 1950
mozart die zauberflöte
seefried/lipp/w.ludwig/kunz/greindl

salzburg 22 august 1950
beethoven fidelio
flagstad/schwarzkopf/patzak/greindl

lucerne 26-27 august 1950
lucerne festival orchestra & chorus
schwarzkopf, vroons, hotter
berlioz la damnation de faust

salzburg 29 august 1950
mozart don giovanni
kupper/rethy/seefried/dermota/
kunz/gobbi

salzburg 31 august 1950
vpo
niedermayer, boskovsky, furtwängler
bach brandenburg concerto 3
bach brandenburg concerto 5
beethoven symphony 3

vienna 16-17 september 1950
vpo
bach brandenburg concerto 3
debussy la mer
brahms symphony 3

stockholm 25 september 1950
vpo
haydn symphony 94
sibelius en saga
strauss don juan
beethoven symphony 5

stockholm 26 september 1950
vpo
bach brandenburg concerto 3
uhl caprice 3
debussy la mer
tchaikovsky symphony 5
j.strauss kaiser-walzer

314

helsinki 27 september 1950
vpo
haydn symphony 94
sibelius en saga
strauss don juan
beethoven symphony 5

helsinki 28 september 1950
vpo
mozart serenade for 13 wind
uhl caprice 3
schubert symphony 8
brahms symphony 2

helsinki 29 september 1950
vpo
haydn symphony 94
debussy la mer
tchaikovsky symphony 5
j.strauss kaiser-walzer

copenhagen 1 october 1950
vpo
cherubini anacreon overture
schubert symphony 8
strauss till eulenspiegel
beethoven symphony 5

copenhagen 2 october 1950
vpo
haydn symphony 94
debussy la mer
brahms symphony 2
j.strauss kaiser-walzer

hamburg 4 october 1950
vpo
cherubini anacreon overture
uhl caprice 3
schubert symphony 8
tchaikovsky symphony 5

hamburg 5 october 1950
vpo
mozart serenade for 13 wind
debussy la mer
beethoven symphony 5

hannover 6 october 1950
vpo
cherubini anacreon overture
schubert symphony 8
strauss till eulenspiegel
brahms symphony 2

amsterdam 7 october 1950
vpo
mozart serenade for 13 wind
schubert symphony 8
strauss till eulenspiegel
beethoven symphony 5

den haag 9 october 1950
vpo
haydn symphony 94
debussy la mer
brahms symphony 2

münster 10 october 1950
vpo
mozart serenade for 13 wind
sibelius en saga
strauss don juan
tchaikovsky symphony 5

münster 11 october 1950
vpo
haydn symphony 94
schubert symphony 8
beethoven symphony 5

wuppertal 12 october 1950
vpo
cherunini anacreon overture
uhl caprice 3
schubert symphony 8
brahms symphony 2

düsseldorf 13 october 1950
vpo
strauss don juan
uhl caprice 3
schubert symphony 8
beethoven symphony 5

wiesbaden 14 october 1950
vpo
haydn symphony 94
schubert symphony 8
beethoven symphony 5

frankfurt 15 october 1950
vpo
mozart serenade for 13 wind
debussy la mer
tchaikovsky symphony 5

heidelberg 16 october 1950
vpo
boskovsky
mozart serenade for 13 wind
schubert symphony 8
beethoven violin concerto
strauss till eulenspiegel

stuttgart 18 october 1950
vpo
cherubini anacreon overture
schubert symphony 8
strauss till eulenspiegel
brahms symphony 2

munich 19 october 1950
vpo
mozart serenade for 13 wind
schubert symphony 8
strauss don juan
beethoven symphony 5

geneva 21 october 1950
vpo
bach brandenburg concerto 3
schubert symphony 8
brahms symphony 2

bern 22 october 1950
vpo
haydn symphony 94
debussy la mer
beethoven symphony 5

berlin 29-30 october 1950
bpo
weber der freischütz overture
bartok concerto for orchestra
brahms symphony 1

rome 5 november 1950
santa cecilia orchestra
stravinsky symphony in 3 movements
beethoven leonore 3 overture
beethoven symphony 3

milan 8-9 november 1950
la scala orchestra
beethoven programme
leonore 2 overture, symphonies 4 & 5

london 13 november 1950
philharmonia orchestra
walton scapino overture
brahms haydn variations
strauss don juan
beethoven symphony 5

london 11 december 1950
philharmonia orchestra
mendelssohn hebrides overture
schubert rosamunde entr'actes
bartok concerto for orchestra
tchaikovsky symphony 5

berlin städtische oper 17 dec 1950
wagner tristan und isolde
büchner/blatter/suthaus/greindl/
metternich

berlin 20, 21 and 22 december 1950
bpo
hedwiq's choir
trötschel, klose, schock, greindl
beethoven symphony 9

vienna 6, 7, 8 and 10 january 1951
vpo
singakademie
seefried, anday, patzak, edelmann
beethoven symphony 9

vienna 15 january 1951
vpo
j.strauss kaiser-walzer
played at philharmonikerball

vienna 20-21 january 1951
vpo
cherubini anacreon overture
bartok concerto for orchestra
bruckner symphony 7

vienna 24-25 january 1951
vso
singakademie
seefried, fischer-dieskau
brahms ein deutsches requiem

basel 29 and 31 january 1951
stadtorchester basel
haydn symphony 101
debussy nuages et fêtes/nocturnes
tchaikovsky symphony 5

london 22 february 1951
philharmonia orchestra
fischer
weber der freischütz overture
bruckner symphony 7
beethoven piano concerto 5

berlin 25-26 february 1951
bpo
mendelssohn hebrides overture
trapp symphony 6 premiere
tchaikovsky symphony 6

berlin 27 february 1951
bpo
schools' concert
mendelssohn hebrides overture
tchaikovsky symphony 6

zürich 5-6 march 1951
tonhalle-orchester
beethoven coriolan overture
beethoven symphony 6
brahms symphony 1

london 9 march 1951
philharmonia orchestra
h.konetzni, treptow, greindl
wagner programme
fliegende holländer overture, parsifal
karfreitagszauber & die walküre act 1

milan la scala 24, 27 & 29 march
and 1 & 4 april 1951
wagner parsifal
mödl/beirer/edelmann/greindl

milan la scala 7 april 1951
gluck orfeo ed euridice
simionato/güden/gabory

milan la scala 11, 13 & 15 april 1951
gluck orfeo ed euridice
barbieri/güden/gabory

cairo 18 april 1951
bpo
haydn symphony 101
strauss tod und verklärung
beethoven symphony 7

cairo 19 april 1951
bpo
rameau la princesse de navarre
debussy nuages et fêtes/nocturnes
berlioz marche hongroise
tchaikovsky symphony 6

cairo 20 april 1951
bpo
weber der freischütz overture
brahms symphony 3
hindemith concerto for orchestra
wagner tannhäuser overture

cairo 21 april 1951
bpo
mozart symphony 40
beethoven leonore 3 overture
beethoven symphony 5

cairo 22 april 1951 morning
bpo
tagliaferro
weber der freischütz overture
schumann piano concerto
tchaikovsky symphony 6

cairo 22 april 1951 evening
bpo
mozart symphony 40
beethoven leonore 3 overture
beethoven symphony 5

cairo 23 april 1951
bpo
borries
bruckner symphony 7
mendelssohn violin concerto
wagner tannhäuser overture

alexandria 24 april 1951
bpo
haydn symphony 101
strauss tod und verklärung
beethoven symphony 7

alexandria 25 april 1951 morning
bpo
brahms symphony 3
debussy nuages et fêtes/nocturnes
wagner meistersinger overture

alexandria 25 april 1951 <u>evening</u>
bpo
brahms symphony 3
debussy nuages et fêtes/nocturnes
wagner parsifal karfeitagszauber
wagner götterdämmerung trauermarsch
wagner tannhäuser overture
berlioz marche hongroise

naples 30 april 1951
bpo
mozart symphony 40
brahms symphony 3
debussy nuages et fêtes/nocturnes

rome 1 may 1951
bpo
bruckner symphony 7
debussy nuages et fêtes/nocturnes
strauss don juan
wagner tannhäuser overture

bologna 2 may 1951
bpo
haydn symphony 101
brahms symphony 3
beethoven symphony 5
wagner tannhäuser overture

turin 3 may 1951
bpo
weber der freischütz overture
debussy nuages et fêtes/nocturnes
strauss tod und verklärung
beethoven symphony 7
wagner tannhäuser overture

paris 5 may 1951
bpo
bruckner symphony 7
beethoven symphony 5
weber der freischütz overture

paris 6 may 1951
bpo
haydn symphony 101
brahms symphony 3
strauss don juan
wagner parsifal karfreitagszauber
wagner tannhäuser overture
berlioz marche hongroise

viersen 8 may 1951
bpo
haydn symphony 88
hindemith concerto for orchestra
bruckner symphony 7

düsseldorf 9 may 1951
bpo
cherubini anacreon overture
brahms symphony 3
tchaikovsky symphony 6

dortmund 10 may 1951
bpo
haydn symphony 101
brahms symphony 3
beethoven symphony 5

essen 11 may 1951
bpo
haydn symphony 101
debussy nuages et fêtes/nocturnes
bruckner symphony 7

bielefeld 12 may 1951
bpo
haydn symphony 101
strauss tod und verklärung
bruckner symphony 7

wolfsburg 13 may 1951
bpo
cherubini anacreon overture
brahms symphony 3
beethoven symphony 5
weber der freischütz overture

hannover 14 may 1951
bpo
haydn symphony 101
debussy nuages et fêtes/nocturnes
berlioz marche hongroise
tchaikovsky symphony 6

hamburg 15 may 1951
bpo
haydn symphony 101
brahms symphony 3
tchaikovsky symphony 6

318

münster 16 may 1951
bpo
haydn symphony 101
brahms symphony 3
strauss don juan
wagner parsifal karfreitagszauber
wagner tannhäuser overture

vienna 19-20 may 1951
vpo
walton scapino overture
franck symphony in d minor
beethoven symphony 5

zürich stadttheater 26-28 june 1951
wagner tristan und isolde
flagstad/cavelti/lorenz/
greindl/schöffler

bayreuth 29 july 1951
bayreuth festival orchestra & chorus
schwarzkopf, höngen, hopf, edelmann
beethoven symphony 9
re-opening of festspielhaus

salzburg 1 and 6 august 1951
mozart die zauberflöte
seefried/lipp/dermota/kunz

salzburg 7 august 1951
verdi otello
martinis/wagner/vinay/schöffler

salzburg 10 august 1951
mozart die zauberflöte
seefried/lipp/dermota/kunz

lucerne 15 august 1951
lucerne festival orchestra
weber der freischütz overture
bartok concerto for orchestra
beethoven symphony 7

salzburg 17 august 1951
mozart die zauberflöte
seefried/lipp/dermota/kunz

salzburg 18 august 1951
verdi otello
martinis/wagner/vinay/schöffler

salzburg 19 august 1951
vpo
fischer-dieskau
mendelssohn hebrides overture
mahler lieder eines fahrenden gesellen
bruckner symphony 5

salzburg 21 august 1952
verdi otello
martinis/wagner/vinay/schöffler

lucerne 25 august 1951
lucerne festival orchestra
varnay, lorenz, rehfuss, greindl
wagner scenes from götterdämmerung

salzburg 29 august 1951
mozart die zauberflöte
seefried/lipp/dermota/kunz

salzburg 30 august 1951
verdi otello
martinis/wagner/vinay/schöffler

salzburg 31 august 1951
vpo
vienna opera chorus
ssefried, wagner, dermota, greindl
beethoven symphony 9

berlin 5 september 1951
bpo
hedwig's choir
grümmer, pitzinger, anders, greindl
gluck alceste overture
beethoven symphony 9
re-opening of schillertheater

berlin 6-7 september 1951
bpo
hedwig's choir
grümmer, pitzinger, anders, greindl
beethoven symphony 9

montreux 5 october 1951
vpo
weber der freischütz overture
schumann symphony 1
tchaikovsky symphony 6

lausanne 6 october 1951
vpo
beethoven coriolan overture
beethoven symphony 6
brahms symphony 4

zürich 7 october 1951
vpo
weber der freischütz overture
schumann symphony 1
tchaikovsky symphony 6

basel 8 october 1951
vpo
beethoven coriolan overture
beethoven symphony 6
brahms symphony 4

paris 9 october 1951
vpo
beethoven coriolan overture
beethoven symphony 6
brahms symphony 4
wagner meistersinger overture

paris 10 october 1951
vpo
weber der freischütz overture
schumann symphony 1
tchaikovsky symphony 6

münster 13 october 1951
vpo
weber der freischütz overture
schumann symphony 1
tchaikovsky symphony 6

hamburg 14 october 1951
vpo
weber der freischütz overture
schumann symphony 1
bruckner symphony 4

hannover 15 october 1951
vpo
beethoven coriolan overture
beethoven symphony 6
brahms symphony 4

dortmund 16 october 1951
vpo
beethoven coriolan overture
beethoven symphony 6
tchaikovsky symphony 6

wuppertal 17 october 1951
vpo
weber der freischütz overture
ravel rapsodie espagnole
bruckner symphony 4

düsseldorf 18 october 1951
vpo
brahms symphony 4
bruckner symphony 4

wiesbaden 19 october 1951
vpo
haydn symphony 88
ravel rapsodie espagnole
bruckner symphony 4

heidelberg 20 october 1951
vpo
weber der freischütz overture
schumann symphony 1
tchaikovsky symphony 6

frankfurt 21 october 1951
vpo
brahms symphony 4
bruckner symphony 4

stuttgart 22 october 1951
vpo
haydn symphony 88
ravel rapsodie espagnole
bruckner symphony 4

london 25 october 1951
philharmonia orchestra
hess
beethoven grosse fuge
beethoven piano concerto 4
brahms symphony 1

hamburg 27 october 1951
nwdr orchestra
roehn, troester
brahms programme
haydn variations, double concerto
and symphony 1

karlsruhe 28 october 1951
vpo
haydn symphony 88
schumann symphony 1
brahms symphony 4

320

munich 29 october 1951
vpo
beethoven coriolan overture
schumann symphony 1
bruckner symphony 4

berlin 30 november and 2-3 dec 1951
bpo
haydn symphony 88
ravel rapsodie espagnole
bruckner symphony 4

rome 10 january 1952
rai roma orchestra
beethoven programme
symphonies 6 and 5

rome 14 january 1952
rai roma orchestra
h.konetzni, treptow, rohr
wagner die walküre act 1

rome 19 january 1952
rai roma orchestra
scarpini
beethoven programme
piano concerto 4 and symphony 3

vienna staatsoper 23 january 1952
wagner die walküre
werth/h.konetzni/milinkovic/
suthaus/frick/herrmann
performance in theater an der wien

vienna 26-27 january 1952
vpo
boskovsky, brabec
brahms programme
haydn variations, double concerto
and symphony 1
27 january was a morning concert

vienna 27 january 1952 evening
vpo
badura-skoda
mozart programme in schloss schönbrunn
piano concerto 22 and
serenade for 13 wind

vienna staatsoper 30 january 1952
wagner tristan und isolde
a.konetzni/milinkovic/suthaus/
frick/herrmann

vienna 2, 3 and 4 february 1952
vpo
singakademie
güden, anday, patzak, poell
beethoven symphony 9

berlin 8, 9 and 10 february 1952
bpo
beethoven grosse fuge
honegger mouvement symphonique 3
schubert symphony 8
brahms symphony 1

milan la scala 29 february 1952
wagner die meistersinger von nürnberg
grümmer/wagner/beirer/herrmann/greindl

turin 3 march 1952
rai torino orchestra
haydn symphony 88
beethoven leonore 3 overture
ravel rapsodie espagnole
strauss tod und verklärung

milan la scala 4 and 6 march 1952
wagner die meistersinger von nürnberg
grümmer/wagner/beirer/herrmann/greindl

turin 7 march 1952
rai torino orchestra
de vito
brahms programme
violin concerto and symphony 1

milan la scala 9 march 1952
wagner die meistersinger von nürnberg
grümmer/wagner/beirer/herrmann/greindl

turin 11 march 1952
rai torino orchestra
de vito
schubert rosamunde overture
schubert symphony 8
mendelssohn violin concerto
wagner tristan prelude & liebestod

milan la scala 12 and 16 march 1952
wagner die meistersinger von nürnberg
grümmer/wagner/beirer/herrmann/greindl

vienna 9, 10 and 11 april 1952
vpo
singakademie
seefried, rössel-majdan, patzak,
braun, wiener
bach matthäus-passion

berlin 18, 19 and 20 april 1952
bpo
beethoven symphony 8
schumann symphony 4
brahms symphony 2

london 24 april 1952
philharmonia orchestra
flagstad
schumann manfred overture
schumann symphony 4
ravel rapsodie espagnole
wagner wesendonk-lieder
wagner götterdämmerung immolation

hamburg 26 april 1952
bpo
weber oberon overture
schumann symphony 4
honegger mouvement symphonique 3
ravel rapsodie espagnole
wagner fliegende holländer overture

kiel 27 april 1952
bpo
beethoven programme
egmont overture, grosse fuge and
symphonies 8 and 5

bremen 28 april 1952
bpo
beethoven egmont overture
beethoven grosse fuge
schumann symphony 4
brahms symphony 2

hannover 29 april 1952
bpo
beethoven cavatina
beethoven grosse fuge
beethoven symphony 5
honegger mouvement symphonique 3
ravel rapsodie espagnole
strauss tod und verklärung

krefeld 30 april 1952
bpo
beethoven egmont overture
beethoven grosse fuge
schumann symphony 4
brahms symphony 2

paris 2 may 1952
bpo
weber oberon overture
schumann symphony 4
honegger mouvement symphonique 3
strauss tod und verklärung
wagner fliegende holländer overture

paris 3 may 1952
bpo
szigeti, fournier
beethoven egmont overture
beethoven grosse fuge
brahms double concerto
brahms symphony 2
wagner meistersinger overture

baden-baden 5 may 1952
bpo
beethoven symphony 8
beethoven cavatina
beethoven grosse fuge
brahms symphony 2

freiburg 6 may 1952
bpo
beethoven egmont overture
beethoven grosse fuge
schumann symphony 4
brahms symphony 2

munich 7 may 1952
bpo
beethoven grosse fuge
brahms symphony 2
ravel rapsodie espagnole
strauss tod und verklärung

stuttgart 8 may 1952
bpo
beethoven cavatina
beethoven grosse fuge
honegger mouvement symphonique 3
strauss tod und verklärung
wagner meistersinger overture

322

landau 9 may 1952
bpo
berlioz carnaval romain overture
ravel rapsodie espagnole
strauss tod und verklärung
beethoven symphony 5

heidelberg 10 may 1952
bpo
berlioz carnaval romain overture
ravel rapsodie espagnole
strauss tod und verklärung
beethoven symphony 7

frankfurt 11 may 1952
bpo
weber oberon overture
ravel rapsodie espagnole
strauss tod und verklärung
beethoven symphony 7

bonn 12 may 1952
bpo
beethoven programme
leonore 3 overture, symphonies 8 & 7

viersen 13 may 1952
bpo
berlioz carnaval romain overture
debussy nuages et fêtes/nocturnes
ravel rapsodie espagnole
brahms symphony 2

essen 14 may 1952
bpo
weber oberon overture
ravel rapsodie espagnole
strauss tod und verklärung
beethoven symphony 5

düsseldorf 15 may 1952
bpo
berlioz carnaval romain overture
schumann symphony 4
brahms symphony 2

bielefeld 16 may 1952
bpo
beethoven symphony 8
beethoven cavatina
beethoven grosse fuge
brahms symphony 2

münster 17 may 1952
bpo
weber oberon overture
brahms symphony 2
ravel rapsodie espagnole
strauss tod und verklärung

berlin 24 may 1952
bpo
menuhin
berlioz carnaval romain overture
debussy nuages et fêtes/nocturnes
mendelssohn violin concerto
beethoven symphony 7

berlin 25 may 1952
bpo
menuhin
haydn symphony 94
bach violin concerto 2
mendelssohn violin concerto
beethoven symphony 7

berlin 26 may 1952
bpo
menuhin
beethoven programme
leonore 2 overture, violin concerto
and symphony 5

turin 31 may 1952
rai torino orchestra and chorus
flagstad, h.konetzni, suthaus, greindl
wagner götterdämmerung act 3

turin 4 june 1952
rai torino orchestra
schneiderhan, mainardi
brahms programme
double concerto and symphony 2

turin 6 june 1952
rai torino orchestra
wagner fliegende holländer overture
wagner siegfried idyll
wagner götterdämmerung rheinfahrt
tchaikovsky symphony 5

zürich stadttheater 29 june 1952
wagner tristan und isolde
grob-prandl/cavelti/lechleitner/
böhm/greindl

furtwängler's 1952 salzburg festival
appearances cancelled due to illness

vienna 29-30 november 1952
vpo
poell
beethoven symphony 1
mahler lieder eines fahrenden gesellen
beethoven symphony 3

berlin 7, 8 and 9 december 1952
bpo
weber der freischütz overture
hindemith harmonie der welt
beethoven symphony 3

frankfurt 16 december 1952
orchestra of hessischer rundfunk
gluck iphigenie in aulis overture
furtwängler symphony 2

turin 19 december 1952
rai torino orchestra and chorus
schwarzkopf, klose, dermota, edelmann
beethoven symphony 9

hamburg 15 january 1953
bpo
beethoven symphony 1
furtwängler symphony 2

bremen 16 january 1953
bpo
beethoven symphony 1
furtwängler symphony 2

duisburg 17 january 1953
bpo
beethoven symphony 1
furtwängler symphony 2

mannheim 18 january 1953
bpo
beethoven symphony 1
furtwängler symphony 2

essen 19 january 1953
bpo
beethoven symphony 1
furtwängler symphony 2

bielefeld 20 january 1953
bpo
beethoven symphony 1
furtwängler symphony 2

performance of beethoven symphony 9
in vienna on 23 january 1953
abandoned due to furtwängler's illness

berlin 8, 9 and 10 february 1953
bpo
bach suite 2
ravel valses nobles et sentimentales
stravinsky suite for small orchestra
brahms symphony 2

vienna 15 and 17 february 1953
vpo
a.konetzni, höngen, suthaus, frick
wagner scenes from götterdämmerung

vienna 21 and 22 february 1953
vpo
gluck iphigenie in aulis overture
furtwängler symphony 2

winterthur 25 february 1953
stadtorchester winterthur
franck symphony in d minor
schoeck sommernacht
tchaikovsky symphony 6

zürich 2 and 3 march 1953
tonhalle-orchester
beethoven programme
symphonies 4 and 3

kassel 24 march 1953
staatskapelle kassel
furtwängler symphony 2
beethoven symphony 1

london 27 march 1953
philharmonia orchestra
beethoven programme
egmont overture, symphonies 6 and 7

berlin 12, 13 and 14 april 1953
bpo
beethoven symphony 8
strauss till eulenspiegel
beethoven symphony 7

hamburg 16 april 1953
bpo
beethoven symphony 8
ravel valses nobles et sentimentales
brahms symphony 2

kiel 17 april 1953
bpo
brahms symphony 2
wagner tristan prelude & liebestod
beethoven symphony 7

dortmund 18 april 1953
bpo
bach suite 2
ravel valses nobles et sentimentales
strauss till eulenspiegel
brahms symphony 2

cologne 19 april 1953
bpo
beethoven symphony 8
strauss don juan
wagner tristan prelude & liebestod
brahms symphony 1

brussels 20 april 1953
bpo
beethoven symphony 8
wagner tristan prelude & liebestod
brahms symphony 1

london 22 april 1953
bpo
bach suite 2
ravel valses nobles et sentimentales
strauss till eulenspiegel
brahms symphony 2

düsseldorf 24 april 1953
bpo
bach suite 2
ravel valses nobles et sentimentales
strauss don juan
brahms symphony 1

essen 25 april 1953
bpo
mendelssohn hebrides overture
ravel valses nobles et sentimentales
strauss don juan
brahms symphony 2

hannover 26 april 1953
bpo
bach suite 2
schoeck sommernacht
wagner tristan prelude & liebestod
brahms symphony 1

paris 28 april 1953
bpo
bach suite 2
ravel valses nobles et sentimentales
strauss till eulenspiegel
brahms symphony 1

paris 30 april 1953
bpo
beethoven symphony 8
beethoven leonore 3 overture
beethoven symphony 7
wagner tristan prelude & liebestod

baden-baden 2 may 1953
bpo
bach suite 2
ravel valses nobles et sentimentales
strauss don juan
beethoven symphony 3

munich 7 may 1953
bpo
menuhin
mendelssohn hebrides overture
beethoven violin concerto
brahms symphony 1

landau 8 may 1953
bpo
mendelssohn hebrides overture
ravel valses nobles et sentimentales
wagner tristan prelude & liebestod
beethoven symphony 7

ludwigshafen 9 may 1953
bpo
brahms symphony 2
beethoven symphony 3

frankfurt 10 may 1953
bpo
mendelssohn hebrides overture
ravel valses nobles et sentimentales
strauss don juan
brahms symphony 2

berlin 17, 18 and 19 may 1953
bpo
schneiderhan
stravinsky baiser de la fée
beethoven violin concerto
brahms symphony 1

vienna 29, 30 and 31 may 1953
vpo
singakademie
seefried/zadek, anday,
dermota, schöffler
beethoven symphony 9
concert given twice on 31 may

linz 1 june 1953
vpo
singakademie
zadek, anday, dermota, schöffler
beethoven symphony 9

salzburg 27 july and 3 august 1953
mozart don giovanni
schwarzkopf/grümmer/berger/dermota/
siepi/edelmann

salzburg 7 august 1953
mozart le nozze di figaro
schwarzkopf/seefried/güden/kunz/
schöffler

salzburg 8 august 1953
mozart don giovanni
schwarzkopf/grümmer/berger/dermota/
siepi/edelmann

salzburg 11 august 1953
mozart le nozze di figaro
schwarzkopf/seefried/güden/kunz/
schöffler

salzburg 12 august 1953
hugo wolf commemoration
furtwängler accompanied schwarzkopf

salzburg 18 august 1953
mozart don giovanni
schwarzkopf/grümmer/berger/dermota/
siepi/edelmann

lucerne 22 august 1953
lucerne festival orchestra
fischer
handel concerto grosso 10
hindemith harmonie der welt
brahms piano concerto 2

lucerne 26 august 1953
lucerne festival orchestra
schumann manfred overture
schumann symphony 4
beethoven symphony 3

salzburg 28 august 1953
mozart don giovanni
schwarzkopf/grümmer/berger/dermota/
siepi/edelmann

salzburg 29 august 1953
mozart le nozze di figaro
schwarzkopf/seefried/güden/
kunz/schöffler

salzburg 30 august 1953
vpo
strauss don juan
hindemith harmonie der welt
schubert symphony 9

munich 4 september 1953
vpo
beethoven programme
egmont overture, symphonies 4 and 3

edinburgh 6-7 september 1953
vpo
beethoven programme
egmont overture, symphonies 4 and 5

edinburgh 9 september 1953
vpo
wagner meistersinger overture
hindemith harmonie der welt
schubert symphony 9

edinburgh 11 september 1953
vpo
menuhin
strauss don juan
bartok violin concerto 2
brahms symphony 1

berlin 15, 16 and 17 september 1953
bpo
schubert programme
rosamunde overture, symphonies 8 & 9

kiel 19 september 1953
vpo
strauss don juan
beethoven symphony 4
brahms symphony 1

vienna staatsoper 12, 15 and 18
october 1953
beethoven fidelio
mödl/jurinac/windgassen/
poell/edelmann
performances in theater an der wien

rome rai 26 october 1953
wagner das rheingold
malaniuk/windgassen/frantz/greindl

rome rai 29 october 1953
wagner die walküre act 1
h.konetzni/windgassen/frick

rome rai 3 november 1953
wagner die walküre act 2
mödl/h.konetzni/cavelti/windgassen/
frick/frantz

rome rai 6 november 1953
wagner die walküre act 3
mödl/h.konetzni/frantz

rome rai 10 november 1953
wagner siegfried act 1
suthaus/patzak/frantz

rome rai 13 november 1953
wagner siegfried act 2
suthaus/patzak/frantz/greindl

vatican city 16 november 1953
private chamber concert for pope
pius XII
furtwängler accompanied de vito
in brahms violin sonata 1

rome rai 17 november 1953
wagner siegfried act 3
mödl/klose/suthaus/frantz

rome rai 20 november 1953
wagner götterdämmerung act 1
mödl/jurinac/klose/suthaus/
poell/greindl

rome 24 november 1953
wagner götterdämmerung act 2
mödl/jurinac/suthaus/poell/greindl

vatican city 26 november 1953
private chamber oncert for pope
pius XII
furtwängler accompanied de vito
in brahms violin sonata 2

rome 27 november 1953
wagner götterdämmerung act 3
mödl/jurinac/suthaus/poell/greindl

berlin 6, 7 and 8 december 1953
bpo
fischer-dieskau
gluck iphigenie in aulis overture
mahler kindertotenlieder
bruckner symphony 5

vienna 12-13 december 1953
vpo
franck symphony in d minor
hindemith harmonie der welt
wagner tannhäuser overture

lieder recitals in london in march
and april 1954, in which furtwängler
was to have accompanied schwarzkopf
and fischer-dieskau, were cancelled

london 12 march 1954
philharmonia orchestra
beethoven programme
leonore 2 overture, symphonies 4 & 5

caracas 19 march 1954
orquesta sinfonica venezuela
handel concerto grosso 10
strauss don juan
wagner tannhäuser overture

caracas 21 march 1954
orquesta sinfonica venezuela
handel concerto grosso 10
strauss don juan
wagner tannhäuser overture
brahms symphony 1

zürich 26 march 1954
tonhalle-orchester
furtwängler symphony 2
beethoven symphony 1

stuttgart 30 march 1954
sdr orchestra
furtwängler symphony 2
beethoven symphony 1

hamburg 1 april 1954
bpo
<u>schubert programme</u>
rosamunde overture, symphonies 8 & 9

hamburg 2 april 1954
bpo
then-bergh
beethoven symphony 2
beethoven leonore 2 overture
brahms piano concerto 1

berlin 4, 5 and 6 april 1954
bpo
then-bergh
beethoven symphony 2
beethoven leonore 2 overture
brahms piano concerto 1

vienna 10-11 april 1954
vpo
bruckner symphony 8

vienna 14, 15, 16 and 17 april 1954
vpo
singverein
grümmer, höffgen, dermota,
edelmann, fischer-dieskau
bach matthäus-passion

berlin 25, 26 and 27 april 1954
bpo
handel concerto grosso 5
brahms symphony 3
blacher concertante musik
strauss don juan
wagner tristan prelude & liebestod

hannover 28 april 1954
bpo
handel concerto grosso 5
brahms symphony 3
beethoven symphony 5

bielefeld 29 april 1954
bpo
weber euryanthe overture
brahms haydn variations
schubert symphony 8

cologne 30 april 1954
bpo
handel concerto grosso 5
brahms symphony 3
beethoven symphony 5

paris 3 may 1954
bpo
handel concerto grosso 5
brahms symphony 3
blacher concertante musik
strauss don juan
wagner tannhäuser overture
wagner tristan prelude & liebestod

paris 4 may 1954
bpo
weber euryanthe overture
brahms haydn variations
schubert symphony 8
beethoven symphony 5

lyon 5 may 1954
bpo
handel concerto grosso 5
brahms symphony 3
beethoven symphony 5

geneva 6 may 1954
bpo
weber euryanthe overture
brahms symphony 3
strauss till eulenspiegel
wagner tannhäuser overture

lausanne 7 may 1954
bpo
brahms haydn variations
schubert symphony 8
beethoven symphony 5

milan 8 may 1954
bpo
brahms haydn variations
schubert symphony 8
beethoven symphony 5
weber euryanthe overture

milan 9 may 1954
bpo
brahms haydn variations
schubert symphony 8
beethoven symphony 5
weber euryanthe overture
wagner tannhäuser overture

florence 10 may 1954
bpo
handel concerto grosso 5
brahms symphony 3
beethoven symphony 7
wagner tannhäuser overture

perugia 11 may 1954
bpo
brahms haydn variations
beethoven symphony 7
strauss till eulenspiegel
wagner tristan prelude & liebestod
wagner tannhäuser overture

rome 12 may 1954
bpo
brahms symphony 3
strauss till eulenspiegel
beethoven symphony 5
wagner tannhäuser overture

turin 14 may 1954
bpo
weber euryanthe overture
brahms symphony 3
strauss till eulenspiegel
wagner tristan prelude & liebestod
wagner tannhäuser overture

lugano 15 may 1954
bpo
lefébure
beethoven symphony 6
mozart piano concerto 20
strauss till eulenspiegel

zürich 16 may 1954
bpo
handel concerto grosso 5
brahms symphony 3
beethoven symphony 5

freiburg 17 may 1954
bpo
brahms haydn variations
brahms symphony 3
beethoven symphony 5

baden-baden 18 may 1954
bpo
cherubini anacreon overture
brahms symphony 3
blacher concertante musik
strauss till eulenspiegel
wagner tristan prelude & liebestod

karlsruhe 19 may 1954
bpo
cherubini anacreon overture
schubert symphony 8
strauss till eulenspiegel
beethoven symphony 7

mannheim 20 may 1954
bpo
beethoven programme
symphonies 6 and 5

kassel 21 may 1954
bpo
brahms haydn variations
brahms symphony 3
beethoven symphony 7

berlin 23, 24 and 25 may 1954
bpo
beethoven programme
symphonies 6 and 5

vienna 30 may 1954
vpo
schubert programme
rosamunde overture, symphonies 8 & 9
furtwängler's final public
concert in vienna

geneva 2 june 1954
suisse romande orchestra
beethoven programme
symphonies 4 and 3

lausanne 3 june 1954
suisse romande orchestra
beethoven programme
symphonies 4 and 3

salzburg 26 and 30 july 1954
weber der freischütz
grümmer/streich/hopf/böhme/poell

salzburg 3 august 1954
mozart don giovanni
schwarzkopf/grümmer/berger/dermota/
edelmann/siepi

salzburg 5 august 1954
weber der freischütz
grümmer/streich/hopf/böhme/poell

salzburg 6 august 1954
mozart don giovanni
schwarzkopf/grümmer/berger/dermota/
edelmann/siepi

bayreuth 9 august 1954
**bayreuth festival orchestra & chorus
brouwenstijn, malaniuk,
windgassen, weber**
beethoven symphony 9

salzburg 10 and 13 august 1954
mozart don giovanni
schwarzkopf/grümmer/berger/dermota/
edelmann/siepi

salzburg 16 august 1954
weber der freischütz
grümmer/streich/hopf/böhme/poell

salzburg 18 august 1954
mozart don giovanni
schwarzkopf/grümmer/berger/dermota/
edelmann/siepi

lucerne 21-22 august 1954
**philharmonia orchestra
lucerne festival chorus
schwarzkopf, cavelti, haefliger,
edelmann**
beethoven symphony 9

lucerne 25 august 1954
philharmonia orchestra
haydn symphony 88
bruckner symphony 7

salzburg 28 august 1954
weber der freischütz
grümmer/streich/hopf/böhme/poell

salzburg 30 august 1954
vpo
beethoven programme
grosse fuge, symphonies 8 and 7

besançon 6 september 1954
orchestre national
beethoven programme
coriolan overture, symphonies 6 & 5

berlin 19-20 september 1954
bpo
furtwängler symphony 2
beethoven symphony 1
furtwängler's final public appearance
and final concert in berlin

BEETHOVEN
Sinfonie No.6
"Pastorale"

BRAHMS
Haydn – Variationen

WIENER PHILHARMONIKER
FURTWÄNGLER

Previously unissued recording
Unveröffentlichte Aufnahme
(1943)

credits

valuable help with the supply of
information or illustration material
came from

Kenzo Amoh   Richard Chlupaty
Siam Chowkwayun   Martin Cotton
David Crighton   Henry Fogel
Paul Geffen   Michael Gray
Syd Gray   Bill Holland
Ken Jagger   Ernst Lumpe
Bruce Morrison   Alan Newcombe
Tatsuro Ouchi   Brian Pinder
Roger Smithson   Ulf Scharlau
Hisashi Takei   Akira Tanaka
Ates Tanin   Peter Taylor
Malcolm Walker   Urs Weber
Ken Wyman

Music and Books published by Travis & Emery Music Bookshop:

Anon.: Hymnarium Sarisburiense, cum Rubricis et Notis Musicis.
Agricola, Johann Friedrich from Tosi: Anleitung zur Singkunst.
Bach, C.P.E.: edited W. Emery: Nekrolog or Obituary Notice of J.S. Bach.
Bateson, Naomi Judith: Alcock of Salisbury
Bathe, William: A Briefe Introduction to the Skill of Song (c.1587)
Bax, Arnold: Symphony #5, Arranged for Piano Four Hands by Walter Emery
Burney, Charles: The Present State of Music in France and Italy (1771)
Burney, Charles: The Present State of Music in Germany, Netherlands... (1773)
Burney, Charles: An Account of the Musical Performances ... Handel (1784)
Burney, Karl: Nachricht von Georg Friedrich Handel's Lebensumstanden (1784)
Burns, Robert: The Caledonian Musical Museum ... Best Scotch Songs (1810)
Cobbett, W.W.: Cobbett's Cyclopedic Survey of Chamber Music. (2 vols.)
Corrette, Michel: Le Maitre de Clavecin (1753)
Crimp, Bryan: Dear Mr. Rosenthal ... Dear Mr. Gaisberg ...
Crimp, Bryan: Solo: The Biography of Solomon
d'Indy, Vincent: Beethoven: Biographie Critique (in French, 1911)
d'Indy, Vincent: Beethoven: A Critical Biography (in English, 1912)
d'Indy, Vincent: César Franck (in French, 1910)
Fischhof, Joseph: Versuch einer Geschichte des Clavierbaues (1853).
Frescobaldi, Girolamo: D'Arie Musicali per Cantarsi. Primo & Secondo Libro.
Geminiani, Francesco: The Art of Playing the Violin (1751)
Handel; Purcell; Boyce et al: Calliope or English Harmony: Vol. First. (1746)
Häuser: Musikalisches Lexikon. 2 vols in one.
Hawkins, John: General History of the Science & Practice of Music (5 vols. 1776)
Herbert-Caesari, Edgar: The Science and Sensations of Vocal Tone
Herbert-Caesari, Edgar: Vocal Truth
Hopkins and Rimboult: The Organ. Its History and Construction.
Hunt, John: Adam to Webern: the recordings of von Karajan
Hunt, John: several discographies – see separate list.
Isaacs, Lewis: Hänsel and Gretel. A Guide to Humperdinck's Opera.
Isaacs, Lewis: Königskinder (Royal Children) A Guide to Humperdinck's Opera.
Kastner: Manuel Général de Musique Militaire
Lacassagne, M. l'Abbé Joseph : Traité Général des élémens du Chant.
Lascelles (née Catley), Anne: The Life of Miss Anne Catley.
Mainwaring, John: Memoirs of the Life of the Late George Frederic Handel
Malcolm, Alexander: A Treaty of Music: Speculative, Practical and Historical
Marx, Adolph Bernhard: Die Kunst des Gesanges, Theoretisch-Practisch (1826)
May, Florence: The Life of Brahms (2nd edition)
May, Florence: The Girlhood Of Clara Schumann: Clara Wieck And Her Time.
Mellers, Wilfrid: Angels of the Night: Popular Female Singers of Our Time
Mellers, Wilfrid: Bach and the Dance of God
Mellers, Wilfrid: Beethoven and the Voice of God
Mellers, Wilfrid: Caliban Reborn - Renewal in Twentieth Century Music

Music and Books published by Travis & Emery Music Bookshop:

Mellers, Wilfrid: François Couperin and the French Classical Tradition
Mellers, Wilfrid: Harmonious Meeting
Mellers, Wilfrid: Le Jardin Retrouvé, The Music of Frederic Mompou
Mellers, Wilfrid: Music and Society, England and the European Tradition
Mellers, Wilfrid: Music in a New Found Land: ... ... American Music
Mellers, Wilfrid: Romanticism and the Twentieth Century (from 1800)
Mellers, Wilfrid: The Masks of Orpheus: ...... the Story of European Music.
Mellers, Wilfrid: The Sonata Principle (from c. 1750)
Mellers, Wilfrid: Vaughan Williams and the Vision of Albion
Panchianio, Cattuffio: Rutzvanscad Il Giovine (1737)
Pearce, Charles: Sims Reeves, Fifty Years of Music in England.
Pettitt, Stephen: Philharmonia Orchestra: Complete Discography (1987)
Playford, John: An Introduction to the Skill of Musick (1674)
Purcell, Henry et al: Harmonia Sacra ... The First Book, (1726)
Purcell, Henry et al: Harmonia Sacra ... Book II (1726)
Quantz, Johann: Versuch einer Anweisung die Flöte traversiere zu spielen.
Rameau, Jean-Philippe: Code de Musique Pratique, ou Methodes (1760)
Rastall, Richard: The Notation of Western Music.
Rimbault, Edward: The Pianoforte, Its Origins, Progress, and Construction.
Rousseau, Jean Jacques: Dictionnaire de Musique
Rubinstein, Anton : Guide to the proper use of the Pianoforte Pedals.
Sainsbury, John S.: Dictionary of Musicians. Vol. 1. (1825). 2 vols.
Serré de Rieux, Jean de : Les dons des Enfans de Latone
Simpson, Christopher: A Compendium of Practical Musick in Five Parts
Spohr, Louis: Autobiography
Spohr, Louis: Grand Violin School
Tans'ur, William: A New Musical Grammar; or The Harmonical Spectator
Terry, Charles Sanford: John Christian Bach (Johann Christian Bach) (1929)
Terry, Charles Sanford: J.S. Bach's Original Hymn-Tunes for Congregational Use
Terry, Charles Sanford: Four-Part Chorals of J.S. Bach. (German & English)
Terry, Charles Sanford: Joh. Seb. Bach, Cantata Texts, Sacred and Secular.
Terry, Charles Sanford: The Origins of the Family of Bach Musicians.
Tosi, Pierfrancesco: Opinioni de' Cantori Antichi, e Moderni (1723)
Van der Straeten, Edmund: History of the Violoncello, The Viol da Gamba ...
Van der Straeten, Edmund: History of the Violin, Its Ancestors... (2 vols.)
Waltern: Musikalisches Lexicon
Walther, J. G.: Musicalisches Lexikon ober Musicalische Bibliothec

Travis & Emery Music Bookshop
17 Cecil Court, London, WC2N 4EZ, United Kingdom.
Tel. (+44) 20 7240 2129

Discographies by Travis & Emery:

Discographies by John Hunt.

1987: 978-1-906857-14-1: From Adam to Webern: the Recordings of von Karajan.

1991: 978-0-951026-83-0: 3 Italian Conductors and 7 Viennese Sopranos: 10 Discographies: Arturo Toscanini, Guido Cantelli, Carlo Maria Giulini, Elisabeth Schwarzkopf, Irmgard Seefried, Elisabeth Gruemmer, Sena Jurinac, Hilde Gueden, Lisa Della Casa, Rita Streich.

1992: 978-0-951026-85-4: Mid-Century Conductors and More Viennese Singers: 10 Discographies: Karl Boehm, Victor De Sabata, Hans Knappertsbusch, Tullio Serafin, Clemens Krauss, Anton Dermota, Leonie Rysanek, Eberhard Waechter, Maria Reining, Erich Kunz.

1993: 978-0-951026-87-8: More 20th Century Conductors: 7 Discographies: Eugen Jochum, Ferenc Fricsay, Carl Schuricht, Felix Weingartner, Josef Krips, Otto Klemperer, Erich Kleiber.

1994: 978-0-951026-88-5: Giants of the Keyboard: 6 Discographies: Wilhelm Kempff, Walter Gieseking, Edwin Fischer, Clara Haskil, Wilhelm Backhaus, Artur Schnabel.

1994: 978-0-951026-89-2: Six Wagnerian Sopranos: 6 Discographies: Frieda Leider, Kirsten Flagstad, Astrid Varnay, Martha Moedl, Birgit Nilsson, Gwyneth Jones.

1995: 978-0-952582-70-0: Musical Knights: 6 Discographies: Henry Wood, Thomas Beecham, Adrian Boult, John Barbirolli, Reginald Goodall, Malcolm Sargent.

1995: 978-0-952582-71-7: A Notable Quartet: 4 Discographies: Gundula Janowitz, Christa Ludwig, Nicolai Gedda, Dietrich Fischer-Dieskau.

1996: 978-0-952582-72-4: The Post-War German Tradition: 5 Discographies: Rudolf Kempe, Joseph Keilberth, Wolfgang Sawallisch, Rafael Kubelik, Andre Cluytens.

1996: 978-0-952582-73-1: Teachers and Pupils: 7 Discographies: Elisabeth Schwarzkopf, Maria Ivoguen, Maria Cebotari, Meta Seinemeyer, Ljuba Welitsch, Rita Streich, Erna Berger.

1996: 978-0-952582-77-9: Tenors in a Lyric Tradition: 3 Discographies: Peter Anders, Walther Ludwig, Fritz Wunderlich.

1997: 978-0-952582-78-6: The Lyric Baritone: 5 Discographies: Hans Reinmar, Gerhard Huesch, Josef Metternich, Hermann Uhde, Eberhard Waechter.

1997: 978-0-952582-79-3: Hungarians in Exile: 3 Discographies: Fritz Reiner, Antal Dorati, George Szell.

1997: 978-1-901395-00-6: The Art of the Diva: 3 Discographies: Claudia Muzio, Maria Callas, Magda Olivero.

1997: 978-1-901395-01-3: Metropolitan Sopranos: 4 Discographies: Rosa Ponselle, Eleanor Steber, Zinka Milanov, Leontyne Price.

1997: 978-1-901395-02-0: Back From The Shadows: 4 Discographies: Willem Mengelberg, Dimitri Mitropoulos, Hermann Abendroth, Eduard Van Beinum.

1997: 978-1-901395-03-7: More Musical Knights: 4 Discographies: Hamilton Harty, Charles Mackerras, Simon Rattle, John Pritchard.

1998: 978-1-901395-94-5: Conductors On The Yellow Label: 8 Discographies: Fritz Lehmann, Ferdinand Leitner, Ferenc Fricsay, Eugen Jochum, Leopold Ludwig, Artur Rother, Franz Konwitschny, Igor Markevitch.

1998: 978-1-901395-95-2: More Giants of the Keyboard: 5 Discographies: Claudio Arrau, Gyorgy Cziffra, Vladimir Horowitz, Dinu Lipatti, Artur Rubinstein.

1998: 978-1-901395-96-9: Mezzo and Contraltos: 5 Discographies: Janet Baker, Margarete Klose, Kathleen Ferrier, Giulietta Simionato, Elisabeth Hoengen.

1999: 978-1-901395-97-6: The Furtwaengler Sound Sixth Edition: Discography and Concert Listing.

1999: 978-1-901395-98-3: The Great Dictators: 3 Discographies: Evgeny Mravinsky, Artur Rodzinski, Sergiu Celibidache.

1999: 978-1-901395-99-0: Sviatoslav Richter: Pianist of the Century: Discography.

2000: 978-1-901395-04-4: Philharmonic Autocrat 1: Discography of: Herbert Von Karajan [Third Edition].

2000: 978-1-901395-05-1: Wiener Philharmoniker 1 - Vienna Philharmonic and Vienna State Opera Orchestras: Discography Part 1 1905-1954.

2000: 978-1-901395-06-8: Wiener Philharmoniker 2 - Vienna Philharmonic and Vienna State Opera Orchestras: Discography Part 2 1954-1989.

2001: 978-1-901395-07-5: Gramophone Stalwarts: 3 Separate Discographies: Bruno Walter, Erich Leinsdorf, Georg Solti.

2001: 978-1-901395-08-2: Singers of the Third Reich: 5 Discographies: Helge Roswaenge, Tiana Lemnitz, Franz Voelker, Maria Mueller, Max Lorenz.

2001: 978-1-901395-09-9: Philharmonic Autocrat 2: Concert Register of Herbert Von Karajan Second Edition.

2002: 978-1-901395-10-5: Sächsische Staatskapelle Dresden: Complete Discography.

2002: 978-1-901395-11-2: Carlo Maria Giulini: Discography and Concert Register.

2002: 978-1-901395-12-9: Pianists For The Connoisseur: 6 Discographies: Arturo Benedetti Michelangeli, Alfred Cortot, Alexis Weissenberg, Clifford Curzon, Solomon, Elly Ney.

2003: 978-1-901395-14-3: Singers on the Yellow Label: 7 Discographies: Maria Stader, Elfriede Troetschel, Annelies Kupper, Wolfgang Windgassen, Ernst Haefliger, Josef Greindl, Kim Borg.

2003: 978-1-901395-15-0: A Gallic Trio: 3 Discographies: Charles Muench, Paul Paray, Pierre Monteux.

2004: 978-1-901395-16-7: Antal Dorati 1906-1988: Discography and Concert Register.

2004: 978-1-901395-17-4: Columbia 33CX Label Discography.

2004: 978-1-901395-18-1: Great Violinists: 3 Discographies: David Oistrakh, Wolfgang Schneiderhan, Arthur Grumiaux.

2006: 978-1-901395-19-8: Leopold Stokowski: Second Edition of the Discography.

2006: 978-1-901395-20-4: Wagner Im Festspielhaus: Discography of the Bayreuth Festival.

2006: 978-1-901395-21-1: Her Master's Voice: Concert Register and Discography of Dame Elisabeth Schwarzkopf [Third Edition].

2007: 978-1-901395-22-8: Hans Knappertsbusch: Kna: Concert Register and Discography of Hans Knappertsbusch, 1888-1965. Second Edition.

2008: 978-1-901395-23-5: Philips Minigroove: Second Extended Version of the European Discography.

2009: 978-1-901395--24-2: American Classics: The Discographies of Leonard Bernstein and Eugene Ormandy.

Discography by Stephen J. Pettitt, edited by John Hunt:

1987: 978-1-906857-16-5: Philharmonia Orchestra: Complete Discography 1945-1987

Available from: Travis & Emery at 17 Cecil Court, London, UK. (+44) 20 7 240 2129. email on sales@travis-and-emery.com .

Lightning Source UK Ltd.
Milton Keynes UK
UKOW041524180812

197744UK00004B/1/P